Driving
Standards
Agency

The **OFFICIAL DSA GUIDE** to
DRIVING
BUSES AND COACHES

London: TSO

Written and compiled by Driving Standards Agency Learning Materials.

First published 1995
Eighth edition Crown copyright 2008
Eighth impression 2013

ISBN 978 0 11 552900 9

A CIP catalogue record for this book is available from the British Library

Other titles in the Driving Skills series

The Official DSA Guide to Driving – the essential skills
The Official DSA Theory Test for Car Drivers
The Official DSA Theory Test for Car Drivers (DVD-ROM)
The Official DSA Guide to Learning to Drive
Prepare for your Practical Driving Test DVD
DSA Driving Theory Quiz (DVD)
The Official Highway Code Interactive CD-ROM

The Official DSA Theory Test iPhone App
The Official DSA Theory Test Kit iPhone App
The Official Highway Code iPhone App

The Official DSA Guide to Riding – the essential skills
The Official DSA Theory Test for Motorcyclists
The Official DSA Theory Test for Motorcyclists (DVD-ROM)
The Official DSA Guide to Learning to Ride
Better Biking – the official DSA training aid (DVD)

The Official DSA Guide to Driving Buses and Coaches
The Official DSA Guide to Driving Goods Vehicles
The Official DSA Theory Test for Drivers of Large Vehicles
The Official DSA Theory Test for Drivers of Large Vehicles (CD-ROM)
Driver CPC – the official DSA guide for professional bus and coach drivers
Driver CPC – the official DSA guide for professional goods vehicle drivers

The Official DSA Guide to Tractor and Specialist Vehicle Driving Tests

The Official DSA Guide to Hazard Perception (DVD)

Acknowledgements

The Driving Standards Agency (DSA) would like to thank the staff of the following organisations for their contribution to the production of this publication:

Astons Coaches   First Midland Red
Barfordian Coaches   The Playbus
Commandry Coaches   VOSA
DRM Bus Services

We're turning over a new leaf.

100% recycled
This book is printed
on 100% recycled paper

RECYCLED
Paper made from
recycled material
FSC www.fsc.org   FSC® C002151

Find us online

> ## GOV.UK – Simpler, clearer, faster

GOV.UK is the best place to find government services and information for

- car drivers
- motorcyclists
- driving licences
- driving and riding tests
- towing a caravan or trailer
- medical rules
- driving and riding for a living
- online services.

Visit **www.gov.uk and try it out!**

You can also find contact details for DSA and other motoring agencies like DVLA at **www.gov.uk**

You'll notice that links to **GOV.UK**, the UK's new central government site, don't always take you to a specific page. This is because this new kind of site constantly adapts to what people really search for and so such static links would quickly go out of date. Try it out. Simply search what you need from your preferred search site or from **www.gov.uk** and you should find what you're looking for. You can give feedback to the Government Digital Service from the website.

Driving Standards Agency

The Driving Standards Agency (DSA) is an executive agency of the Department for Transport. You'll see its logo at theory and practical test centres.

DSA aims to promote road safety through the advancement of driving standards, by

- establishing and developing high standards and best practice in driving and riding on the road; before people start to drive, as they learn, and after they pass their test
- ensuring high standards of instruction for different types of driver and rider
- conducting the statutory theory and practical tests efficiently, fairly and consistently across the country
- providing a centre of excellence for driver training and driving standards
- developing a range of publications and publicity material designed to promote safe driving for life.

The Driving Standards Agency recognises and values its customers. It will treat all its customers with respect, and deliver its services in an objective, polite and fair way.

www.gov.uk/dsa

The Driver and Vehicle Agency (DVA) is an executive agency within the Department of the Environment for Northern Ireland.

Its primary aim is to promote and improve road safety through the advancement of driving standards and implementation of the government's policies for improving the mechanical standards of vehicles.

dvani.gov.uk

Contents

05 Preparing for the driving test

06 The PCV driving test

07 Additional information

About this book

This book will help you to

- understand what's expected of a passenger-carrying vehicle (PCV) driver
- prepare for your practical PCV driving test
- prepare for and maintain your Certificate of Professional Competence (CPC) qualification.

The information in this book should be read in conjunction with the general driving advice given in *The Official Highway Code* and *The Official DSA Guide to Driving – the essential skills,* which provide valuable information on driver skills in general.

You'll need this information in addition to the specific skills regarding driving PCVs detailed in section 4 of this book.

You can buy official DSA learning materials online at **tsoshop.co.uk/dsa** or by calling our expert publications team on **0870 850 6553**.

DSA publications are also available from bookshops and online retailers. DSA apps can be downloaded from the iPhone app store and eBooks are available from your device's eBook store.

The important factors

Reading this book should help you to appreciate the principles of driving PCVs and so lead you to become a safer driver. However, this book is only a guide; it shouldn't be taken as a training manual. It's just one of the important factors in your training. The others are

- having a good instructor
- getting plenty of practice
- having the right attitude.

Once you've obtained your PCV licence you should take pride in your driving. Your professionalism will be seen and appreciated by other road users.

Driving is a life skill.

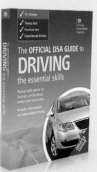

section **one**
GETTING STARTED

This section covers

- Applying for your licence
- The theory test
- Medical requirements
- Bus operator organisation
- Professional standards
- Driver Certificate of Professional Competence
- Responsibility
- Attitude
- Passengers
- Manual handling techniques
- Diet and driving ability

A message from the chief driving examiner

This book provides detailed professional guidance for the safe driving of buses and coaches. As the driver of a vehicle carrying passengers, you must accept responsibility for their safety. Whether you drive a minibus with eight passengers or a double-deck coach with 88, each one is relying on you to get them to their destination safely.

The starting point for a professional driver is having the correct attitude and approach to your driving, together with a sound knowledge of safe, modern driving techniques. You should set an example by showing courtesy and consideration to other road users, and make allowances for the mistakes and errors of other drivers. A professional driver will have a sound knowledge of driving theory, coupled with the ability to apply that theory in an expert manner.

This book provides the officially recommended syllabus for learning how to drive a bus or coach, plus a structured approach to training that should help you to progress to a professional standard. Studying *The Official DSA Guide to Driving Buses and Coaches* will help you to achieve a better understanding of the skills and attitudes that combine to make for higher driving standards.

Included in this edition is lots of information to help prepare for the extended theory and practical tests that link to the Driver Certificate of Professional Competence (Driver CPC), which was introduced in September 2008.

Put the information this book contains into practice and you should be able to reach the higher standards demanded. Having passed your test, you'll have demonstrated the skills necessary to become a bus or coach driver and, above all, to continue to follow DSA's slogan of *'safe driving for life'*.

Lesley Young

Chief Driving Examiner

9

Applying for your licence

In order to drive passenger-carrying vehicles (PCVs), you must apply to the Driver and Vehicle Licensing Agency (DVLA), Swansea (DVA in Northern Ireland) for provisional PCV entitlement to be added to your full car (category B) licence, unless you've held the entitlement before. You **MUST NOT** drive a PCV until you've received your licence with the proper category added. An application form is available online from DVLA or at DVA test centres, local vehicle licensing offices or post offices.

www.gov.uk   nidirect.gov.uk/motoring

To be issued with a licence to drive PCVs you must

- be at or above the minimum age for the category of vehicle that you intend to drive – see the relevant table on page 324
- have a full category B licence – you can't take a driving test on a bus before passing a car test

- meet the medical requirements
- pay the fee.

You can obtain a driving licence application form (D2) from

- traffic area offices
- vehicle registration offices
- DVLA Customer Enquiries Unit, Swansea, SA6 7JL

or visit **www.gov.uk**

In Northern Ireland, the form (DL1) can be obtained from

- MOT centres
- local vehicle licensing offices
- post offices.

Read the notes that accompany the form carefully and fill in all the relevant parts. If you leave anything out, the form may have to be returned to you, and there could be a delay in issuing your licence.

If you need advice about completing the form, ring the enquiry numbers for DVLA or DVA listed at the back of this book.

For more information about becoming a PCV driver and applying for a PCV licence, visit **www.gov.uk** and in NI visit **nidirect.gov.uk/motoring**

Send the completed application form and

- your category B licence, or a provisional car driving licence and a valid driving test pass certificate (form D10) (in NI, the certificate is a DL8)
- a completed medical report form (D4), signed by a doctor (in NI, the form is a DLM1)
- the appropriate fee

to DVLA, Swansea (DVA, Coleraine in NI). The current fees and ways to pay are listed on the application form.

The rules for lorry and bus driving licences (categories C, C+E, C1, C1+E, D, D+E, D1 or D1+E) changed on 19 January 2013. If you drive a lorry or bus, your licence is now valid for a maximum of five years, and you'll have to sign a medical declaration each time you renew your entitlement up to age 45. After age 45, you'll need to send a medical examination report to DVLA (DVA). For full details, visit **www.gov.uk** or **nidirect.gov.uk**

Automatic transmission

Vehicles with fully automatic, semi-automatic, pneumo-cyclic, electronically controlled or pre-select gearboxes with a gear-change pedal are all classified as automatic.

If a vehicle has a clutch pedal it's classified as having a manual gearbox. To drive a PCV with a manual gearbox you'll have to pass a test in a bus or coach with a manual gearbox.

The theory test

All new drivers wishing to drive PCVs will first have to pass a PCV theory test before taking the practical driving test. You can start your lessons before passing the theory test, but you must pass before a booking for a practical test can be accepted.

The theory test pass certificate has a two-year life. If you don't pass your practical test within that time you'll have to retake your theory test and pass it before a booking for a practical test can be accepted.

Additional notes

- A category D licence is required to drive articulated buses (described in the UK as bendy buses).
- It won't be necessary to obtain a category D1 or D1+E licence before applying for a category D test.
- If a trailer with a maximum permitted weight of more than 750 kg is to be towed, a category D1+E or D+E licence may be required, as appropriate. A trailer weighing 750 kg or less may be towed by any of the vehicles in these licence categories.
- Passengers **MUST NOT** be carried in any trailer.

If you're unsure of the category of licence entitlement that you need, see the charts on pages 323–325 at the back of this book.

As a learner you **MUST** be accompanied by a qualified driver who has held a full licence, for the last three years, in the category of vehicle being driven (see page 231).

A DVD entitled *The Official DSA Guide to Hazard Perception* for all drivers and riders will help candidates prepare for the hazard perception part of the theory test. This DVD can be obtained by mail order by calling **0870 850 6553**. Alternatively, it can be purchased from good bookshops or online at **tsoshop.co.uk/dsa**

Medical requirements

Eyesight

All drivers, regardless of vehicle category, **MUST** be able to read a number plate in good daylight at 20.5 metres (67 feet), or 20 metres (about 66 feet) if the narrow font letters have been used on the number plate. If glasses or contact lenses are needed to do this, then they **MUST** be worn when driving. In addition, any applicant for a PCV licence must have a visual acuity of at least

- 6/9 in the better eye
- 6/12 in the other eye

when wearing glasses or contact lenses, if needed. There must also be normal vision in both eyes (defined as a 120° field) and no evidence of double vision (diplopia). Satisfactory uncorrected visual acuity is also a requirement.

All applicants must have an uncorrected visual acuity of at least 3/60 in each eye. This visual field requirement is the normal binocular field of vision. Your doctor or optician will use the standard Snellen test card to test your eyesight. If you only have eyesight in one eye you must declare this on the relevant medical form. A licence-holder who held a PCV or LGV licence before 1 January 1997 and whose eyesight

doesn't meet the required new standard should contact

Drivers Medical Group
DVLA
Swansea, SA99 1TU
Tel **0300 790 6807**
Email **eftd@dvla.gsi.gov.uk**

If you require any further general or medical information you should contact DVLA on **0300 790 6801** or visit **www.gov.uk**

For Northern Ireland call DVA on **0845 402 4000** or visit **nidirect.gov.uk**

Remember, if you normally wear glasses or contact lenses, always wear them whenever you drive.

Medical examination and form D4 (DLM1 in NI)

Driving a PCV carries a serious responsibility towards all other road users so it's vital that you meet detailed and specific medical standards.

Consult your doctor first if you have any doubts about your fitness. In any case, if this is your first application for PCV entitlement, a medical examination must be carried out by a doctor.

You'll need to send off a medical report form with your application. You'll also need to send a report if you're renewing your PCV licence and you're aged 45 or over, unless you've already sent one to DVLA (or DVA) during the last 12 months.

In order to complete form D4 (form DLM1 in Northern Ireland) you'll need to undergo a medical examination. You should only complete the applicant details and declaration (section 8 on the forms) when you're with your doctor at the time of the examination. Your doctor has to witness you doing this. The other sections on the form will be completed by your doctor. The medical report will cover

- vision
- nervous system
- diabetes mellitus
- psychiatric illness
- general health
- cardiac health
- medical practitioner details.

When using form D4, there's an explanatory leaflet available (INF4D) to help you. It contains necessary information and useful reference notes, which explain what needs to be done. You should retain this leaflet for future reference. Both form D4 and the leaflet can be found at post offices or downloaded online at **www.gov.uk**

Form DLM1 (used in Northern Ireland) can be obtained from DVA centres local vehicle licensing offices and post offices. It contains some reference notes on pages 1 and 2, which include sections explaining what you and your doctor need to do. Send in your application to DVA Licensing, Vocational Medical Records Section – the full address is given at the back of this book.

The medical examination isn't available free under National Health Service (NHS) rules. Your doctor is entitled to charge the current fee for this medical examination, and you'll be responsible for paying it. The fee can't be recovered from DVLA or DVA, and it isn't refundable if your application is refused.

The completed form must be received by DVLA or DVA within four months of the date your doctor signed it.

Change in health

It's your responsibility to notify the Drivers Medical Unit at DVLA, Swansea (DVA in Northern Ireland) immediately if you have or develop any serious illness or disability that's likely to last more than three months and that could affect your driving.

Medical standards

You may be refused a PCV driving licence if you suffer from any of the following

- liability to epilepsy/seizure*

- diabetes requiring insulin (unless you held a licence on 1 April 1991 and the traffic commissioner who issued that licence had knowledge of your condition)

- eyesight defects (see eyesight requirements on page 13)

- heart disorders

- persistent high blood pressure (see notes on form DLM1 in NI, or on leaflet INF4D if using form D4)

- a stroke within the past year

- unconscious lapses within the last five years

- any disorder causing vertigo within the last year

- major brain surgery or severe head injury with serious continuing after-effects

- Parkinson's disease, multiple sclerosis or other chronic nervous disorders likely to affect the use of the limbs

- mental disorders

- alcohol/drug problems

- serious difficulty in communicating by telephone in an emergency.

An applicant or licence-holder failing to meet the epilepsy, diabetes or eyesight regulations must by law be refused a licence.

*Remember, a driver who remains seizure-free for at least 10 years (without anticonvulsant treatment within that time) may be eligible for a licence, but with restricted entitlement. Contact DVLA (DVA in NI) for further information.

Bus operator organisation

Bus services outside London were deregulated in 1985; this meant that bus operators were broadly free to run services wherever they saw a commercial opportunity, but still had to be licensed and conform to the associated safety regulations. The vast majority of local bus services – about 80% – are now run on a commercial basis, and decisions on matters such as fare levels, routes operated and frequency of services, are essentially decided by the individual bus companies.

Decisions on bus policy for England are divided between the Department for Transport (DfT; responsible for bus policy outside London) and Transport for London (TfL; responsible for bus policy inside London). Traffic commissioners are responsible for administering the system of operator licensing and local bus service registration and may take disciplinary action against operators that fall foul of the legislative requirements.

Local authorities have a duty to secure the provision of bus services that would not otherwise be provided, and which the local authority judges to be socially necessary. Local authorities have the power to subsidise socially necessary services.

Regulation of the bus industry

The bus industry is subject to two principal regulatory regimes:

Public service vehicle operator licensing This governs operating standards for buses and coaches. All vehicles that are used to carry fare paying passengers (legal term: 'hire or reward') are classed as public service vehicles (PSVs), but are more commonly known as passenger-carrying vehicles (PCVs). Except in special circumstances, their operators must obtain a PSV operator's licence from the relevant traffic commissioner. The traffic commissioner may disqualify an operator from holding an operator's licence, place conditions on its licence prohibiting the use of specified vehicles, or require it to conduct safety inspections at regular intervals.

The operator licence disc must be displayed alongside the vehicle excise licence (tax disc) on the front nearside of the windscreen. Make sure neither disc nor anything else obstructs your view. Discs must be able to be clearly read (in daylight) from outside the vehicle. It's an offence to write on, or alter, a disc in any way.

Bus registration This deals with local services and routes. Bus operators that run local services are required to register them with the traffic commissioner. The primary objective is to ensure that all services are run by properly licensed operators and to provide an element of stability to the bus network – operators must give notice to the traffic commissioner if they wish to vary individual registrations. Once a service has been registered, operators are required to run it in accordance with the registered details. Failure to run a service in accordance with the registered details may result in an operator being investigated by the traffic commissioner.

Bus services in London

The Mayor of London has responsibility for the provision of bus services in the capital. Services are provided by private bus companies under contract to London Buses (part of Transport for London (TfL)), which plans routes and sets fares.

Concessionary fares

A concession came into force on 1 April 2008, that gives people who are

- resident in England (not applicable to NI)
- aged 60 or over
- eligible disabled people

free travel on local buses from 9.30 am until 11.00 pm on weekdays, and all day on weekends and bank holidays, across England. (Times may vary with local services.)

Around 11 million older people and those with special needs are guaranteed free off-peak local bus travel.

On top of the statutory England-wide concession, local authorities can choose to pay for additional benefits. These will only apply locally and, as a general rule, will only be available to the local authority's residents.

More information about concessionary fares in England, Scotland and Wales can be found at **www.gov.uk** For Northern Ireland visit **nidirect.gov.uk**

Passenger percentages

In 2010, buses and coaches had a 5% share of all passenger miles travelled, while journeys by rail accounted for a further 9%.* Non-local buses and coaches have a slightly bigger share of passenger miles than local buses, because of the longer distances travelled by coaches.

Bus passenger journeys in England increased by around 15% between 2004/05 and 2008/09, but have remained broadly flat since then, with an increase in London offset by decreases outside London.*

There were 4.6 billion bus passenger journeys in England in 2010/11. This is a 0.1% increase from the 2009/10 level.*

Journeys in London increased by 1.4% over this period and now account for nearly half (49%) of all bus passenger journeys in England.*

* Taken from dft.gov.uk statistics, 2010–11.

17

In 2010/11, 60% of all buses in Great Britain were issued with an accessibility certificate and a further 25% had low floor access (but no certificate).* The government target agreed with the bus industry, that 50% of buses should be low-floor by 2010, was therefore exceeded well before the due date.

The Disability Discrimination Act (Public Service Vehicles Accessibility Regulations 2000) requires all service buses to be low-floor by 2016 (single deck) and 2017 (double-deck). Any buses constructed since 2000 meet this requirement.

A double-deck bus can carry as many passengers as 20 cars. Buses help the environment and ease congestion by

• cutting down the number of vehicles on the road

• providing a means of transport for those who can't afford their own vehicles.

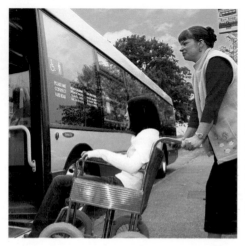

Some examples of different activities of passenger carriage by bus are

• local bus services run on a stagefare basis

• express buses for longer-distance travel on scheduled services

• door-to-door and dial-a-ride services, including those for people with disabilities or visual impairments

• park-and-ride schemes providing a bus service from an out-of-town car park

• excursions such as pre-arranged day trips or coach holidays

• community bus services to provide a local bus service on a voluntary non-profit basis where there would otherwise be no public transport

• minibus services to provide a service to members of organisations such as those concerned with education, religion, recreation, etc.

In 2010/11, 69% of all buses in Great Britain were fitted with CCTV and 63% of buses in Great Britain were fitted with global positioning systems and automatic vehicle location devices for measuring bus punctuality.*

The government believes that smart and integrated ticketing has the potential to revolutionise the way passengers use public transport, and improve end-to-end journeys. Currently, in 2010/11, an estimated 33% of buses in Great Britain had smart-card readers.*

* Taken from dft.gov.uk statistics, 2010–11.

Professional standards

In order to drive a bus, coach or minibus safely you'll need

- a comprehensive knowledge of The Highway Code, including the meaning of traffic signs and road markings (especially those that indicate restrictions for large vehicles)

- a thorough knowledge of the regulations that apply to your work

- a high level of driving skill

- the ability to plan well ahead.

You must appreciate the differences between driving larger and smaller vehicles. Some of these aspects will be obvious from the moment you first start to drive a larger vehicle. Other features will only become apparent as you gain more experience.

As a professional driver, you have a responsibility to use your vehicle in a manner that's sympathetic to the environment. For more information, see pages 205–212.

Always apply the professional driving techniques described in this book. You must never allow safety to be put at risk.

The Safe and Responsible Driving (Category D) Standard™ sets out the knowledge, skills and understanding that DSA believes are required to be a safe and responsible driver of a category D vehicle. To read or download the National Driving Standards, please visit **www.gov.uk**

Remember, no risk is ever justified.

Driver Certificate of Professional Competence

The Driver Certificate of Professional Competence (CPC) is a qualification that all professional bus, coach and lorry drivers in the EU must have in addition to their vocational licence. Benefits include improvements to road safety and enhanced professionalism. Additional advantages include a reduction in fuel consumption and emissions resulting from a better knowledge of environmentally friendly driving techniques.

You can get full and up-to-date information on Driver CPC at **www.gov.uk** or from DSA (GB) or DVA (Northern Ireland). Contact details are given on page 22.

How you get your Driver CPC will depend on whether you're already a professional driver or a newly qualified driver. New drivers will need to pass additional theory and practical tests and then maintain their knowledge with 35 hours of periodic training in each five-year period after that. A new CPC will automatically be issued, provided that the periodic training has been delivered and recorded in accordance with regulations. The syllabus for these training courses covers safe and fuel-efficient driving, legal requirements, health, safety, service and logistics.

Existing drivers will have 'acquired' rights. This means that a driver who already holds a vocational driving licence on the relevant start dates will be deemed to hold the Driver CPC. They won't need to take any new tests, but they'll need to undertake 35 hours of periodic training every five years to maintain their Driver CPC.

This training can be taken at any time within the five years, as one block or split into periods of at least seven hours, which can be further split into two parts as long as the second part starts within 24 hours of the first part finishing. The first five-year period started on 10 September 2008. This means that any professional driver who was originally given acquired rights on that date **must** complete the required 36 hours of periodic training by 9 September 2013 in order to keep and maintain their Driver CPC qualification.

The second five-year period starts on 10 September 2013. From that date, drivers will then have another five-year period in which to complete a further 35 hours of required periodic training, in order to retain their Driver CPC qualification **after** 9 September 2018.

You can check your Driver CPC periodic training hours online at **www.gov.uk**

The tests

Theory Test (module 1) The test is very similar to the current driving theory test. It's split into two parts that can be taken consecutively or at different times. The multiple choice part has 100 questions and the hazard perception part has 19 clips (with 20 scorable hazards). In total the two parts take about two hours and 30 minutes.

Driver CPC Case Studies (module 2)
In addition to passing the theory test (module 1), drivers wishing to obtain their Driver CPC and drive professionally will also need to pass the case studies test (module 2). Each case study will be based on a real-life scenario that you may encounter in your working life, and aims to test your knowledge and basic understanding, as well as how you put this knowledge into practice.

Questions will be based on this scenario and you'll be asked to answer in a number of different ways, such as selecting from multiple choice answers, clicking on an area of a photograph or image, listening to audio information, or giving a short text answer. There will be between six and eight case studies, each with between five and ten associated questions. You'll need to answer 50 questions in total and the test will take about one hour and 30 minutes.

Practical Driving Test (module 3) This is the practical driving test, which all new bus and coach drivers will need to pass. It's slightly longer than it was before the CPC was introduced to allow you to show the examiner how you drive in various situations and types of road. You'll be assessed on your ecosafe driving during the test. At the end of the test, the examiner may also provide a leaflet that gives further information to help you develop your skills.

Driver CPC Practical Demonstration Test (module 4) This is also a practical test but it's for new professional drivers only, who require the Driver CPC. It assesses your knowledge and abilities on matters of safety and security; for example, safe use of the vehicle, the security of the vehicle and yourself, preventing criminal acts and trafficking, assessing emergencies and preventing risks.

The EU Driver CPC Directive requires DSA to test your knowledge and awareness of dealing with special needs passengers. Modern vehicles are now fitted with specialised equipment to comply with the Disability Discrimination Act (DDA). You'll be asked to demonstrate the use of this equipment and will need to show a good understanding of

- your bus stop parking procedure, to allow special needs passengers to get on and off the bus safely

- how and where to secure a wheelchair passenger or pushchair

- how to identify different vehicle types and their passenger access facilities, eg wheelchair access ramp.

If the vehicle you present for test isn't compliant with the DDA, we will ask you to demonstrate and explain your knowledge by showing you a range of pictures.

Periodic training

On completion of 35 hours of training, drivers who hold a GB photocard licence will be automatically issued with a Driver Qualification Card (DQC) at no additional cost. The DQC will be sent to the address that's on the driving licence, so it's very important that drivers keep DVLA (DVA in Northern Ireland) informed of their current address. Your DQC must be carried with you at all times when driving professionally.

Legal issues

It's an offence for an operator to cause or permit a driver who needs a Driver CPC or DQC to drive without one and there are penalties for drivers and operators who do this. You're guilty of an offence if you're

- a driver and you knowingly drive a large vehicle without a CPC DQC
- an operator and you cause a driver to drive a large vehicle without a CPC DQC.

Both driver and operator can be fined up to £1000, if convicted of an offence.

Paper licence and other EU licences

Any qualifying GB paper licence holders opting to upgrade to a photocard licence will automatically receive their DQC without any need for a further DQC application process or fee.

A newly qualified driver with a GB photocard licence will get their DQC automatically when they've passed all four parts of the driving test – a similar process to the automated driver licence issue.

Contact details

See the CPC information at **www.gov.uk**

Great Britain
PO Box 280
Newcastle upon Tyne
NE99 1FP
Email **drivercpc@dsa.gsi.gov.uk**

Northern Ireland
Driver and Vehicle Agency (Licensing)
Castlerock Road
Coleraine BT51 3TB
Driver CPC helpline
Tel **028 7034 6960**
Email via **dvani.gov.uk**

Responsibility

You must show responsibility towards all other road users, as well as to your passengers. If you act hastily you risk endangering others.

- Drive properly, and your passengers will arrive safely at their destination.
- Drive carelessly or dangerously, and you risk the safety of your passengers and other road users.

When a bus or coach is involved in a collision it's bound to lead to damage, injury or loss of life. As a professional driver you have a part to play in making sure road traffic incidents don't happen.

Human error is the main cause of most collisions on the road. High-quality training should help you to avoid making such errors and reduce your risk of being involved in road traffic incidents.

Sometimes incidents are caused by the mechanical failure of vehicle components. The way you drive can affect the life of these components. Drivers who demonstrate a high degree of expertise reduce the risk of incidents happening. So, be responsible for driving your vehicle safely and sensibly at all times.

Mobile phones and public address systems

It's illegal to operate a hand-held mobile phone or similar device while driving. No driver should use a mobile communication device while in control of a moving vehicle. Many companies consider the wearing of headphones or earpieces (including portable media players such as iPods) while driving to be a disciplinary offence.

Your professionalism is important – being seen using a mobile while driving undermines the bus company's image, and could also make your passengers feel uncomfortable and unsafe. Most operators will encourage drivers to keep a mobile on silent – messages or missed calls should be checked at the end of a route or at a terminus point.

You should be aware that if you do use a mobile phone or similar device while driving and you're caught by the police, you'll be prosecuted and could ultimately lose your PCV licence entitlement to drive buses and coaches.

Even using a hands-free system can divert your attention from the road. It's far safer not to use any such equipment until you've found a safe place to stop. If you have to use one in a genuine emergency, 'keep it short and simple' (KISS).

Don't be tempted to use a public address (PA) system while driving. Find a convenient stopping place first. The only time a PA system should be used while the vehicle is in motion is if a courier travelling with you makes the announcements.

Any activity that reduces concentration while driving is dangerous. Be sensible, be professional and only listen to messages at safe and appropriate stops in your schedule.

Attitude

The sheer size, noise and appearance of a PCV can be intimidating to cyclists, pedestrians and even car drivers. Never use the size of your vehicle in an aggressive way. The general public tend to see the bus or coach driver either as

- a skilful professional who manoeuvres a large vehicle in difficult spaces and delivers passengers safely to their destination, or

- an impatient person determined to make other road users, and his or her passengers, do precisely what he or she wants.

A PCV driver should create the best possible image by setting a good example for others to follow.

Driving large vehicles can be very enjoyable – even more so when you can be proud that you're doing it well.

Tailgating

Tailgating means following dangerously close behind another vehicle, at speed, perhaps even only a few feet apart. It often happens on motorways.

Not only are tailgating and driving in close convoy with other PCVs bad driving habits, but they often have serious consequences. Some police forces are so concerned at the number of incidents involving tailgating vehicles that they now video the offence and prosecute offenders.

If you're tailgating, your view of the road ahead is seriously restricted and it's impossible to stop in the distance between your vehicle and the one in front. If a vehicle in front brakes heavily you need time to react and move your foot to the brake pedal. At 50 mph (80 km/h) you'll have travelled 15 metres (49 feet – more than the length of a coach) before you start to brake. During that time the vehicle in front could have reduced its speed to below 40 mph (64 km/h).

Always maintain your safety margins. Considerate drivers also allow the drivers behind them ample time to react.

Intimidation

Never use the size, weight and power of your vehicle to intimidate other road users. Even the repeated hiss of air brakes being applied or released while your vehicle is stationary gives the impression of 'breathing down the neck' of the driver in front.

Retaliation

Everyone makes mistakes or misjudgements at times, which may cause others to take avoiding action. This is especially true of learner drivers. How you react is important, in terms of the safe control of your vehicle and the safety and wellbeing of your passengers. In areas where there are side roads or parked vehicles obstructing your view, be particularly alert. If something happens that means you to have to stop quickly, be tolerant, remain calm and learn from the experience. You must resist the temptation to get upset or retaliate in order to 'teach someone a lesson'.

Always drive

- courteously
- with anticipation
- calmly, allowing for other road users' mistakes
- in full control of your vehicle.

You can't act hastily when driving a PCV without the possibility of serious loss of vehicle control.

The horn

PCVs are often equipped with powerful horns and their use should be strictly confined to the guidance set out in The Highway Code – to warn other road users of your presence. Never use the horn

- aggressively
- between 11.30 pm and 7.00 am in a built-up area
- when stationary, unless a moving vehicle poses a danger.

See page 159 for more information on using the horn.

The headlights

There's only one official use of flashing the headlights described in The Highway Code: to let other road users know that you're there.

- Never repeatedly flash the headlights while driving directly behind another vehicle.
- To avoid dazzle, don't put headlights on full beam when behind another vehicle.
- Don't switch on auxiliary lights (such as fog lights) fitted to your vehicle unless weather conditions require them, and remember to switch them off when the conditions improve.

Misleading signals

Neither the horn nor the headlights should be used to rebuke or to intimidate another road user. By using unauthorised 'codes' of headlight or indicator flashing, you may be misunderstood by others. This in turn could lead to an incident.

When driving abroad, headlight flashing is used purely as a warning. Any other intention won't be understood.

Hazard warning lights

These lights can be used to warn others if

- you're causing a temporary obstruction to traffic
- you've broken down
- you become aware of an obstruction ahead when on a motorway.

As a bus driver, you're also allowed to use them when your vehicle is stationary and children are getting on or off a school bus. Never use your hazard warning lights as an excuse to park illegally.

Speed

You can never justify driving too fast just because you have to reach a given location by a specific time. Don't be tempted to drive faster when you've fallen behind schedule. If an incident happens and you injure someone there's no possible defence for your actions.

Road speed limiters

Specific requirements relating to speed limiters for PCVs can be found on page 134.

Types of speed limiter

There are two main types of speed limiters. One type works by the mechanical or electrical actuator, while the other works through the vehicle's engine management system.

Principles of operation

The speed limiter works by receiving a road speed signal either from the tachograph or a sensor fitted to another system on the vehicle, such as the anti-lock braking system (ABS). Occasionally a specific sensor for the speed limiter system may be fitted. Most vehicles are fitted with speed limiters that take the speed signal from the tachograph.

Irrespective of the type of sensor used, the information is transmitted to the electronic control unit (ECU), which, in turn, controls the equipment used to regulate the power output or revolutions of the vehicle's engine. This is normally achieved by reducing the amount of fuel supplied to the engine.

Parts

The system will consist of a road speed sensor (this may or may not be part of the tachograph system), an electronic cable, an electronic control unit (this may or may not be part of the vehicle's engine management system), an actuation device (this may be a pump, relay or valve) and a plate that's fitted to the vehicle to show the set speed.

Connections

Only authorised speed limiter centres can carry out installation, repairs and calibration. These centres will seal all connections between the speed sensor, electronic control unit and the actuation device to ensure the system is tamper-proof.

Maintenance

No day-to-day maintenance is required, although any failure of the road speed limiter must be reported to the operator of the vehicle, who should arrange for the repair at the end of the journey upon which the vehicle is engaged.

As a result of the fitting of speed limiters set to 100 km/h (62 mph), buses and coaches may not use the far right-hand lane on a motorway. The restriction doesn't apply to 'A' class roads with three lanes.

Effects of your vehicle

As a competent PCV driver you must always be aware of the effects your vehicle and your driving have on other road users.

You must recognise the effects of the turbulence or buffeting your vehicle causes when overtaking

- pedestrians
- horse riders (on the road or grass verge)
- cyclists
- motorcyclists
- cars
- vans and car-derived vans
- cars towing caravans
- other buses and lorries.

Smaller, lighter vehicles are also affected when they overtake you at speed, especially on motorways.

On congested roads, particularly in shopping areas, or when near ice cream vans or mobile shops, take extra care when you need to drive close to the kerb. Be aware of

- pedestrians stepping off the kerb
- the danger of your nearside mirror striking the head of a pedestrian standing at the edge of the kerb
- cyclists moving up on the nearside of your vehicle in slow-moving traffic.

Passengers

Your job is to deliver your passengers to their destinations safely, on time, efficiently and courteously.

Caring for your passengers is as important a part of PCV driving as the individual driving skills. As the driver, you're responsible for your passengers. Remember, you're the representative of the company. How well you perform this role is a measure of your professionalism.

Many companies have rules governing standards of behaviour required, of both you and your passengers. These are in addition to the more general statutory laws that drivers of PCVs must obey. Make sure that you know the rules and enforce them when necessary.

At some point you'll find yourself driving to a timetable. This can exert pressure on you to rush. Resist the temptation to hurry and don't become impatient.

It's important that drivers try to adhere to the scheduled timetable, although it's not always possible to avoid running late.

Running earlier than scheduled can result in complaints from customers. This, in turn, can result in less revenue from passenger fares, damage to the company's reputation and, in extreme cases, loss of the operator licence.

Offering a courteous apology to passengers for any deviation in schedule that was beyond your control may help alleviate any feelings of frustration.

Customer care

- Be on the lookout for passengers. Those waiting might not be able to see or hear the bus coming. When driving through bus stations, look out for people leaving other buses. Take care and keep your speed down.

- Make sure you know the carrying capacity of your vehicle – this can be found on a plate inside the vehicle, near the front (see page 89).

- Eliminate gaps from the kerb. Many passengers find it difficult to board or get off the bus if it pulls up too far away from the kerb. Stop well in to the kerb to help them.

- Make eye contact and listen to each passenger. Looking directly at them when you speak is important, especially if they have hearing difficulties and need to lip-read.
- Check that passengers have given you the correct fare, and issue tickets while stationary at bus stops. **Do not** start to move off while you're still taking fares, giving change and issuing tickets.
- Give passengers time to get seated before you move off. A few extra seconds at this point will add very little to journey times but demonstrates good customer care.

- Use the internal mirror system to check the stairs on double-deck vehicles, particularly when stopping, moving off or cornering. These manoeuvres can affect a person's balance, causing them to stumble or fall. Stay aware of anyone on the top deck or using the stairs.
- Before moving off from a standstill, always make a final check for passengers who may be attempting to get on or off the bus at the last minute.

- Always make sure the doors are shut before moving off. If your bus has an open platform, you mustn't allow passengers to ride on it while the vehicle is moving. Anyone doing so would be at risk, especially if the driver has to brake suddenly or take a corner at speed.

Good customer care is important for maintaining business. Drivers are the first point of contact with passengers. If passengers complain, drivers should be sympathetic and not seem disinterested. Most companies will expect drivers to explain their service standards and complaints procedures. In many cases a written copy will be available on the vehicle to give to passengers.

Ultimately, and with a good standard of customer care always in mind, you should

- acknowledge customers promptly and politely, and speak to them in a way that promotes confidence in your organisation
- give customers information that's within your own limits of authority
- refer customers to other appropriate people if you don't have the knowledge to help them, or if their need goes beyond your responsibilities
- follow approved procedures and policies for promoting customer service
- record, accurately and completely, information from customers that relates to your business

- identify and report, to the appropriate person, possible difficulties that could affect customers.

During special planned excursions or specific day trips where you may be taking passengers to a specific event or location, it's good practice for drivers to have a knowledge of other attractions in the vicinity. This may be useful if the attraction they're going to see is closed on arrival.

Buses taking children to school

Many bus or coach companies throughout the country are responsible for transporting children to and from school during term time. Drivers have often complained about the stress caused by the children's behaviour and the responsibility of having up to 80 children on the bus at one time. Many children consider the driver to be a miserable person who moans all the time and think that the buses are overcrowded and of poor quality.

Bus companies are looking into ways of improving the situation for both drivers and children. Research has been undertaken to find the best way to approach this problem and the Department for Transport (DfT) has created a training programme for bus drivers. Copies of the report 'The school run: A training programme for bus drivers focusing on conflict resolution with school pupils' are available from

DfT Publications
Tel: 0300 123 1102

Alternatively, the report can be downloaded from **www.gov.uk/dft**

The report includes problems from the drivers' point of view. Many thought that

- children's behaviour had deteriorated and they were unmanageable
- children didn't show drivers any respect.

Pupils' views were also highlighted in the report; for example, they thought that

- a degree of high spirits was acceptable
- drivers had forgotten what it was like to be young.

However, pupils also recognised that high spirits could easily get out of hand and lead to unacceptable behaviour.

The training programme suggests ways to make the situation more tolerable and less stressful for all concerned. Effort is needed on both sides for the working relationship between driver and pupils to be successful.

Difficulties encountered on buses taking children to and from school may be dealt with in different ways. Bus and coach companies will have guidance and advice set out by their management teams that should be followed. Examples of good practice include the following.

- Consider the safety of yourself and other bus and highway users: the safety of schoolchildren and other members of the public must be your priority.

- Avoid all physical contact with schoolchildren under any circumstances other than
  - genuine self-defence
  - a medical emergency
  - to prevent a serious offence or threat to safety.
- Schoolchildren may not, in words or actions, be told to get off the bus or be refused entry.
- Racist or other offensive or abusive language won't be tolerated or permitted from any driver.
- Don't make any threats; instead give warnings along the lines of *The School Children Bus Contract*
- Drivers shouldn't react to bell-ringing or verbal abuse.

If there's a risk of a disruptive young person or young people causing damage to the vehicle or endangering the safety of themselves, other passengers or you, the driver, you should take the following steps.

- Bring the bus to a halt.
- Ask them to calm down.
- If there's no response, read out loud from the card issued to all drivers for use in such instances.
- If the disruptive behaviour continues, call for help.

It's essential that you remain calm during any situation and avoid doing or saying anything that implies you're asking them to leave the bus. Act in a confident manner and keep your behaviour in proportion to the provocation. You should

- think about your approach
- minimise the 'audience' effect: young people find it harder to back down if they're being watched by their peer group
- be aware of warning signs and think ahead
- show that you're willing to listen
- avoid body language that could inflame the situation, such as pointing of fingers
- inform the school and your management of any persistent problems.

It has been found that using a dedicated driver for a particular school run enables a long-term relationship to develop between the driver and passengers. This helps reduce the need for young people to test the boundaries of what's acceptable.

Revised legislation

Buses carrying children must display a distinctive yellow reflective sign on the front and rear, unless running a scheduled service for use by the general public. This need only be displayed during the morning and afternoon journeys between school and home. Buses displaying the sign are permitted to use hazard warning lights when stationary and when children are boarding or alighting.

Since February 1998 all minibuses and coaches must have seat belts fitted if they're used for the carriage of three or more children on an organised trip.

The '3 for 2' concession, which allowed three children under 14 years to sit in seats fitted with two seat belts, has been discontinued. See page 53 for more information on seat belt requirements.

Legal lettering

The following information **MUST** be clearly displayed on the bus at all times

- seating and standing capacity
- emergency exit location
- fuel cut-off switch (if fitted)
- electrical isolator switch.

You need to make sure that nothing masks or obscures this information at any time, in the interests of safety.

Professional service

Operators often publicise journeys as being

- comfortable
- convenient
- fast
- trouble-free.

Courtesy and consideration are the hallmarks of a professional driver. You, your company and your profession will be on display every time you drive. Therefore, you should show a good example of skill, courtesy and tolerance. Be a credit to yourself, your company and your profession, and aim for the highest standards.

Commercial pressure

There's a lot of competition among operators for passengers. Such competition helps to ensure that high-quality services are available. However, competition also means that operators need to have tight cost controls to ensure efficient and effective use of their resources. But cutting corners on safety isn't acceptable and could be a recipe for disaster. Remember, safety must be your priority.

- You must not drive a vehicle with a serious defect.
- If you're delayed, do your best to make up time, but don't speed or take risks.
- Obstructing or racing another operator's vehicle is inexcusable.

Carriage of older people and those with disabilities

Since 2000, all new buses and coaches must be accessible to people with disabilities, including wheelchair users. To make them easier for people with disabilities (and others such as those travelling with small children) to use, they must have ramps, priority seating and colour contrast between adjacent surfaces for maximum clarity.

It's equally important that staff on buses and coaches recognise, understand and are responsive to the needs of people with disabilities. Attitudes can have a massive effect on the perception that a person with a disability has of public transport and a positive experience can make all the difference.

Since 2002, drivers of accessible buses and coaches have had to ensure that people with disabilities, including wheelchair users, are able to board and alight their vehicles easily and safely. You should

- ensure that the vehicle is parked close to the kerb, in neutral gear with the parking brake applied
- kneel the bus if necessary (see page 38) or if requested to do so, ensuring an adequate angle to allow safe usage
- provide reasonable assistance to passengers with disabilities

- allow a wheelchair user to board the vehicle, providing the wheelchair isn't too large, and the designated space is unoccupied or can be made available.

Ramps or lifts should be lowered on request or manual ramps provided, and you must ensure that wheelchair users are correctly positioned within the wheelchair space (also called docking or securement areas).

These areas have straps or securing devices that connect to the wheelchair, to prevent its movement while in transit. You should secure these yourself but, if the passenger prefers to do this themselves, then you must also inspect the fixings to make sure they're secured safely. Passengers in wheelchairs usually sit with their back to the direction of travel, and the chair brakes must also be applied.

After helping an older/infirm passenger, wheelchair user or a pushchair user to board safely, you should then

- ensure that the 'kneeling' facility or wheelchair ramp is safely secured
- ensure all doors are closed
- ensure all passengers have reached a safe and secure position
- check the nearside mirror for any late passengers before moving away.

Occasionally, machinery such as boarding devices will break down, despite best efforts to service it. You won't have failed in your statutory duties if the boarding device breaks down and there's no other means of assisting the passenger.

You can refuse to carry out any particular duty, if it's considered unreasonable to do so, on the grounds that it might risk the health and safety of the person with a disability, other passengers, yourself or the security of the bus or coach. Also, you must take care not to overload the vehicle by exceeding the seating and standing capacity as this could be dangerous.

You're permitted to refuse entry to a person in a wheelchair if the wheelchair space on your bus is occupied by standing passengers and their luggage. This would be the case on a bus almost full to capacity, where it would be unreasonable to expect standing passengers to move out in order to make way for the wheelchair-bound passenger.

On 4 December 2006, laws came into force giving people with disabilities a right of access to transport services as they already have to other services such as shops and banks. It's illegal for bus and coach operators to

- discriminate against people with disabilities; for example, by refusing to allow someone to board a vehicle simply because they have special needs
- treat people with disabilities less favourably; for example, by charging them more for a service

- fail to make a reasonable adjustment to the way they provide that service; for example, by ensuring that any ramp or lift is in working order.

What can you do to assist?

- Ensure that all facilities such as lifts, ramps, etc are present and in working order before leaving the depot.
- Pull up as close to the kerb as possible – this will assist all passengers.
- Avoid sudden braking and acceleration.

When dealing with passengers who have disabilities remember

- that some passengers won't be able to see or hear the bus approaching – be on the look out for them
- that people with disabilities aren't all the same, so don't make assumptions or generalisations
- to give less mobile passengers time to get to their seats before moving off
- to avoid being patronising.

Passengers with mobility difficulties

'If someone smiles and takes the money with a little bit of patience it makes the world of difference.'

'Just speaking carefully, looking at the person and giving them attention – not feeling rushed – matters a lot. The feeling that you're holding up a queue of people is a very anxiety-producing situation.'

These are comments from passengers about their local bus service. They're the sort of people you might carry every day – regular customers, in fact. Yet both of them have a problem that may be hard to recognise: they're disabled.

Some disabilities are very obvious. A person carrying a white stick, a long white cane or accompanied by a guide dog is visually impaired. If the stick has a red ring or red and white checks painted on it, or the dog has a red and white harness, they also have impaired hearing. Remember that there's no limit to the number of guide or assistance dogs that can travel on a bus at any one time.

It's also easy to see that someone with crutches, a walking frame or any other aid to movement has a disability – perhaps only temporarily. Showing a little consideration goes a long way with most people – whether they have special needs or not. Don't make them feel rushed, and make sure they've all reached a secure and safe position. Check the nearside mirror for any late passengers before you move away.

Try to imagine what assistance you would like if you were in the position of a person with mobility difficulties. Be patient and considerate. Always respect their wishes: disabled people want to retain their independence. If someone tells you they can manage – let them. But be prepared to offer help if they appear to need it, or ask for it. You'll have your own problems to cope with – such as trying to keep to time, busy traffic conditions, inconsiderate behaviour by other road users – but you should do your best to offer courtesy and a smooth ride to those with special needs.

Also, think about the everyday problems faced by people trying to manage with children, pushchairs or shopping trolleys. Allow time for pushchairs to be stowed away in the correct place. This will prevent them being thrown forward in the event of an incident. You should also make sure they're not left in a place that would endanger other passengers attempting to get past.

Blind and partially sighted people

There are around 360,000 people registered as blind or partially sighted in the UK.* Only a small proportion are totally blind, but you may not be able to tell by their appearance. Visually impaired people often depend on their local bus service for mobility. And remember, most partially sighted people find it hard to read a destination display or timetable.

'There's a problem of explaining that we can't see very well ... we want to do as much as we can for ourselves and just be helped with the tiny bit that we can't do ...'

People who are deaf or hard of hearing

'I usually ask the fare and, if I don't hear how much it is, sometimes I bluff and just offer £1 and hope to get the right change. If the bus driver seems to be a pleasant, approachable person I don't mind asking him to repeat it, but some drivers are under pressure and appear not to be aware of you or don't look at your face ...'

It's common courtesy to look at people when you speak to them. Just doing that will allow most deaf or hearing-impaired people to understand you. Good communication also saves time.

Physical disabilities

People with arthritis, stiff joints, artificial limbs or conditions such as multiple sclerosis will often put up with extra pain (and the impatience of other passengers) rather than ask for extra consideration on a bus. For them, courtesy and a smooth ride are important.

'Nobody wants to shout to the rest of the world "I am having trouble", but if the driver could just wait until you're sitting down before they pulled away ...'

'If letting the clutch out or moving away is done too violently it hurts every inch of the way ...'

'If the driver was to go round corners a little more slowly it would probably be less painful ...'

* Figure taken from rnib.org.uk/aboutus/research/statistics/Pages/statistics.aspx

Lifts, ramps and 'kneeling' buses

Make sure that you're thoroughly trained in the safe use of passenger lifts, ramps and securing devices. If you drive a vehicle fitted with this equipment, never let untrained people operate it. Watch out for the safety of others at all times.

Some buses are equipped with air or hydraulic systems that allow the step level to be raised and lowered. These 'kneeling' buses improve access for disabled and older passengers. It's essential that you're thoroughly trained in the use of such systems and are aware of the principles of safe operation. Don't forget to raise the step again before moving off.

Learning disabilities

Customers with learning disabilities may appear fit and active, but they may also find bus travel a special problem and a challenge. It may be hard for them to understand other people or to make themselves understood. Also, any unexpected problems can sometimes produce a sense of panic.

Those with learning disabilities are increasingly being encouraged to go out to work, to go shopping or visit friends. With patience and understanding you can contribute towards their confidence and sense of achievement.

Manual handling techniques

More than a third of all over-three-day injuries reported each year are caused by manual handling – the transporting or supporting of loads by hand or by bodily force.

To reduce the risk of an injury of this nature, make sure that you

- follow appropriate systems of work which are laid down for your safety

- make proper use of any equipment provided

- inform the relevant person if you identify any hazardous handling activities

- take care to ensure that your activities don't put others at risk.

Good techniques for lifting

Here are some practical points to remember when lifting a load.

Think before lifting/handling Plan the lift. Can you use handling aids? Where are you going to place the load? Will you need any help with the load? Remove any obstruction beforehand. For a long lift, consider resting the load midway, to change grip.

Keep the load close to your waist
Keep the load close to your body for as long as possible while lifting. Keep the heaviest side of the load next to your body. If a close approach to the load isn't possible, try to slide it towards your body before attempting to lift it.

Adopt a stable position Your feet should be apart with one leg slightly forward to maintain balance (alongside the load, if it's on the ground). Be prepared to move your feet during the lift to maintain stability. Avoid tight clothing or unsuitable footwear, which may make this difficult.

Get a good hold Where possible, hug the load closely to your body. This may be better than gripping it tightly with hands only.

Start in a good posture At the start of the lift, slight bending of the back, hips and knees is preferable to fully flexing the back (stooping) or fully flexing the hips and knees (squatting).

Avoid twisting or leaning sideways, especially while your back is bent
Keep your shoulders level and facing in the same direction as your hips. Turning by moving your feet is better than twisting and lifting at the same time.

Keep your head up when handling
Look ahead, not down at the load, once you're holding it securely.

Move smoothly Don't jerk or snatch the load as this can make it harder to keep control and can increase the risk of injury.

Adopt a stable position

Start in a good posture

Don't lift or handle more than you can easily manage There's a difference between what people can lift and what they can safely lift. If in doubt, seek advice or get help.

Put down, then adjust If precise positioning of the load is necessary, put it down first, then slide it into the desired position.

Good techniques for pushing and pulling

Here are some practical points to remember when pushing or pulling loads.

Handling devices Aids such as barrows and trolleys should have handle heights that are between the shoulder and waist.

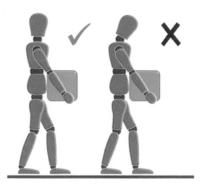

Keep your head up

Avoid twisting or leaning sideways

Force As a rough guide, the amount of force that needs to be applied to move a load over a flat, level surface, using a well maintained handling aid, is at least 2% of the load weight. For example, if the load weight is 400 kg, then the force needed to move the load is 8 kg. The force needed will be larger, perhaps a lot larger, if conditions aren't perfect (eg wheels not in the right position or a device that's poorly maintained). Try to push rather than pull when moving a load, provided you can see over it and control steering and stopping.

Slopes Enlist the help of another person if you have to negotiate a slope or ramp, as pushing and pulling forces can be very high. For example, if a load of 400 kg is moved up a slope of 1 in 12, the required force is over 30 kg even in ideal conditions – good wheels and a smooth slope. This is above the guideline weight for men and well above the guideline weight for women.

Uneven surfaces Moving an object over soft or uneven surfaces requires higher forces. On an uneven surface, the force needed to start the load moving could increase to 10% of the load weight, although this might be offset to some extent by using larger wheels. Soft ground may be even worse.

Stance and pace To make it easier to push or pull, keep your feet well away from the load and go no faster than walking speed.

Ergonomic considerations

How comfortable you are when driving is as important as manual handling. Remember that you may be spending considerable time in the same restricted position – what's comfortable for five minutes may feel very different after 90 minutes. You should check for, and make, any adjustments necessary before you start any journey, especially if you are to drive an unfamiliar vehicle for the first time. Never adjust your seat while the vehicle is moving. Before starting the vehicle, you should carefully check the driver's seat to ensure that

- the seat feels comfortable for you and is locked in position

- the angle of the seat back provides suitable support for good posture

- the head restraint is in the correct position for your safety and comfort

- you can reach all the controls without straining or overreaching in any way

- you can see the road ahead clearly – the seat or steering wheel may also be adjustable for height or angle

- the mirrors are correctly adjusted to meet your particular requirements

- the seat belt is comfortable and in the right position across your body.

If you find any of the above can't be adjusted sufficiently to meet your needs, you should speak to your operator or the company health and safety representative for advice.

Diet and driving ability

Medical standards are more stringent for LGV and PCV drivers than for car drivers. Many common conditions in middle age, such as heart disease and diabetes, are linked to poor eating habits. A sensible approach to food, fluid and caffeine intake can benefit your driving performance and safety in the short term and improve your health in the longer term. This will reduce the risk of an early end to your time working as a driver, either from death or disability, or from withdrawal of your driving licence on medical grounds.

Long-term health effects from bad eating habits

One of the key factors for ensuring long-term general good health is a well-balanced diet. A pattern of poor eating habits will increase your risk of developing serious long-term health problems in middle age, such as obesity, diabetes and heart disease. These diseases will increase your risk of sudden incapacity at the wheel, as well as making you more likely to develop serious illness at other times and increase your probability of an early death.

Other factors such as smoking and lack of exercise also increase these risks.

The development of these serious diseases takes many years and your dietary habits in earlier years will contribute to your risk of disease when you're between 40 and 70 years of age. The following are the main ways in which your diet can contribute to future serious ill-health.

- **Excessive calorie intake from any source, but commonly from sugars and fat** This can lead to obesity; not only does this impair your physical performance but it's also linked to an increased risk of late-onset diabetes, raised blood pressure and heart disease.

- **Intake of saturated fats** These are usually the hard fats in butter and lard rather than in liquids such as sunflower and olive oil. Packaged foods will normally give information on the levels present. High levels of intake are associated with an increased risk of arterial disease, leading to a heart attack or stroke.

- **Salt** While your body needs salt in small amounts, most western diets contain far more than is essential and this can lead to high blood pressure and an increased risk of heart disease and stroke.

It isn't always easy to detect the presence of these undesirable components in food. Savoury pies may be very high in both salt and saturated fat but these are hidden by the taste and texture of the pie. Cakes, while tasting sweet, also contain large amounts of fat, which isn't apparent.

Soft drinks, when they don't use non-sugar sweeteners, often contain very large amounts of sugar which is hidden by the acidity of other ingredients. Labelling allows you to identify ingredients and to make choices that will help you avoid those which are undesirable.

Proteins are essential components of diet but aren't needed in vast quantities by adults, although their presence makes for slow digestion and prolonged satisfaction after eating. However, care is needed to ensure that you don't eat excessive amounts of foods such as eggs and cheese.

Protein-based foods should be included as part of a healthy eating plan. However, eating them in large quantities can add extra unnecessary fat or salt to your diet, which can contribute to an increase in cholesterol levels. Recommended protein portion sizes vary according to sources, but a general approximation of a single portion would be any one of the following

- 4 oz (100 g) meat, fish or poultry
- approx 1 oz (30 g) of hard cheese or nuts
- two whole eggs.

Many traditional ways of serving proteins, such as frying, battering and cooking in pies and puddings can add unnecessary calories. Any fats added should be unsaturated ones, such as sunflower and olive oils or products such as spreads manufactured from them.

Fibre in fruit, vegetables and unrefined cereals also prolongs post-meal satisfaction and may to an extent be protective against several forms of ill-health. There's a recommendation that five portions of fruit/vegetables/salad should be eaten each day. Eating five portions a day will help towards a healthy balanced diet and contribute to your long-term health.

Diet and performance while driving

Concentration, and therefore safe driving, will be improved by regular, light, balanced meals, timed to fit into rest breaks rather than continuous snacking while on the move.

Regular meals are preferable to snacks when trying to control diet as, with the exception of fruit, most snack foods are high in sugar, fat or salt.

Meals based around protein-containing foods (such as meat, fish, eggs, cheese, peas or beans) and slowly digested calories (such as bread, rice, pasta and vegetables) will keep you satisfied and prevent hunger for longer than those high in sugar which give an immediate energy boost.

When driving through the night or on late-evening or early-morning shifts you need to consider the following points.

- An additional meal is desirable at the start and in the middle of the period of work.

- At the start of night work, after a period when night-time sleep would be customary, digestion is likely to be less efficient and you may need to adjust the amount and type of food eaten to take account of any feelings of discomfort.

- If it isn't possible to find a meal other than one containing a high fat content or quick-release calories, it may be better to prepare your own food in advance.

- Take care to balance your eating patterns for the rest of the day to avoid an excessive intake of calories.

Fluid intake

Your fluid requirements will depend, in part, on the temperature of your cab and the physical demands of your job during loading and unloading. You should carry water in case of delays on the journey, especially in summer.

Water is the ideal drink; it quenches thirst for longer than drinks such as tea and coffee, which increase urine production. The only advantage of bottled waters over tap water in developed countries is their convenience. A large amount of hidden sugar and hence calories can be consumed in bottled and canned drinks that aren't marked as low in calories or sugar.

The amount of caffeine in purchased hot drinks is very variable. Caffeine from coffee, and to a lesser extent from tea, doesn't reduce sleepiness; it masks sleepiness and can only prolong alertness for an hour or so, usually with a rebound increase in tiredness and sleepiness afterwards. Tea and coffee without sugar provide fluid and caffeine with few calories, although large amounts of caffeine can cause jitteriness and anxiety.

Branded caffeine-containing soft drinks provide a more reliable source, but usually also contain a lot of sugar, so try to go for sugar-free or artificially sweetened options. Caffeine-rich drinks should only be considered as a short-term emergency countermeasure rather than as a way to prolong the amount of time at the wheel.

In addition to what's already mentioned on alcohol and driving elsewhere, don't drink alcohol when driving as it will seriously affect your judgement and abilities, as well as being illegal.

> **Remember,** if you're feeling sleepy, stop driving and sleep; don't rely on caffeine.

section **two**

PASSENGER-CARRYING VEHICLES

This section covers

- Forces at work
- Maintaining control
- Vehicle sympathy
- Seat belts
- Types of PCV
- Vehicle maintenance
- Other auxiliary systems

Forces at work

You should understand something of the various forces that act on a vehicle and its passengers. The effects of these forces can seriously undermine your control, so it's important to be aware of them and to act appropriately.

A bus, coach or minibus travelling in a straight line under gentle acceleration is relatively stable.

When a vehicle

- accelerates
- brakes
- changes direction

forces are applied to it and its load. The more violent or sudden the change, the greater the forces. Sudden, excessive or badly timed steering, braking and acceleration will introduce forces that can result in loss of control.

Steering should always be

- planned
- smooth
- controlled
- accurate.

Braking should always be

- progressive
- correctly timed
- smooth
- sensitive.

Acceleration should always be

- progressive
- used to best economic advantage
- well planned
- considerate.

Most of the forces described here act on a vehicle in motion. If you disregard them you'll probably lose control, so allow for them in your driving.

Driving new or unfamiliar vehicles

Before driving any vehicle, you should be familiar with all its controls and operating systems. This is especially important if it's

- a new vehicle
- a type which you haven't driven before
- one with which you aren't familiar.

Friction

The resistance between two surfaces rubbing together is called friction. A tyre's grip on a road surface depends on friction, and is essential when

- moving away or accelerating
- turning/changing direction
- braking/slowing down.

The amount of grip will depend on

- the weight of the vehicle
- the vehicle's speed
- the condition of the tyre tread
- the tyre pressure

- the type and condition of the road surface
  - loose
  - smooth
  - anti-skid
- weather conditions
- any other material present on the road
  - mud
  - wet leaves
  - diesel spillage
  - other slippery spillages
  - inset metal rails
- whether the vehicle is braking or steering sharply
- the condition of steering and suspension components.

Sudden acceleration or braking can lead to loss of grip between the tyre tread and the road surface. Under these conditions the vehicle may

- lose traction (wheelspin)
- break away on a turn (skid)

- not stop safely (skid)
- overturn.

The same will happen when changing into a lower gear if you're travelling too fast or if the clutch is suddenly released, because the braking effect will only be applied to the driven wheels.

Gravity

When a vehicle is stationary on level ground the only force acting upon it is the downward pull of gravity (ignoring wind forces, etc). On an uphill gradient the effects of gravity will be much greater so that

- more engine power is needed to move the vehicle forward and upward
- less braking effort is needed and the vehicle will stop in a shorter distance.

On a downhill gradient the effects of gravity will tend to

- make the vehicle's speed increase
- require more braking effort to slow down or stop the vehicle
- increase stopping distances.

The vehicle's centre of gravity is the point around which all of its weight is balanced. All passenger vehicles are tilt-tested to ensure that the design is stable. But violent steering, acceleration or braking shifts the centre of gravity and places excessive forces on the vehicle's tyres and suspension, and on the passengers.

Heavy braking while cornering can bring components very close to their design limits and will be uncomfortable for passengers. Catching a kerb or raised drain cover with a tyre under such conditions could result in a blow-out and the vehicle going out of control or even overturning.

Cornering force

When a vehicle takes a curved path at a bend the forces acting upon it tend to cause it to continue on the original, straight course. This is known as cornering force. If a bus or coach takes a bend too fast, cornering force will cause the passengers to be thrown towards the outside of the bend. The vehicle may even skid, especially if the road surface is at all slippery.

Don't take a bend too fast; this could cause passenger discomfort and may cause loss of control.

Inertia and momentum

A stationary bus with 70 or 80 passengers on board may weigh up to 18 tonnes. It requires a great deal of force to begin to move it, even on a flat road, but it takes relatively little power to keep it rolling at a constant speed. Resistance to change in a vehicle's state of motion is called inertia, and the force that keeps the vehicle rolling is called momentum.

Modern buses and coaches have engines with a high power output to

- give good acceleration
- overcome inertia.

Passengers are also affected by these forces. In order to avoid harsh braking, look and plan well ahead so that you can take early action. Sudden braking will cause passengers to be thrown forward towards the front of the bus. Equally, sudden acceleration can cause passengers to be thrown backwards towards the rear of the vehicle. Both situations are dangerous and could cause injury. Therefore, all acceleration and braking should be smooth, controlled and as progressive as possible. The main advantages of progressive braking are improved passenger safety and comfort, lower fuel consumption and reduced tyre wear.

Kinetic energy

The energy that's stored up in the vehicle and its passengers when travelling is known as kinetic energy. This is converted into heat at the brake shoes and drums when braking occurs.

Continuous use of the brakes results in them becoming over heated and losing their effectiveness (especially on long downhill gradients). This effect is known as 'brake fade'.

Much more effort is needed to stop a fully laden PCV than an ordinary car travelling at a similar speed. It's important, therefore, to avoid harsh braking. Plan ahead and take early action.

Maintaining control

You can't alter the severity of a bend or change the weight of the bus and its passengers. Similarly, you can't alter the design and performance characteristics of your vehicle and its components. But you do have control over the speed of your vehicle and hence the forces acting upon it.

If you ask too much of your tyres by turning and braking at the same time, you'll lose some of the available power and grip. When the tyres slide or lift you'll no longer be in full control of the vehicle. To keep control you should ensure that all braking is

- controlled
- in good time
- made when travelling in a straight line, wherever possible.

Reduce speed in good time by braking, if necessary, before negotiating

- bends
- roundabouts
- corners.

Avoid braking and turning at the same time, unless manoeuvring at low speed. Reduce your speed first and look well ahead to assess and plan.

When making short stops, particularly on hills, always apply the parking brake when the vehicle comes to a standstill.

If your vehicle has automatic transmission, you should apply the footbrake before you engage 'D'. This will stop the vehicle creeping forward or rolling back, which could be dangerous, especially if there are other road users close behind, or pedestrians in the area.

To avoid the possibility of 'pedal confusion' or 'unintended acceleration', before releasing the parking brake you need to ensure that you're aware of the position of your foot in relation to the accelerator and brake pedals. Pedal confusion or unintended acceleration has been known to cause drivers to press the accelerator believing it to be the brake, consequently losing control of their vehicle, sometimes with catastrophic consequences. This problem generally occurs at slow speed usually when the vehicle has moved off from rest and there has been some movement of the driver, perhaps by twisting in his or her seat or similar. Drivers using vehicles where the pedals may be in a slightly different position are also susceptible to this.

Vehicle sympathy

There are many different types of PCVs and each type will require specific handling. Adapt your driving to suit the vehicle and develop what's known as 'vehicle sympathy'.

For example, drivers need to take corners slowly in order to keep their passengers comfortable. Yet it's difficult to define what 'slowly' means for all vehicles on all occasions. A safe, comfortable speed will depend on the sharpness of the corner and any other hazards there might be. The vehicle's design might dictate when the speed is comfortable. New coaches have very sophisticated air-suspension levelling systems, which allow relatively fast cornering while maintaining the body almost level. These systems help with passenger care by keeping the vehicle at an even height while manoeuvring. This gives passengers a safer and more comfortable journey.

The implementation of the Disability Discrimination Act means more buses and coaches will have wheelchair users travelling on them, so their comfort must be considered.

Information on the types of licence needed to drive the different types of PCV is given on page 323. This section discusses some of the basic characteristics of the various types of PCVs. However, it's up to you to develop your own vehicle sympathy when driving.

You should always make yourself aware of any possible overhangs or projections that may be evident on the type of vehicle you are to drive. Overhangs can sweep over kerbs when turning – they can also collide with street furniture, pedestrians and other vehicles, as can any mirror projections. Care should be taken at all times; good all-round observation is required, as well as extensive use of mirrors, to also check for any rear-end sweep.

When turning a long vehicle it might be necessary for you to straddle lanes, in order to avoid mounting the kerb. Use your mirrors to check all around your vehicle. Other traffic might try to move up into the gap you've left and vulnerable road users such as cyclists may be difficult to see, so be sure this area is clear before you start your turn. Take up your position in good time and signal your intentions clearly.

Stay aware of the angle (camber) of the road surface. A steep camber can affect your bus, particularly if it's a double-deck vehicle. You may need to leave extra room when passing near shop awnings, trees and street furniture such as lampposts or traffic signs/lights. Remember, to passengers on the top deck, these things can seem to come frighteningly close.

Seat belts

Seat belts save lives and reduce the risk of injury. Legislation was introduced in 1998 which requires that when three or more children aged between three and 15 years (inclusive) are carried on an organised outing in a minibus, larger minibus or coach, they must be provided with, as a minimum, a forward-facing seat fitted with a lap belt. An organised outing includes the school run, even when driven by parents.

Minibuses include less obvious types of vehicles such as large domestic vehicles with more than eight and not more than 16 seated passengers.

In all buses, coaches and minibuses, the driver and all front seat passengers (ie those parallel to the driver) **MUST** use an adult seat belt, where it's fitted. For the driver specifically, the only exceptions to this rule are while the vehicle is being reversed or when a valid medical exemption certificate is held. Children under three years **MUST** use the correct child restraint (ie baby/child seat) in the front – if there's no child restraint, they **MUST** travel in the rear. Those aged three years up to the height of 135 cm in the front **MUST** use a child restraint (ie child seat/booster) if available otherwise the adult seat belt **MUST** be worn. Children aged 12 and 13 years **MUST** use adult seat belts. If there are no seat belts then children may not travel in the front.

All rear passengers in a minibus (ie a vehicle of up to 2540 kg unladen weight) are required to use seat belts where they're fitted. Children aged three years to 135 cm in height **MUST** use a child restraint if available, otherwise the adult seat belt **MUST** be used.

In larger vehicles, rear-seat passengers aged 14 years and above (ie including adults) **MUST** use adult seat belts where fitted.

Regulations don't force a child under three years to use an adult belt (the only alternative) in any of these vehicles if there's no child restraint available – but parents may want to bring their own to see whether it will fit. Don't permit an adult to put one adult seat belt around both themselves and an infant on their lap. That could result in severe injuries to the child in the event of a crash. There's nothing to prevent child restraints being used on bus and coach seats if they're suitable. However, it should be borne in mind that child restraints are designed to fit on car seats and may not be suitable for buses and coaches.

Finally, the regulations require that passengers **MUST** be advised that seat belts **MUST** be worn where they're fitted. This can be by signs, pictograms (most commonly used) or announcements by the driver/courier. It's good practice for drivers to make sure that any passengers who may be unable to read or understand signs are advised of the legal requirements relating to seat belt use.

Types of PCV

Minibuses

A minibus is generally defined as a motor vehicle with more than eight and not more than 16 passenger seats. They're often based on van bodies and have been adapted by specialist coach-building firms, although some manufacturers produce purpose-built vehicles. The controls are usually similar to those on cars.

Few minibuses are built as full public service vehicles. The regulations for PSVs require higher minimum standards for items such as

- headroom
- access
- seating
- safety precautions
- equipment
- markings.

Driving minibuses

Driving a minibus is often a lot like driving a car. However, you need to be aware that despite having power-assisted steering and braking, and possibly an automatic gearbox, a minibus can be more demanding and tiring to drive than a car.

You're strongly advised to seek professional training if you intend to drive minibuses. Various bodies run courses, but if you have difficulty finding one locally, contact RoSPA, whose address and telephone number are given on page 322.

Other information at the back of this book tells you about licence requirements dependent on usage. Vehicles that are operated under a community or minibus permit scheme are subject to special rules.

When driving a minibus you'll need to think about

- **weight**
  - greater stopping distances are needed
  - they're slower to accelerate and to overtake
  - more effort is needed for steering
- **height**
  - there's greater body roll, pitch and sway
  - they're more susceptible to crosswinds, etc
- **noise levels**
  - these can be high, especially in van-derived models
  - passenger noise can be loud and distracting
- **speeds**
  - it's more difficult to maintain high average speeds
  - when fully laden, speed may be lost rapidly on uphill stretches of road
- **passengers' comfort**
- **distances travelled**
  - is the vehicle suitable for long journeys?
  - would the use of a larger vehicle, possibly hired with a driver, be more appropriate?
- **time**
  - plan your journey and estimate realistically how long it will take
  - allow plenty of time for the journey, thus putting yourself under less pressure
  - you'll need to take adequate breaks.

Never drive for more than four and a half hours without taking a break of at least 45 minutes. If you're subject to drivers' hours regulations, you'll find that this rule, and others, are legal requirements. To avoid fatigue it's advisable to have a break after two hours' driving.

Treat minibus driving as you would other work, even if it isn't your normal job. You need to be alert and to concentrate. Refer to the rules in section 3 of this book, which apply to professional drivers, and consider the advice given within the officially recommended syllabus in section 5.

Ultimately, consider carefully before each journey whether

- you need someone else to drive
- a second driver is advisable.

See page 53 for information on seat belt requirements.

Midibuses

There's no legal definition of a midibus. However, the term is commonly used within the industry to describe any single-deck vehicle that's bigger than a minibus but smaller than a 40+ seat coach or bus.

Virtually all are purpose-built and many have bus or coach controls, equipment and other systems. Some midibuses are specialist vehicles with wheelchair lifts and securing equipment. Many are used on normal services, where demand isn't sufficient to justify the use of full-size buses.

Seat belts

For information on seat belts, refer to the seat belt section on page 53.

Depending on the use and seating capacity, drivers require one of the following licence entitlements

- D
- D1
- D+E or D1+E, if a trailer over 750 kg is to be towed.

See pages 323–325 for more information on licence entitlements and requirements.

Some midibuses operated under the community minibus and large bus permit schemes can be driven with a category B (car) licence. The rules are explained in booklet PSV 385, available from traffic area offices or it can be downloaded from **dft.gov.uk/vosa**

It's essential that you fully understand the vehicle controls and, wherever possible, undergo 'type' training.

Many of the points relating to minibuses also apply to midibuses, as do many of the topics covered in the sections on buses and coaches. In particular, you'll need to consider

- blind spots and restricted vision
- standing passengers
- careful use of automatic gearboxes, where fitted
- body roll.

Single-deck service buses

These vehicles are generally designed for local bus service use and have basic passenger equipment. They may also have a limited amount of seating and a higher proportion of space for standing passengers. Most are operated by one person.

Newer vehicles are built to the Disabled Persons Transport Advisory Committee (DPTAC) specification and may incorporate kneeling suspension, wide doors and other design features to cater for passengers with disabilities. Because of the stop–start nature of the journeys, most of these vehicles have semi-automatic or fully automatic gearboxes, although some buses with manual gearboxes are still in use. All have relatively low gearing, with only four or five gears, or are coupled to low-ratio drive axles to give greater flexibility at low speeds. As a result they may have lower top speeds.

Single-deck service buses require skill and sensitivity on the part of the driver if they're to be driven smoothly. While these vehicles and double-deck buses are generally exempt from the requirement to fit seat belts, be aware that some contracts, particularly those with schools, may require vehicles fitted with seat belts to be provided for passengers. See page 53 for more information on seat belt requirements.

Route and destination displays

The correct route number and destination **MUST** be displayed on the vehicle and **MUST** be illuminated between sunset and sunrise. Where it isn't possible to display the route destination in the usual way, eg on a temporary route, then a temporary sign should be displayed on the front or nearside of the bus, as near as possible to the front door. These temporary signs don't need to be lit at night. (This information is also applicable to double-deck and articulated service buses.)

Double-deck service buses

These are high-capacity vehicles used primarily for local bus services. Many are fitted with dual doors and fare-collection equipment in order to allow for effective one-person operation. (Also see destination display information on page 57.)

Additional internal mirrors are positioned to allow the driver to observe entrances, exits, stairs and the upper deck. To ensure high standards of passenger care and safety, drivers should make full use of these mirrors.

Automatic and semi-automatic gearboxes are frequently fitted to these vehicles. Make sure that you know how to make smooth gear changes and to use the gearbox correctly when moving off and pulling up. Vehicle manufacturers give advice for each type of vehicle.

Drivers need to balance safe driving techniques with the comfort of passengers and the need to keep to timetables. Smooth, skilful driving is essential

during peak periods when there will be more passengers standing, climbing the stairs and moving about the bus.

Most modern double-deck vehicles have underfloor or rear-mounted engines. Therefore, you're less likely to know if the engine is overheating, so you'll have to make full use of instruments and warning lights to ensure early action should a fault develop.

On double-deck buses the driving position and front entrance are generally ahead of the front axle, while the position of rear axles varies considerably. The wheelbase of the bus will dictate the appropriate course to take when cornering. This means that you must take care with overhangs and be aware of the danger of tyre damage on kerbs, etc.

Read the information on vehicle height on pages 92–95 and take extra care when driving open-top double-deck buses, such as sightseeing tour buses and those operated in seaside towns.

Articulated buses

Articulated buses, also known as 'bendy buses', consist of a lead unit coupled to a single-axle rear section by means of floor- and roof-level pivots and a flexible shroud. They offer high-capacity urban transport on routes where double-deck buses are less practical. (Also see destination display information on page 57.)

Trials with articulated buses have taken place in a number of areas in the UK, and their numbers are increasing. They're more common in other countries, particularly in Europe, where height limits of 4 metres (13 feet) exist. In this country, their length – up to 18 metres long (59 feet) – can present problems when they're used on urban streets.

Additional care is needed when driving these vehicles. Always be aware of the 'swept path' the vehicle is taking. Also, remember, the rear section may not follow the same path as the lead section.

'Type' training is essential before driving an articulated bus.

When negotiating road junctions and pulling into lay-bys, you must remember to make allowances for the additional length of the vehicle. Make sure you don't obstruct other road users.

Try to avoid getting into situations where you need to reverse the vehicle. Only reverse when special video reversing equipment is fitted or a reliable person is standing in your view to guide you back.

New drivers of vehicles towing trailers will need to take a category D+E test if the trailer is over a maximum authorised mass of 750 kg. An articulated bus isn't deemed to be a bus towing a trailer and can therefore be driven on a category D licence.

Category D and D1 test vehicles must be fitted with an anti-lock brake system and a tachograph. For full information on test vehicle requirements see pages 326–327.

Single-deck coaches

Coaches are designed to carry passengers for longer distances, in greater comfort and with improved facilities. Many have sophisticated heating and air conditioning systems, toilets, catering areas and crew seats. Most modern vehicles are fitted with rear or underfloor engines, to limit noise levels and to enable more luggage to be carried.

Coach journeys are longer and frequently involve motorways, so manual gearboxes remain the norm, but they often have six or more gears. Semi-automatic and fully automatic vehicles are also in use, and there's an increasing trend towards air suspension systems.

Coaches are often downgraded to dual-purpose or service-bus use after several years of operation. In addition, some rural bus operators use coaches so that their passengers travel in greater comfort. In such instances, lower specification running gear may be fitted to the vehicles to make it easier for the driver (less gear-changing, etc).

For seat belt information, see page 53.

If vehicles are fitted with television and video equipment for passenger use, it's illegal for their screens to be visible to the driver while they're in use.

Special regulations apply to the charging, use, location and emptying of water and toilet systems fitted to road vehicles. See the relevant advice in the officially recommended syllabus in section 5 of this book.

Double-deck coaches

The first double-deck coaches were introduced in the UK in the 1950s. They were based on bus body shells, but were fitted with more powerful engines and higher gearing. Coach seats were added to provide high-capacity, luxury vehicles able to compete with other modes of long-distance passenger transport.

Since then there have been considerable developments, not least in the facilities double-deck coaches now offer. Nearly all are now specially designed and purpose-built. Comfort and customer service are the biggest selling points. Although some double-deck coaches provide 70 or more seats, passenger-carrying capacity isn't always the key attraction to customers.

These coaches may be fitted with

- toilets
- refreshment facilities
- lounges
- tables
- telephones and fax machines
- audiovisual equipment
- crew sleeping accommodation.

A number of double-deck coaches have a courier service and some specialist vehicles are designed to carry as few as 12 passengers, with full sleeping or conference facilities provided.

The regulations governing video and television equipment and waste water disposal are similar to those for single-deck coaches: these are covered in more detail in the syllabus in section 5 of this book.

These coaches are among the most sophisticated vehicles on the road, with high-power engines; versatile manual, automatic, semi-automatic or electronic gearboxes; air suspension; and power-assisted controls.

Make sure that you understand all the systems fitted to the vehicle and are fully competent to operate them.

For seat belt information, see page 53.

Driving positions may be unusual in these vehicles, so

- the driver may not be able to see what's happening inside the coach
- video or electronic sensor systems may be fitted to help with manoeuvring and to add to the view given by the rear-view mirrors
- additional mirrors may be fitted to show the driver what's happening below their field of vision at the front of the coach.

Use all these aids when driving to help you to drive safely.

Tri-axle buses and coaches

Higher vehicle weight has meant that air suspension is increasingly being fitted to all but the lightest PCVs to improve passenger comfort. It helps counter the damaging effects on roads and bridges and assists the dynamic handling of the vehicle. Another recent development has been the addition of a third rear axle to further distribute vehicle loads.

Handling isn't greatly different from that of two-axle vehicles, except that punctures and blow-outs are sometimes difficult to detect. Therefore, frequent tyre checks are advised.

The course that the wheels take on tight corners should be observed and allowed for when driving. Very low speed is advisable when the steering is on full lock in order to minimise any possible scrubbing effect on the rearmost tyres.

Follow the seat belt instructions given on page 53 if your tri-axle coach is fitted with seat belts.

Mobile project and playbuses

More than 500 double- and single-deck buses and coaches have been converted for community use in the UK. As their primary purpose is for recreational, vocational or educational use, they aren't regarded as PCVs.

There are particular rules for their use and licensing requirements (see section 7 in this book). They may, in some cases, be driven by category B (car) licence-holders. However, the driving requirements for these large vehicles are the same whether an additional driving test has to be taken or not. If you drive one of these vehicles, it's essential that you're fully aware of your responsibilities.

This book tells you what's expected of professional PCV drivers, but the advice applies to anyone who drives buses or coaches. A book can teach you the basic facts and theory about driving, but you should always seek professional guidance

before driving on public roads. You can't expect to drive a bus, whatever its use, without adequate training.

Most mobile project and playbuses are older buses that are 'life expired' for PCV operations. The importance of safety checks and adequate maintenance is greater as a result. Drivers must be able to identify faults and understand procedures for putting them right.

Operators and drivers of mobile project and playbuses need to consider the safe

- stowage of equipment when the bus is being driven
- manoeuvring of the bus when arriving at, or departing from, sites
- installation and stowage of any heating, lighting or cooking equipment, including gas cylinders
- operation of generators and fuel storage.

Detailed guidance is available from Working on Wheels (the working title of the National Playbus Association), whose contact details are given on page 322.

Historic buses and coaches

Enthusiasts have ensured that many historic buses and coaches have been preserved and are shown at rallies.

Some of these historic vehicles may be driven on a category B (car) licence provided certain rules are observed. These are

- the driver must be over 21
- the vehicle must carry no more than eight passengers plus the driver
- the vehicle must be used for non-commercial use only.

Drivers with category D entitlement may drive historic buses and coaches as they would any other PCV.

You should seek professional training if you intend to drive historic buses and coaches. For example, you need to know how to double-declutch (see page 330) to use crash or part-synchromesh gearboxes. These are special techniques that you should practise after they've been explained and demonstrated to you. Also, if the vehicle you drive has air or vacuum brakes, make sure that you understand the meaning of any warning signals.

When you drive a historic vehicle for the first time, start by mastering steering, gear-changing and braking techniques

- off the road
- under supervision
- without passengers.

Older buses and coaches are more difficult to drive than modern counterparts. Generally, there's no power-assisted steering, air-assisted clutches or semi-automatic gearboxes to make driving easier.

When driving these older vehicles

- think how your slower speed affects other road users
- pull over to let others pass, when you can do so safely
- treat the vehicle with respect and ask for advice if you come across controls or warning systems that are unfamiliar
- make sure that you have full control.

It's important that you never drive a preserved vehicle unless you're certain that it's fully roadworthy. Carry out all the checks advised in sections 2 and 3 and also make sure that you're competent to drive the vehicle.

Passenger and general safety

Never drive a bus in which you have no contact with passengers (eg a bus with a half-cab layout where the driver is segregated), without one designated, responsible person in charge of the passenger saloon(s). The exceptions to this are when no passengers are carried and when access to the vehicle is prevented by means of a door, chain, strap or other barrier. In addition, never

- allow passengers to board or alight from the vehicle, unless the parking brake is applied
- allow passengers to ride on open platforms or with open doors
- operate the doors while the vehicle is in motion
- allow more passengers to be carried than the vehicle is designed for, or the law allows
- allow bells to be used other than in the accepted way. In half-cab vehicles this is the only means of communication between the passenger saloon(s) and the driver.

The use of conductors has diminished and nowadays they may only be seen occasionally. If you're required to use bell codes, ensure that they're understood. As a driver, be aware that passengers may use the bell incorrectly. The bell codes are

- one bell – stop when safe
- two bells – move off when safe
- three bells – bus full
- four bells – emergency on bus.

Always take great care on rally sites when pedestrians are close to moving vehicles. Drive only at walking pace, or slower, and use marshals or other responsible people to help you to manoeuvre safely.

Emergency doors

Remember that the emergency door and any other emergency exits should be kept unlocked at all times when passengers are on the vehicle and when the vehicle is in service or on a journey.

If an emergency exit door is found locked at a roadside check, the driver would be prosecuted. For further information on VOSA roadside checks, see page 132.

Sudden faults

Occasionally, faults occur that can't be anticipated. It's important to take immediate action to correct these in the interests of safety for your passengers as well as yourself. For example, if you begin to smell fuel or exhaust fumes in the vehicle while travelling, or if a passenger reports such odours, you must stop immediately and arrange to have the fault put right before continuing.

Light rail (or rapid) transit (LRT) systems

Trams, LRTs or 'metros' are being introduced in large towns and cities to provide a more efficient, environmentally friendly public transport system. They reduce town traffic, noise pollution and run on electricity. Tram systems are common throughout Europe and there are plans to introduce them to more cities in the UK.

In some areas, the trams operate completely segregated from other traffic, but in other areas may also run on roads that are open to other traffic. As tram vehicles run on rails, they're fixed in their routes and can't manoeuvre around other vehicles and pedestrians. They may run singly or as multiple units, and may be up to 60 metres (about 200 feet) long.

The area occupied by a tram (the 'swept path') is marked by paving or markings on the road surface. This area must always be kept clear. Other road users must avoid blocking tram routes. Be aware of the following

- In some towns and cities certain roads are restricted to buses and trams only.
- Tram drivers and vehicles are subject to all the normal rules of the road, as well as specific rules about tram operation.

Drivers are only permitted to operate supertrams after extensive training. All UK LRT and traditional tram operators have dedicated training schools and staff to ensure high safety standards.

When a tram approaches, other vehicles (and pedestrians) must

- keep away from the swept path area
- obey yellow box junction rules and not block junctions
- anticipate well ahead and never stop on or across the tracks
- obey all traffic light signals and never jump lights that show the tram has priority.

Hazards

Open-top buses shouldn't be driven beneath overhead LRT power supply lines. Also, whenever possible, drivers of non-tram vehicles should avoid driving directly along metal rails, especially in wet weather, to avoid the risk of skidding. Take extra care when

- running close to the kerb in order to pick up or set down passengers
- lines move from one side of the road to the other.

Extra care

Take extra care when you first encounter trams until you're accustomed to dealing with the different traffic system.

Crossing points

Deal with these in exactly the same way as normal railway crossings. Bear in mind the speed and silent approach of trams.

Reserved areas

Drivers mustn't enter reserved areas for the trams, which are marked with white line markings, or a different type of surface, or both.

Tram stops

Where a tram stops at a platform, either in the middle or at the side of the road, follow the route shown by road signs and markings. At stops without platforms, don't drive between a tram and the left-hand kerb when a tram has stopped to pick up or set down passengers.

Warning signs and signals

Obey all warning signs or signals controlling traffic. Diamond-shaped signs give instructions to tram drivers only. Where there are no signals, always give way to trams.

White light signals may be provided for tram drivers.

Do

- watch out for additional pedestrian crossings where passengers will be getting on and off trams. You **MUST** stop for them
- make allowances for other road users who may not be familiar with tram systems
- be especially aware of the problems of cyclists and motorcyclists. Their narrow tyres can put them at risk when they come into contact with slippery rails.

Don't

- try to pass a tram where the road space is insufficient for both vehicles side by side. Remember that the ends of the vehicle sweep out on bends
- overtake trams at tram stops in the street
- drive between platforms at tramway stations. Follow the direction signs
- park so that your vehicle obstructs the trams or would force other drivers to do so.

Examples of relevant signage are shown below.

Towing trailers

Considerable care is needed when towing a trailer, especially when reversing. Extensive training and practice are strongly recommended.

When you tow a trailer make sure that

- access to emergency exits aren't obstructed or unnecessarily restricted
- you know and comply with the speed limits that apply to vehicles towing trailers
- you don't carry passengers in the trailer.

Any unattended trailer is a road hazard, especially at night or in poor visibility, such as foggy conditions.

New EC regulations are now in force covering the towing of trailers by motor vehicles. The information in section 7 of this book details how this will affect drivers of PCVs.

When uncoupling a trailer, select a suitable site. It should be safe and on firm and level ground. Make sure that you apply the trailer parking brake (handbrake) before commencing the uncoupling procedure (see page 310).

Vehicle maintenance

Preventative maintenance

It's important to keep your vehicle well maintained; breaking down while on the road can have road safety implications. Follow manufacturer's guidelines for service intervals. In addition to this, being aware of components wearing out or requiring replacement will help prevent costly breakdowns for your company.

The vehicle handbook will explain what work or maintenance can be carried out by the driver. Workshop manuals are also available for detailed technical advice.

Neglecting the maintenance of vital controls and fluids such as brakes, steering and lubricants is dangerous; they need to be checked regularly. Having your vehicle serviced according to its maintenance schedule helps the engine work more efficiently, thereby saving fuel and reducing the effect on the environment by cutting emissions. Causing excessive smoke is an offence, and also contributes

to the possibility of causing an incident or collision. If you notice thick black smoke coming from the exhaust, stop in a safe place and get help.

Ensuring that daily walk-round checks are carried out will enable you to find any defects that could become a problem and cause the vehicle to break down or be driven while illegal. The time taken to complete a thorough check will be less than that required to organise repair or replacement while out on the road.

Checks need to be made before you start up the vehicle or begin a journey. The consequences are too great to risk driving a vehicle with defective parts.

Daily checks

You need to check the following regularly to ensure your vehicle is well maintained and not in need of attention. Check

- there are no fuel or oil leaks, including missing or broken fuel caps
- the filler cap is securely shut before starting any journey
- the security and condition of your battery
- tyres and wheel fixings
- spray-suppression equipment (if fitted)
- steering
- excessive engine exhaust smoke
- brake hoses
- coupling security (if applicable)
- brakes.

See also the daily walk-round checks on page 131; they'll help you to notice if any part of your vehicle needs maintenance. Always refer to the handbook for your individual vehicle before carrying out any maintenance tasks and follow any safety guidance it may contain.

Drivers should wear gloves when checking oil reservoirs, fuel caps, emptying waste systems, etc to help eliminate the risk of infections or conditions such as dermatitis or eczema. Your hands will remain clean and this will also preserve a smart appearance for customers.

Don't forget to wear a high-visibility vest or jacket when making any check of the outside of your vehicle. For your own protection, it's vital to ensure that you're clearly visible. This is especially important if you have to work in an area where other traffic is still moving.

Technical support

Traffic commissioners and the Vehicle and Operator Services Agency (VOSA) will provide advice and assistance to operators on safety inspection intervals. VOSA offers a brake performance check service, headlight alignment and an emission check at all its full-time heavy goods vehicle testing stations.

Construction and functioning of the internal combustion engine

There are two main types of internal combustion engine

- spark ignition (petrol) – the fuel and air mixture is ignited by a spark
- compression ignition (diesel) – the rise in temperature and pressure during compression causes spontaneous ignition of the fuel and air mixture.

During each revolution of the crankshaft there are two strokes of the piston: the piston travels both up and down the engine cylinder. Both types of engine can be designed to operate using a two-stroke or four-stroke principle. Almost all modern passenger-carrying vehicles use the four-stroke principle.

The four-stroke operating cycle

- **Induction stroke** The open inlet valve enables the piston to draw in a charge of air when travelling down the cylinder. With spark ignition engines the fuel is usually pre-mixed with air.
- **Compression stroke** Both inlet and exhaust valves close and the piston travels up the cylinder. As the piston approaches the top, ignition occurs. Compression ignition engines have the fuel injected towards the end of the compression stroke.

- **Expansion or power stroke** Combustion created throughout the charge raises the pressure and temperature and forces the piston down. At the end of the power stroke the exhaust valve opens.
- **Exhaust stroke** The exhaust valve remains open, the piston then travels up the cylinder and remaining gases will be expelled. When the valve closes, residual exhaust gases will dilute the next charge.

Most diesel engines have pre-heaters, which head the glow plugs in the cylinders to assist in starting when cold. The starter should only be operated when the indicator light goes out.

Diesel fuel system

Compression ignition, commonly called diesel, engines are now almost universally used for large goods vehicles and passenger-carrying vehicles.

The fuel injection system functions by delivering a fine spray of a precisely controlled amount of fuel at very high pressure and at the correct time into the engine cylinder combustion chamber.

Many engines are turbo-charged, where the exhaust gas drives a turbine, which compresses the incoming air and effectively delivers more air to the engine. For a given size engine the power is increased and torque is both increased and maintained over a wider engine speed range than the non-turbocharged or normally aspirated engine. Both result in improved vehicle performance. A defective injector can have a detrimental effect on the engine, causing it to run erratically and lose power.

Never use poor-quality diesel fuel. This may lead to increased wear of the injection pump and early blockage of fuel injector nozzles. In winter the composition of diesel fuel is altered by the use of additives to lower the temperature at which waxing or partial solidifying of the fuel occurs. If waxing happens, the engine may not even start or, if it does, it may run unevenly or stop. Winter-grade fuels should be perfectly satisfactory in all but very severe conditions. Electrically powered fuel line heating systems are available if required.

Open the water drain valve, usually fitted to the base of the fuel filter, at least at the intervals recommended by the vehicle manufacturer.

Bleeding of fuel systems

It may become necessary to 'bleed' the fuel system to remove any trapped air if

- the engine is new or has been renovated
- the fuel system has been cleaned or the filter changed
- the engine hasn't been run for a long time
- the vehicle has been driven until the fuel tank is empty.

Engine lubrication system

The engine uses a pressure-fed, full-flow, wet sump system. The oil filter, which is normally disposable, contains a bypass valve, which operates if the filter becomes blocked. A pressure relief valve controls the oil pressure; this is situated in the oil pump housing. The oil pump is driven directly from the engine.

Oil is drawn from the sump to the oil pump via a wire mesh pre-filter. The oil circulates from the pump through the main filter, which collects sediment from the oil. The oil then passes to the engine bearings and other moving parts. Having completed its circle, the oil drains back into the sump.

Always use the recommended type and viscosity of lubricant as suggested by the manufacturer. The oil should also be changed at the required recommended intervals. Friction and wear will reduce the life expectancy and the performance of a vehicle. Friction increases when there's direct metal-to-metal contact between sliding parts. Lubrication helps prevent such contact by reducing wear from friction and heat on working parts within the engine. A film of lubrication covers the various surfaces to keep them apart and maintain fluid friction rather than a dry friction.

Lubrication prevents corrosion of the internal components in the engine. It removes the heat generated in the bearings or caused by combustion and absorbed by metal components.

It's also able to seal piston rings and grooves against combustion leakage.

Checking oil levels

You need to check the oil frequently: make sure the vehicle is parked on a level area not on a slope. Check the oil while the engine is cold for a more accurate result. If your vehicle is fitted with automatic transmission there may be an additional dipstick for transmission oil level checks.

You shouldn't run the engine when the oil level is below the minimum mark on the dipstick. Don't add so much oil that the level goes above the maximum level; this creates excess pressures that could damage the engine seals and gaskets and cause oil leaks. Moving internal parts can hit the oil surface in an over-full engine causing possible damage and loss of power.

If the oil pressure warning light on your instrument panel comes on when you're driving, stop and check the oil level as soon as it's safe to do so. If the level is satisfactory, there may be a more serious problem such as failure of the oil pump, which would lead to severe engine damage.

Lubrication oil – engine

The oil in your engine has to perform several tasks at high pressures and temperatures up to 300°C. Lubrication resists wear on moving surfaces and combats the corrosive acids formed as the hydrocarbons in the fuels are burnt in the engine. Engine oil also helps to keep the engine cool. Use the lubricant recommended in the vehicle handbook.

Lubrication oil – gearbox

Most vehicles have a separate lubricating oil supply for the gearbox; it's especially formulated for gearbox use. Follow the instructions in the vehicle handbook.

Engine coolant

It's generally recognised that using an approved coolant solution, containing an anti-freeze additive, throughout the year will give you the best protection. Coolants ensure the cooling system will be protected from freezing in cold weather.

In addition to the anti-freeze agent, coolant contains a corrosion inhibitor, which reduces oxidation and corrosion in the engine and prolongs the life of the cooling system. The anti-freeze additive is an inhibitor called ethylene glycol that has a boiling point of 195°C compared to water at 100°C. The coolant solution is usually diluted with the same volume of water to give maximum protection.

Check the coolant level frequently; if you need to top up regularly it might indicate a leak or other fault in the cooling system that will require checking. Never remove the radiator cap to refill when the engine is hot, always allow the engine to cool before adding further diluted coolant. Don't overfill the system, as the excess will be expelled as soon as the engine warms up.

Transmission system

All transmission systems are vehicle-specific and you should check the vehicle handbook. However, to help you drive in the most efficient way, most vehicles are colour-coded on the rev counter (sometimes called the tachometer). This gives an easy guide as to the optimum use, with green showing the section giving adequate torque/power and optimum fuel efficiency. As a general rule you should normally keep the rev counter within the green band when driving.

Other sections may also be coded and colours may differ, but you should refer to your vehicle handbook as variations occur depending on the manufacturer. As a general guide

- **green band** normal use, adequate power and optimum fuel efficiency
- **amber band** occasional use when accelerating firmly
- **blue band** optimum use of engine braking
- **red band** avoid driving within this section as the engine could get damaged.

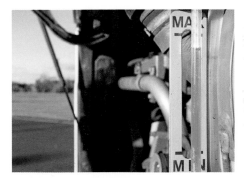

If the fuel is regulated by an engine management system, as it is on most modern vehicles, you don't need to press the accelerator to give additional revs when turning the ignition to start the engine. This causes excessive fuel injection and will waste fuel.

Manual transmission

A manual transmission system is made up of the clutch, gearbox and driveshafts. The torque is transmitted from the engine to the road wheels via the clutch and gearbox. The normal form of clutch is referred to as a friction clutch.

The clutch

This temporarily disconnects/connects the drive between the engine and gearbox. It enables the drive to be taken up gradually.

The three main components of a clutch are the driven plate, sometimes referred to as the clutch plate or friction plate, plus the pressure plate and release bearing. The driven plate is clamped between the pressure plate and the engine flywheel by spring pressure.

The engine creates the turning motion or torque, which is transmitted from the crankshaft to the flywheel. The driveshaft, attached to the friction plate, transmits the torque to the gearbox. Depressing the clutch pedal operates the release bearing to relieve the spring clamping pressure and free the driven plate.

The life of a clutch can be prolonged by careful use and avoidance of slipping or riding the clutch. Replacement should be done before the driven plate becomes too worn, as further use could cause the flywheel to become scored.

The gearbox

The purpose of the gearbox is to

- multiply the torque (driving force) being transmitted by the engine

- provide a means of reversing the vehicle

- provide a permanent position for neutral.

The gears contained in the gearbox allow the driver to vary the speed of the road wheels corresponding to any particular engine speed. This also results in varying the tractive effort, which is applied through the tyre to the road, to overcome the resistance to the movement of the vehicle while moving off from rest, accelerating and hill climbing.

It's common for around six gear ratios to be used in the gearboxes of PCVs and there's widespread use of semi-automatic and automatic gearbox systems,

to assist the driver and improve vehicle performance. In many systems, there's no need for a normal clutch pedal and vehicle movement from rest is achieved in response to movement of the accelerator pedal. Gear changing may be controlled by the driver (semi-automatic), be controlled hydraulically or, increasingly, by the use of electronic systems, to change gear according to the requirements of the vehicle use situation.

Older vehicles used to be fitted with gearboxes that required a driver to double-declutch when changing gear (see pages 64 and 330). On modern vehicles fitted with synchromesh transmission, there's no need to double-declutch when changing gear as this can waste fuel and cause unnecessary extra wear to the clutch.

Electrical system

Much progress has been made regarding the systems within vehicles so that most mechanical units are now controlled by electricity. The wiring requirements are so extensive in some vehicles that a system called multiplexing is used. This system is computer controlled; it uses a cable carrying electronic messages to switch equipment on or off. A power bus cable carries the main electric current to operate the equipment.

PCV and LGV vehicles commonly use 24 volt lead/acid batteries to provide the power to start the vehicle. Once the engine is running, the alternator takes over and provides the electrical power needed while also recharging the battery. The alternator generates electrical current and is usually directly driven by the engine via a belt. A controlled current is directed to the battery, which enables it to remain charged and provide current for other electrical systems of the vehicle, such as the lighting system. If the ignition light comes on when you're driving, this indicates an electrical fault of some kind. Get it checked as soon as possible.

Fuses of varying ratings, dependent on the power consumption, protect the different circuits within the vehicle. They prevent excess current from overloading the system, which may cause electrical fires. It's advisable to carry spare fuses, but make sure that you use the correct rating and find out why the fuse blew before replacing it.

Care should be taken when checking batteries as explosive gases build up and the dilute sulphuric acid used as an electrolyte will burn skin. Always follow the manufacturer's recommendations when dealing with batteries. There's a leaflet available free from HSE, 'Using electric storage batteries safely', which warns of the dangers of charging batteries, and gives help and advice on the correct way to deal with them (see page 321 for contact details). Alternatively it can be downloaded from the HSE website at **hse.gov.uk/pubns/indg139.pdf**

Tyres

All tyres on your vehicle and any trailer must be in good condition. They need to be checked weekly for damage or wear and to ensure that they're at the correct pressure. Follow manufacturer's recommendations for the correct pressure required. Neglecting tyre pressures is a major cause of tyre failure: check your tyre pressures when the tyres are cold; that is, before the vehicle is used. Ensure that all tyres are suitable for the loads being carried. PCV tyres have codes indicating the maximum load and speed capability. These must be suitable for the vehicle's conditions of use.

The life of a tyre will depend upon the load, inflation pressure and the speed at which the vehicle is driven. Under-inflated tyres will increase wear of the outer edge of the tread area of the tyre. Over-inflated tyres will distort the tread and increase wear in the centre of the tread area of the tyre.

Incorrectly inflated tyres can cause a vehicle to lean to one side and result in a dangerous loss of steering control.

You should also consider the dangers of colliding with 'street furniture', including lampposts, shop awnings, trees and signs. Double-deck and high vehicles are particularly at risk.

Radial ply tyres have textile cords arranged radially across the tyre almost at right angles to the width of the tread. The tyre walls are quite supple and a rubber-covered steel mesh belt, which runs around the tyre underneath the tread rubber, braces the tread area. The belt keeps the tread in flat contact with the road to improve traction and grip. Energy-saving tyres have a reduced rolling resistance so they contribute to better fuel economy.

Tyres should be checked regularly for damage or bulges, tread wear, and correct pressure. Any serious fault such as a lump or bulge in the tyre wall, exposed ply or cord, or deep cuts more than one inch (25 mm) long will make that tyre illegal for a large vehicle.

Some PCVs are designed to have different sized wheels on the front and the rear, but sizes should never be mixed on the same axle.

Keeping tyres correctly inflated will help prevent failure and also improve fuel consumption: using radial ply tyres can improve consumption by 5–10%.

The tread depth of tyres used on PCVs with more than eight passenger seats must be at least 1 mm across three-quarters of the breadth of the tread, and in a continuous band around the entire circumference.

Check wheels and tyres for balance to avoid uneven wear. When a wheel and tyre rotate they're subject to centrifugal forces. If the mass of the wheel and tyre is dispersed uniformly then the wheel is balanced. Clip-on balance weights are used to rectify any imbalance.

Commercial vehicles with tubeless tyres use metal valve stems fitted to the wheel rim. Either an O-ring or a flat-flanged rubber washer makes the sealing airtight. Vehicles fitted with tube tyres have an adaptor, which is moulded to a rubber patch and vulcanised to the inner tube. The valve-stem casing is then screwed on to the tube adaptor.

Changing a tyre

Great care must be taken when changing the tyre of a large vehicle and it's often better to call out a professional tyre fitter. If you're forced to change a tyre you should

- select a firm, flat surface
- check that the parking brake is applied
- ensure the passengers or other personnel are clear of the area in which you're working
- check the wheel isn't damaged and that another tyre can be fitted to it
- deflate the tyre before attempting to remove the wheel
- not loosen or unscrew the clamping nuts if they're connected to divided wheel rims
- take care not to damage the flanges and locking rings when taking the tyre off.

Fitting a new tyre

As a driver, it's unlikely that you'll ever have to fit a new tyre. However, it's still useful for you to be aware of the procedure involved.

Having checked the condition of the wheel before replacing with a correctly sized tyre, you should

- renew the complete valve whenever a tubeless tyre is being replaced
- fit the wheel to the tyre while the wheel is lying flat on the ground. This will enable the tyre to fit the rim and obtain a good airtight seal
- inflate commercial tyres in a cage or similar safety cell
- inflate the tyre to 1 bar level with the valve core removed
- insert a valve core
- inflate the tyre to manufacturer's recommendation

- fully tighten the wheel nuts, to the torque recommended by the vehicle manufacturer, using a calibrated torque wrench. Tighten the wheel fixings gradually and alternately diagonally across the wheel. Recheck the torque after about 30 minutes if the vehicle remains stationary or after 40 to 80 km (25 to 50 miles), if used.

Power tools aren't recommended for tightening wheel fixings. It's recommended that pressure gauges are checked frequently for accuracy. When leaving areas with loose debris, check between the tyres for bricks or other large objects that could damage your tyres or those of traffic behind you should they fall out.

Fitting wheels

As a driver you're unlikely to have to change a wheel. Many companies will only allow specialist fitters and breakdown organisations to change wheels. However, the following information may be useful.

- Never attempt to change a wheel by yourself on a motorway, dual carriageway or in a busy location.
- Be aware of the danger of other traffic.
- Ensure the vehicle is parked on level, firm ground and that no passengers remain on the bus during the procedure.
- The jack or lifting device should be suitable for the height and weight of the vehicle.
- When re-fitting the wheel, fully tighten the wheel nuts to the torque recommended by the manufacturer, using a calibrated torque wrench.
- Where possible get someone to assist you.

Please note that wheel nuts may need retightening after a short distance.

Coupling system

The coupling system is a device used to connect the PCV to a trailer. It permits articulation between the units. Guidance on the correct way to uncouple or recouple a unit can be found on page 310.

Maintenance

The coupling must be maintained properly to ensure safety. You should refer to your vehicle/trailer manual for maintenance intervals and lubricants.

Braking system

There are three braking systems fitted to PCV: the service brake, the secondary brake and the parking brake (also referred to as the 'handbrake').

The service brake

- The principal braking system used.
- Operated by the foot control.
- Used to control the speed of the vehicle and to bring it to a halt safely.
- May incorporate an anti-lock braking system (ABS).

The secondary brake

- May be combined with the footbrake control or the parking brake.
- For use in the event of a failure of the service brake.

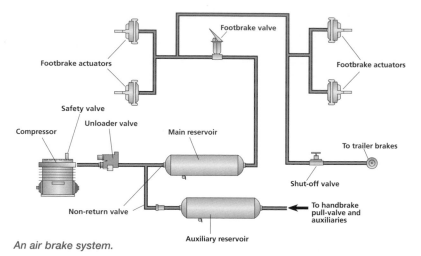

An air brake system.

- Normally operates on fewer wheels than the service brake and therefore has a reduced level of performance.

The parking brake (handbrake)

- Usually a hand control. It must be a mechanical device, which may be applied or released with power assistance. Most vehicles have spring brake chambers acting on the rear axle. These can't be released until there's sufficient air pressure (normally exceeding 60 psi) in the appropriate reservoir.

- May also be the secondary brake but should normally only be used when the vehicle is stationary.

- Must always be set when the vehicle is left unattended. (It's an offence to leave any vehicle without applying the parking brake.)

The minimum legal braking performance permitted for each system is

- service brake – 50% efficiency
- secondary brake – 25% efficiency
- parking brake – 16% efficiency.

Anti-lock braking systems

Some vehicles are fitted with anti-lock braking systems (ABS). Wheel-speed sensors in these systems detect the moment during braking when a wheel is about to lock. Just before this happens the system reduces the braking effort and then rapidly re-applies it.

This action may happen many times a second to maintain brake performance.

Preventing the wheels from locking means that the vehicle's steering and stability is also maintained, leading to safer stopping. But remember, ABS is only a driver aid. It doesn't remove the need for good driving practices, such as anticipating events and assessing road and weather conditions.

Anti-lock braking systems are commonly used on large PCVs and are required by law on some. It's important to ensure that an ABS is functioning before setting off on a journey. Driving with a defective ABS may constitute an offence.

The satisfactory operation of the ABS can be checked from a warning signal on the dashboard. The way the warning light operates varies between manufacturers, but with all types the light comes on with the ignition. It should go out no later than when the vehicle has reached a road speed of about 10 km/h (6 mph).

Note
ABS is the registered trade mark of Bosch (Germany) for Antiblockiersystem.

Endurance braking systems
Buses and coaches are also frequently equipped with endurance braking systems (commonly called retarders). These systems provide a way of controlling the vehicle's speed without using the wheel-mounted brakes.

Retarders operate by applying resistance, via the transmission, to the rotation of the vehicle's wheels. This may be achieved by

• increased engine braking

• exhaust braking

• transmission-mounted electromagnetic or hydraulic devices.

Endurance braking systems can be particularly useful on the descent of long hills, when the vehicle's speed can be stabilised without using the service brake.

Braking generates heat, and at high temperatures braking performance can be reduced. Proper use of endurance braking systems can prevent this from happening.

Using these braking systems will significantly reduce brake lining wear during intensive stop–start urban operation. However care must be taken to check the depletion of the air pressure in the service reservoirs due to the frequent application and release of the service brake. On long descents, the air volume usage often exceeds the replenishment rate of the compressor. This causes the service reservoir air pressure to drop below the normal maximum at which the service brake may operate.

The system may be operated with the service brake (integrated) or by using a separate hand control (independent). Retarders normally have several stages of effectiveness, depending on the braking requirement. With independent systems the driver has to select the level of performance required.

When operating independent retarders while driving on slippery roads, care must be exercised if wheel locking is to be avoided. Some retarders are under the management of the ABS system to help avoid this problem.

Safety
Air brake systems are fitted with warning devices that are activated when air pressure drops below a pre-determined level in one or more air reservoirs. In some

circumstances there may be sufficient pressure to release the parking brake even though the warning is showing. Under these circumstances the service brake may be ineffective. Therefore, you should never release the parking brake when the brake pressure warning device is operating.

On some vehicles a special brake may be automatically applied when the vehicle is brought to a stop. This is designed to prevent the vehicle moving until the accelerator is used to move off. This isn't a parking brake, however, so you shouldn't leave your seat until the parking brake has been applied.

Inspection and maintenance

You aren't expected to be a mechanic; however, some braking system checks are your responsibility. Before starting a journey, check the brake system warning lights. If the ignition switch on your vehicle doesn't operate these lights, look for a 'check' switch on the dashboard.

Action in the event of brake failure

In vehicles fitted with either full air brakes or air-assisted hydraulic brakes, in the event of loss of air pressure, there would be a warning light and/or buzzer to alert you, with sufficient reserves of air pressure remaining to allow you to pull up safely.

Some steep hills have an escape lane for traffic – particularly larger vehicles – travelling downhill. These lanes are most commonly used on long downhill stretches of road and are for use in the event of brake failure. They're designed to safely slow or stop the vehicle by use of an uphill gradient and/or gravel-filled arrester bed, either alongside or adjacent to the carriageway. These areas are not to be used for ordinary parking.

Emergency refuge areas (ERAs) are different to escape lanes and are more commonly found on motorways. They are defined as a 'place or facility where drivers can stop in an emergency'. Again, these areas are not to be used for ordinary parking.

Types of braking systems

Large vehicles mainly have full air-braking systems, or air-assisted brakes (hydraulic system with air assistance). Smaller vehicles have hydraulic braking systems (sometimes called a hydraulic vacuum servobrake circuit).

Hydraulic brakes

With hydraulic brakes, if the brake pedal travel increases or reduces, this could indicate a system malfunction.

For vehicles fitted with hydraulic brakes and air-assisted brakes, you should check the brake fluid level (and the brake fluid warning light, if fitted) as part of your daily walk-round check.

Before you move off, press the brake pedal to get a feel for it. If it's too hard, it suggests a loss of vacuum or that the vacuum pump is faulty. If the brake pedal gives too little resistance and goes down too far, it suggests a loss of fluid or that it's badly out of adjustment. If there are any problems, you should get the system checked by a qualified mechanic before moving off.

In addition test the brakes every day as you set out. Choose a safe place to do this. If you hear any strange noises or the vehicle pulls to one side, consult a qualified mechanic immediately.

Air reservoirs

Air braking systems draw their air from the atmosphere, which contains moisture. This moisture condenses in the air reservoirs and can be transmitted around a vehicle's braking system. In cold weather this can lead to ice forming in valves and pipes and may result in air pressure loss and/or system failure. Some air systems have automatic drain valves to remove this moisture, while others require daily manual draining. You should establish whether your vehicle's system reservoirs require manual draining and, if so, whose responsibility it is to make sure it's done.

Controls

Before each journey make sure that all warning systems are working. ABS warning signals will operate as soon as the ignition is switched on. Brake pressure warning devices may operate when the ignition is turned on (before starting the engine) or may be activated by using a special check switch. Never start a journey with a defective warning device or when a warning is showing. If the warning operates when you're travelling, stop as soon as you can do so safely and seek expert assistance. Driving with a warning device operating may be very dangerous and is an offence.

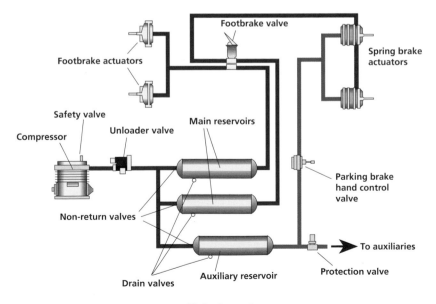

Air brake system

Other auxiliary systems

Auxiliary air systems

Modern PCVs may be equipped with air-operated accelerators, clutches, gear-change mechanisms, wipers, doors, suspension, ramps, lifts or 'kneeling' devices.

Drivers should familiarise themselves with the function and effect of these systems and be aware of any 'interlinks' that may be fitted. For example, air-operated accelerators may be disabled when the passenger doors are open.

Power-assisted steering

Older and smaller vehicles often rely on the driver's own effort when turning the steering wheel to steer the vehicle's front wheels. So that this effort is reasonable, a gearing system is used. The driver may need to turn the steering wheel several times to reach full lock (the tightest turn the vehicle can make). With historic buses it's necessary to drive more slowly round corners in order to give yourself enough time to turn the wheel.

To reduce the effort required and the amount that the driver has to turn the steering wheel, many modern minibuses, buses and coaches are fitted with a power-assisted steering (PAS) system. The power assistance is often incorporated within the steering box.

PAS reduces the driver's efforts when turning. However, it only operates when the engine is running. If a fault develops you can retain control of the steering, but much greater effort is needed to turn the steering wheel. Movement at the steering wheel may also be felt as a series of jerks.

Don't attempt to drive a vehicle fitted with PAS

• without the engine running – that is, coasting

• if the system is faulty.

If a fault develops while travelling, stop as soon as you can safely do so and seek expert assistance.

Underinflated tyres mean your engine is working harder. Keeping them at the right pressure burns less fuel and cuts your CO_2 emissions. For more about CO_2, visit www.gov.uk

section **three**
LIMITS AND REGULATIONS

This section covers
- Basic knowledge
- Environmental issues
- Drivers' hours and records
- Other issues
- Your health and conduct
- Your vehicle
- Your driving
- Anti-theft measures

Basic knowledge

The passenger transport industry is subject to a wide range of regulations and requirements relating to

- drivers
- operators
- companies
- vehicles
- passengers
- workshops.

The first thing you'll need to know about is your vehicle. The various aspects to consider are its

- weight (restrictions)
- height (clearances, etc)
- width (restrictions)
- length (lay-bys, corners)
- ground clearance (for hump bridges, grass verges, kerbs, etc).

Seating and standing capacity should be clearly marked on the inside of the vehicle.

You'll also need to know the various speed limits that apply to your vehicle and the speeds at which it will normally travel and cruise.

Weight

Weight limits are imposed on roads and bridges for two reasons

- the structure may not be capable of carrying greater loads
- to divert larger vehicles to more suitable routes.

Sometimes buses and coaches are exempt from the notified limits by means of a plate beneath the weight limit sign. This normally refers to PCVs in service or requiring to use that particular road for access. If you can use another route, do so. Remember, try to be considerate towards local people and the environment.

You should be aware of, and understand, the limits relating to any vehicle you drive. Certainly you should make sure that you know what your vehicle weighs. The unladen weight should be displayed on the nearside of the vehicle.

In many cases, weight limits apply to the maximum authorised mass (MAM). It's important that you never overload your vehicle or exceed this limit. To arrive at this figure, add about 1 tonne per 15 passengers to the unladen weight shown on your vehicle, plus an allowance for fuel (roughly 100 litres per 15 passengers) and any luggage you may be carrying (roughly 330 kg per 15 cases). The tables on the opposite page give three example calculations.

75-seat double-deck coach*

Type	Weight	
	Tonnes	Kg
75-seat double-deck coach	12	12,000
75 passengers	5	5,000
75 cases	1.5	1,500
500 litres of fuel	0.5	500
Total	**19**	**19,000**

16 passenger-seat minibus

Type	Weight	
	Tonnes	Kg
16 passenger-seat minibus	2.5	2,500
15 passengers	1	1,000
15 cases	0.33	330
100 litres of fuel	0.1	100
Total	**3.93**	**3,930**

45-seat coach*

Type	Weight	
	Tonnes	Kg
45-seat coach	10	10,000
45 passengers	3	3,000
45 cases	1	1,000
250 litres of fuel	0.25	250
Total	**14.25**	**14,250**

The weight difference between an unladen and a fully laden coach may be as much as 7 tonnes. The loading and distribution of large amounts of luggage can also affect axle weights and stability.

Definitions of terms to do with weight limits can be found in the glossary.

* If your vehicle has water storage tanks, you'll also need to know, and allow for, the total weight of the tank plus liquid content.

Height

If you're the driver of any vehicle of which the overall travelling height is more than 3.0 metres (9 feet 10 inches) you **MUST** ensure that the overall travelling height is conspicuously marked on a notice in the driving cab where it can be read by you

- in feet and inches, or in feet and inches and in metres so that there's no more than 50 mm difference between the height specified in feet and inches and the height specified in metres
- in figures at least 40 mm high, which can be read by you, the driver, when in your normal driving position.

You **MUST** know the overall travelling height of your vehicle before setting off. In addition, you should ensure that

- any height displayed on the notice in the cab isn't less than the overall travelling height of the vehicle
- no other information, which may be interpreted as the overall travelling height, is shown on the notice.

A driver may drive a vehicle higher than 3.0 metres (9 feet 10 inches) without displaying a notice showing the vehicle's height if there's a document in the driving cab, accessible to the driver, describing the route or giving information as to the height of bridges under which the vehicle may pass on the route.

On any journey, always stop and seek advice on an alternative route if you

- are diverted from your planned route
- realise that your route is obstructed by a bridge lower than the height of your vehicle.

Overhead clearances

Drivers of any vehicle exceeding 3.0 metres (9 feet 10 inches) in height should exercise care when entering

- loading bays
- bus and coach stations
- depots
- refuelling areas
- service station forecourts
- any premises that have overhanging canopies

or when driving under or negotiating

- bridges
- overhead cables
- overhead pipelines
- overhead walkways
- road tunnels

or when negotiating level crossings on lines with overhead electrification.

If you need to move to the centre of the road in order to pass under a low-arch bridge, stay aware of other road users who may not understand this manoeuvre. Be sure your way is clear before proceeding.

The normal maximum permitted overall travelling height of any PCV with fixed bodywork is 4.57 metres (15 feet). Many countries in the EC don't allow PCVs in excess of 4.0 metres (13 feet) unless an exceptional vehicle permit has been applied for, and issued, in advance.

Be aware of overhanging tree branches, particularly on roads rarely used by high vehicles, in case upper-deck windows are broken. Trees on regularly used routes are generally kept trimmed. If in doubt, slow right down and, if necessary, stop, get out and check.

In addition, most roads have a slope (camber) to help with drainage, and this can sometimes cause problems. For example, on roads with a severe camber, the top of a double-deck bus can lean up to 250 mm (around 10 inches) further over than the wheels. This situation could be made worse when pulling up at bus stops, if the nearside wheels drop into the gutter. Lampposts, traffic signs, shop awnings, bus shelters, etc are within this danger zone, so watch out for these hazards.

Low bridges

Every year a significant number of incidents occur involving vehicles or their loads hitting railway bridges. Bridge strikes occur for several reasons such as

- drivers not reading or obeying road traffic signs or the road ahead
- drivers relying totally on satellite navigation systems that don't include locations of low bridges

- drivers going off the set route, including under supervision
- drivers operating 'not in service' and taking a short cut
- drivers normally used to single-deck vehicles who may be driving a double-deck vehicle
- engineers with insufficient route knowledge returning a vehicle to the depot for maintenance.

You should always plan your route before your journey, unless you're supplied with a route already planned by your operations manager.

An impact with any bridge can have serious consequences. Collisions involving buses can kill or injure passengers and/or the driver, not to mention damaging the bridge. Striking a railway bridge with your vehicle puts the safety of road and rail users as well as yourself and your passengers at risk, because structural damage may be caused to the bridge. When a railway bridge is involved, such a collision will disrupt rail traffic and could lead to a major disaster. Your company will be liable for costs for bridge examination, possible repairs and delays to rail traffic, as well as damage to the bus and injuries to your passengers. There will also be costs to the community due to disruption resulting from the strike.

Signs showing height restrictions are generally provided at, and in advance of, bridges with headroom of 5 metres (16 feet 6 inches) over public roads in the UK. Where the overhead clearance is arched this is normally **only** between the limits marked and will reduce towards each kerb, so you may need to use the centre of the road when passing under the arch. Oncoming traffic may restrict the road width available, so give way until there's space for you to use the centre of the road in order to pass under the bridge. You mustn't swerve to avoid an oncoming vehicle when under the arch as you'll strike the bridge. Stop and, unless you can reverse, wait for the other vehicle to reverse.

Plan your route and read any signs. Never rely on a satellite navigation system alone, as even those designed for large vehicles may have out-of-date or incomplete information at any given time.

If you're not sure of the safe height of a railway bridge, stop and call the railway authority. To avoid problems

- plan your route carefully
- don't rely on satellite systems alone, even those specifically designed for large vehicles
- slow down when approaching bridges
- know the height of your vehicle
- keep to the centre of arched bridges
- wait for a safe gap to proceed if there's oncoming traffic.

If your vehicle collides with any bridge, **stop**. Your first responsibility is to your passengers, so check that there are no injuries. If there are, take appropriate action (see the advice on first aid on pages 225–227).

THIS IS BRIDGE EGM1/001

Saughton Road

between Haymarket and Edinburgh Park

In the event of any road vehicles striking this bridge please phone

THE RAILWAY AUTHORITY on 0141 335 3399

as quickly as possible. The safety of trains may be affected.

You **MUST** report the collision to the police. If a railway bridge is involved, report it to the railway authority as well, by calling the number shown on the bridge identification plate or, if no plate is provided, call **999**.

Do this immediately, to avoid a possible serious incident or loss of life.

Give your name and telephone number, as well as information about

- the road name, identification number and bridge location
- the time that the strike occurred
- any damage caused to the bridge
- whether the vehicle is wedged under the bridge and if persons are trapped
- the vehicle registration number and owner's name
- your insurance details as the driver.

The strike **MUST** be reported to the police via 999 as it's also a road traffic collision. Failure to notify the police is an offence. If there's no plate at the bridge giving a telephone number, the police will advise the railway authority. The railway authority will take action, depending on the bridge, to protect the safety of the railway so it needs to be able to identify the bridge involved. Arrangements will also be made for the bridge to be examined to establish the damage caused and the requirements for repair.

You must also inform your employer as they must report to the traffic commissioners any incident in which road traffic offences have been committed.

You **MUST** know the height of your vehicle: don't guess. If in doubt, measure it or look at the information shown in the cab.

Always be on the lookout for height restrictions shown on

• traffic signs

• road markings

• warning lights.

Stay alert to the dangers.

Effects of a bridge strike

Striking bridges is potentially dangerous and expensive. You could

• be killed or seriously injured

• cause death or serious injury to another road user or your passengers

• lose your job

• suffer serious economic loss

• cause serious disruption to the community.

Your company may lose its operator's licence and it will also be liable for the costs of bridge examination and repair.

Height guide	
Metres	**Feet/inches**
5.0	16 6
4.8	16
4.5	15
4.2	14
3.9	13
3.6	12
3.3	11
3.0	9 10
2.7	9

Electric cables

Overhead electricity lines crossing public roads will normally be clear for a vehicle of 5 metres (16 feet 6 inches) in height; (6.1 metres (20 feet) on DfT-designated high vehicle routes), but away from public roads, a clearance of only 4.4 metres (14 feet 6 inches) is available. As high-voltage electricity can 'jump' across a gap, the wire will be positioned higher than this to allow for a safe electrical clearance. This clearance **MUST NOT** be compromised. Height restrictions under overhead electrified cables may be temporary or permanent and may warn of a permanent restriction in advance of railway level crossings.

The power supply conductors for railways and tramways on public roads will normally allow clearance for a vehicle of 5 metres (16 feet 6 inches) in height unless the signage on the approach indicates otherwise.

At level crossings where the safe height is less than 5 metres, a height barrier will be provided in the form of a wire supporting bells. If your vehicle won't pass under this barrier it's not safe to pass under the electric line. You **MUST** obey the safe height warning road signs and you **MUST NOT** continue forward if your vehicle touches any height barrier or bells.

Open-top buses **MUST NOT** pass under the electric wires of tram systems or over railway level crossings with overhead electrical conductors.

Width

You must always be aware of the road space your vehicle occupies. This is particularly important where road width is restricted because of parked or oncoming vehicles, or in narrow roads.

Many local authorities now use traffic-calming measures, which often include road width restrictions. Watch out for these.

If you know of roads with such restrictions, try to avoid them, unless you're following a scheduled service route of course.

The majority of buses and coaches in the UK are 2.5 metres wide (8 feet 3 inches) but the legal maximum width is 2.55 metres (8 feet 5 inches). Mirrors and exterior trim can also add to a vehicle's width.

Where space is limited, take particular care when meeting other large vehicles. If necessary, stop first and, only if you're certain there's enough space, manoeuvre past slowly. Keep a lookout all around and especially watch out for mirrors hitting each other or lampposts, etc. A broken mirror means that your vehicle is unroadworthy and, therefore, illegal. It could also cause injury to you or others.

Length

You need to know the length of your vehicle, as well as its width, so that you can judge the space you need on the road. You'll also need to know these dimensions to comply with regulations that affect your vehicle.

Other than traffic-calmed zones, places where there are restrictions on vehicle length are comparatively rare. Examples are

- road tunnels
- level crossings
- ferries.

The usual maximum length for a bus or coach is 12 metres (39 feet 4 inches). Articulated buses may be up to 18 metres long (59 feet). At some level crossings, you may need to phone for permission to cross.

Drivers of long vehicles must be careful when

- turning left or right

- negotiating roundabouts or mini-roundabouts
- emerging from premises or exits
- overtaking
- parking, especially in lay-bys
- driving on narrow roads where there are passing places
- negotiating level crossings.

Be aware of the amount of space you need to turn (the turning circle) and the way that your vehicle overhangs kerbs and verges (the swept area). Take great care when turning, to ensure that any overhang on your vehicle doesn't come into contact with pedestrians, traffic lights, street furniture, posts or fences.

You must be particularly aware of the risk of grounding; for example, on a hump bridge, and you should look out for appropriate traffic warning signs.

Environmental issues

Vehicle designers, bus operators and maintenance staff all have a part in helping to reduce the effects that vehicles have on the environment. You can also help. You should be aware of the effects your vehicle, and the way in which it's driven and operated, can have on the environment around you.

The bus and coach industry has a major role to play in limiting the total number of vehicles on our roads. One double-deck bus can carry the occupants of 20 cars. Therefore, only one engine could be running instead of 20. However, a badly maintained or poorly driven bus can cause unnecessary pollution, perhaps as much as several cars.

There are many things **you** can do to help.

- Follow manufacturer's recommendations for servicing.
- If you do your own maintenance, make sure you take your old oil, batteries and used tyres to a garage or local authority site for recycling or safe disposal. It's illegal and harmful to pour oil down a drain.
- Make regular checks of your vehicle and ensure that any defects are reported and sorted out.
- Check excessive exhaust smoke (the public are encouraged to report vehicles emitting excessive fumes).
- Check uneven running, which may be caused by fuel pump or injector faults.
- Check brake faults, which can cause drag.
- Have correct tyre pressures.
- Make sure filters are changed regularly.
- Check suspension system faults, which may result in road damage.

Always drive with fuel economy in mind.
Operators keep careful checks on vehicle
running costs, and fuel economy is a key
factor for profitability as well as reducing
waste.

You should

- plan routes to avoid congestion
- anticipate well ahead
- avoid the need to make up time
- avoid over-revving (if a rev counter is
  fitted try to keep in the green band as
  much as possible)
- drive smoothly. This can reduce fuel
  consumption by 15%. Avoid rapid
  acceleration as this leads to greater fuel
  consumption, wear and tear
- avoid using the air-conditioning
  continuously as this increases fuel
  consumption by about 15%
- consider the use of cruise control where
  fitted, as this will help reduce fuel costs

- brake in good time (all braking wastes
  energy in the form of heat)
- make good use of regenerative
  retarders, where fitted. This is a braking
  system which allows the use of the
  vehicle's drive motor, or motors, to
  convert the vehicle's kinetic energy into
  electrical energy during deceleration.
  Also, by using this system instead of the
  footbrake, brake lining life is extended
- switch off your engine when stationary
  for some time, especially where noise
  and exhaust fumes cause annoyance
- allow air pressure to build up with the
  engine on tick over rather than revving up.

If your vehicle has a fuel consumption
readout display on the instrument panel,
use it to monitor the fuel used during
the journey.

Select for economy and low emissions

Consider the following points

- Vehicles with automatic transmission use about 10% more fuel than those with manual transmission.

- Consider using ultra-low sulphur fuel, such as city diesel, as it reduces harmful emissions.

- When replacing tyres, consider buying energy-saving types. These have reduced rolling resistance, and they increase fuel efficiency and also improve grip on the road.

Members of the public are encouraged to report any vehicle emitting excessive exhaust fumes.

Further information and publications can be found on the Energy Saving Trust's website, **energysavingtrust.org.uk**

Traffic management

Continuous research has resulted in new methods of helping the environment by easing traffic flow.

Traffic flow

Strict parking rules in major cities and towns help the traffic flow. Red Routes in London have improved the traffic flow considerably.

Speed reductions

Traffic-calming measures, including road humps and chicanes, help to keep vehicle speeds low in sensitive areas. Drive slowly over road humps and don't speed up between them. There's an increasing number of areas with a 20 mph (32 km/h) speed limit in force.

When buses are crossing road humps, the discomfort experienced by bus passengers can increase substantially as speeds increase from 15 mph towards 20 mph. To minimise discomfort, bus operators should consider adopting an operation speed of 15 mph or less when crossing road humps. You should check with your operator to ask about any specific company instructions.

For general enquiries about traffic-calming measures, visit **www.gov.uk**

Road-friendly suspension

Large heavy vehicles have the most impact on road surface and its condition. It's important that the vehicle's air suspension system is working properly at all times. Bumping over kerbs, verges and pavements damages your vehicle and can also affect underground services. Repairs can be costly. Many PCVs are fitted with air suspension to reduce wear on road surfaces. These systems cut down on vibration, which also helps reduce damage to things like bridges and historical buildings.

Damage to your vehicle's tyres, which may not be immediately obvious, can also be the result of poor driving and bad suspension. Subsequent tyre failure may have serious consequences, possibly to another driver and his or her passengers. Make sure that you drive responsibly and with due care, even if your vehicle is fitted with road-friendly suspension.

Fuels

Take care to avoid spillages when you refuel your vehicle. Diesel fuel is slippery and can be very dangerous if stepped on (especially in garage areas). On the road it can create a serious risk to other road users, especially motorcyclists. It's a legal requirement that you check all filler caps are properly closed and secure before driving off.

Exhaust emissions

Fuel combustion produces carbon dioxide, a major greenhouse gas, and transport accounts for about one fifth of the carbon dioxide we produce in this country.

MOT tests now include a strict exhaust emission test to ensure that all vehicles are operating efficiently and causing less air pollution.

If you're driving a vehicle that's emitting lots of exhaust smoke, you're breaking the law and risk being reported. If you become aware of excessive exhaust smoke from your vehicle, you should take steps to have the problem dealt with as soon as possible.

Diesel engines

These engines are more fuel-efficient than petrol engines. Although they produce higher levels of some pollutants (nitrogen oxides and particulates), they produce less carbon dioxide (a global warming gas). They also emit less carbon monoxide and fewer hydrocarbons.

Alternative fuels

To improve exhaust emissions even further, ultra-low sulphur diesel or city diesel fuels can be used. These have been formulated so that the sulphur content is very low. Sulphur is the main cause of particulates in exhaust emissions and it also produces acidic gases. The lower the content of sulphur in fuel, the less damage to the environment.

Electricity

Trials have been taking place with electric vehicles for a number of years, but it's only recently that advances have been made in overcoming the problems of battery size and capacity.

Fuel cells

These operate like rechargeable batteries and produce little or no pollutants, but have greater range and improved performance than most battery electric vehicles.

Compressed natural gas (CNG)

While there are improvements in the quality of exhaust emissions produced, some of the technical disadvantages relate to the size and design of the fuel tanks required.

Hybrid vehicles

These offer the advantages of electricity without the need for large batteries. The combination of an electric motor and battery with an internal combustion engine gives increased fuel efficiency and greatly reduced emissions.

Hydrogen

This is another possible fuel source for road vehicles that's being studied. However, technical problems include storage of this highly inflammable gas.

Liquefied petroleum gas (LPG)

This consists mainly of methane, produced during petrol refining. Vehicles can run on LPG alone or both LPG and petrol (known as dual fuel). Benefits include low cost, lower emissions and reduced wear and tear to engine and exhaust systems. Disadvantages include cold start problems and valve-seat wear.

Methane

Because of the naturally occurring renewable sources of this fuel, it's also being considered as a possible alternative to diesel oil, which is a finite resource.

Solar power

Needing only daylight to function, solar vehicles are small, light, slow and silent. They produce no emissions at all; however, they're very expensive as yet and improvements are needed so they can store energy for use in the dark.

Audible warning systems

Some vehicles are fitted with systems which warn people that the vehicle is reversing, such as

- bleepers
- horns
- voice warnings.

These **MUST NOT** be allowed to operate on a road subject to a 30 mph speed limit between 11.30 pm and 7.00 am. Remember, using an audible warning device doesn't take away the need to practise good, all-round effective observation. Get someone to guide you if you can't see all around when reversing. Large vehicles have more blind spots than smaller vehicles so always check carefully.

Also, take care when setting vehicle alarm systems. There are restrictions on the length of time that the warning may sound. Environmental health officers are empowered to enter vehicles and disable the system if a nuisance is caused.

Drivers' hours and records

Drivers' hours are controlled in the interest of road safety, drivers' conditions and fair competition. European regulations set maximum limits for driving times and minimum requirements for rest breaks. These are known as EC rules. Breaking these rules will result in heavy fines and you may lose your licence. It's illegal to tamper with, or alter with intent to deceive, drivers' hours records.

Analogue tachographs

When driving within the EC rules, drivers' hours and rest periods are recorded by means of a chart that's inserted into a tachograph. A tachograph is a device that records hours of driving, other work, breaks and rest periods. It can also record the distance covered and the speed at which the vehicle travels.

The tachograph should be properly calibrated and sealed by an approved vehicle manufacturer or calibration centre. These must be checked at a Department for Transport (DfT) (or DVA in Northern Ireland) approved calibration centre every two years and recalibrated every six years. A plaque either on or near the tachograph will say when the checks were last carried out.

If there's anything wrong with the tachograph it should be replaced or repaired by a DfT-approved centre as soon as possible. If the vehicle can't return to base within seven days of failure of the tachograph or of the discovery of its defective operation, the repair must be carried out during the journey. While it's broken you must keep a written manual record either on the charts or on a temporary chart to be attached to the charts.

Charts

You must carry enough charts with you for the whole of your journey. You'll need one for every 24 hours. You should also carry some spares with you in case the charts become dirty or damaged or if your chart is retained by an authorised inspecting officer. Your employer is responsible for giving you enough clean charts, of an approved type, for the tachograph installed in the vehicle.

You, the driver, must ensure that the correct information is recorded on the charts. You must enter on the chart

- your surname and first name (you should do this before departure)
- the date and the place where use of the chart begins (before departure) and ends (after arrival)
- the registration number of the vehicles driven during the use of the chart (this should be entered before departing in a different vehicle)
- the odometer reading at the start of the first journey and at the end of the last journey shown on the chart (and the readings at the time of any change of vehicle)
- the time of any change of vehicle.

Recording information

The tachograph will start recording onto the chart as soon as it's inserted.

You must ensure that the time recorded on the chart is the official time of the vehicle's country of registration and that the mode switch is in the appropriate position. The modes are shown as symbols.

- Driving (this is automatically recorded on some tachographs)

- Other work

- Periods of availability (POA) (only when length is known in advance)

- Break or rest.

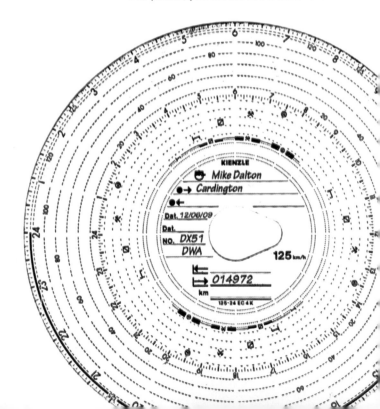

Under 'other work' you should include time spent on vehicle daily walk-round checks, attending training courses, loading and unloading and travelling (when requested by the employer) to join or leave the vehicle.

The above list is **not** exhaustive. If you're driving more than one vehicle in one day you must take your chart with you and use it in the next vehicle. If for some reason the equipment in the other vehicle isn't compatible, you should use another chart.

If you're working away from the vehicle and can't leave a chart in the tachograph (eg because the vehicle is likely to be used by someone else), or you have left a chart in but have changed work mode while away from the vehicle, you must make a manual entry on the reverse of the chart; eg OW 09.15–10.20. If your chart is dirty or damaged you should start another and then attach it to the damaged one.

Ensure that all the information for the day is entered on your chart(s). The obligation to record the complete information correctly falls on you, the driver, as well as on the operator. Heavy fines are imposed for the misuse or falsification of charts.

Chart inspections

Your tachograph records must be available for inspection at the roadside by the enforcement authorities. You must carry the record sheet (and printouts) for the current day and for the previous 28 days. (Note: you should also carry and be able to produce your digital tachograph driver card if one has been issued to you.) You'll be committing an offence if you don't, even if you're pulled over while driving a vehicle equipped with an analogue tachograph. If your records are kept by an enforcement officer you should ask the officer to endorse the replacement chart with his or her name and telephone number. The officer should also state the number of charts retained. Alternatively, he or she may provide you with a receipt.

To ensure that all records are kept up-to-date and available for inspection by enforcement

staff, you must give the completed charts to your employer within 42 days. This requirement must be complied with even when a driver changes employer. If you're working for more than one employer, you must provide each with sufficient information to make sure the rules are being met.

Mobile workers (see glossary on page 331) who work for more than one employer are responsible for notifying an employer in writing of any time worked for another employer. This information should be kept for a statutory period. Both the employer and the mobile worker share the responsibility for complying with the regulations. If the rules are broken, both parties are liable for prosecution.

The law says that employers must keep the tachograph records and printouts (where applicable) in chronological order and in a legible form for at least one year from the date of their use. They must be submitted to enforcement officers as required. Also, if a driver requests it, employers must provide copies of the records as well as, if requested, copies of downloaded data from the driver card. There are various methods of storing the charts (eg on pegs, in envelopes, in folders, and either under vehicle registration or under each driver's name).

Working time records

The law says that employers must keep a record of the hours worked by all employees, including mobile workers. This can be in a very simple form, such as through the normal payroll system.

These records should be stored/filed for at least two years after the end of the period covered. Employers must be able to give employed drivers and other workers copies of the records of hours worked if requested.

Digital tachographs

Digital tachographs became mandatory on all new PCVs 'in-scope' of EU drivers' hours rules on 1 May 2006.

These convert the signal into encrypted electronic data stored in both the vehicle unit (VU) and the **driver smart card**. The VU records the vehicle movement as well as the drivers who use the vehicle. The driver smart card records all the driver's activities as well as details of the vehicle driven. Digital tachographs have to be calibrated before use and every two years from the previous calibration or after each repair, whichever is the earlier (and also if tyre sizes are changed). A plaque either on or near the tachograph will say when the last calibration was carried out.

The digital tachograph records all movement of the vehicle along with a record of driver(s) and crew who have inserted their card into the tachograph when driving or conducting other duties. Unlike the analogue tachograph, which will only record activity onto a paper chart, the digital tachograph will record the date, time and duration of all driving activity irrespective of whether a driver smart card has been inserted into the tachograph. You must be able to take prints from the VU

when requested so you should ensure that you carry sufficient print roll. If the card and VU are correctly functioning but you haven't entered any periods of work that occurred prior to inserting the driver card or after removing the driver card, or if you breach drivers' hours rules because of unforeseen circumstances, then you must take a print of your activities that day and make a manual entry on the reverse of the print roll.

The tachograph also records within its own memory a record of events and faults such as driving without a driver card inserted, speeding, power disconnections, security breach attempts etc, as well as a detailed speed trace for the last 24 hours of actual driving. Downloading and storing of data should be carried out frequently enough for the operator to be able to monitor the driver's hours and record-keeping and at least as frequently as regulations require.

As with analogue tachographs, if the digital tachograph becomes faulty, drivers may continue to use the vehicle, but must make a manual temporary record. This should contain data enabling the driver to be identified (driver card number and/or name and/or driving licence number) including their signature, plus all information for the various periods of time, which can no longer be recorded or printed out correctly by the recording equipment.

Drivers should take a print at the start and end of the day. They can continue to drive without a driver card for a maximum of 15 calendar days. If they don't have a replacement card by then they must cease driving vehicles equipped with digital tachographs.

Driver smart cards

These are compulsory – a driver cannot legally drive a vehicle 'in-scope' of EU Drivers' Hours Regulations equipped with a digital tachograph unless he or she has first been issued with a driver smart card. Driver cards for digital tachographs are issued by the Driver and Vehicle Licensing Agency (DVLA), Swansea. Apply for a digital tachograph driver smart card at **www.gov.uk**

Replacement cards can be collected from a local DVLA office or a VOSA testing station. In Northern Ireland, the cards are issued by the Driver and Vehicle Agency (DVA). The card, like a driving licence, belongs to the Secretary of State for Transport.

The driver smart card is intended to prevent drivers' hours offences. Cards are personalised to the driver and include

- identification information
- expiry date
- driving licence number
- a photograph of the driver

- copy of the driver's signature
- the unique issue number of the card.

Information is held electronically on the card chip as well as being printed on the card. If, on reporting for work and intending to drive a vehicle equipped with a digital tachograph, you find you've left your card at home, you should return home to collect it.

Drivers aren't allowed to have more than one valid driver smart card issued to them. Cards are valid for a maximum period of five years. You should receive a reminder about three months before the expiry date. However, it's your responsibility to make sure that you apply for a new card at least 15 days before the old one expires.

The driver smart card should be inserted into the digital tachograph whenever the driver takes charge of a vehicle equipped with one. The tachograph will then prompt the driver to manually enter a record of any work activities undertaken since the card was last removed from a digital tachograph. Where the driver conducts both 'in-scope' and 'out-of-scope' driving this also can be recorded by a manual entry.

The driver smart card allows for a record normally spanning a period covering 28 days on which driving and other activities have been recorded (this is based on 97 activity changes per day). The card will start to over-write the earliest records once full so it's a legal requirement that data is downloaded from driver smart cards and stored before this occurs.

Drivers, when in charge of a vehicle, are currently required to be able to provide records of their activities covering the current day and the previous 28 days, ie driver smart card together with any analogue charts.

Irrespective of whether drivers have driven a digital tachograph equipped vehicle during this period, if they've been issued with a driver smart card they must carry the card at all times when driving to enable inspection and checking of the data record by VOSA (DVA in NI) or the police.

Lost or stolen driver smart cards

As a professional driver, you have a responsibility to report any loss or theft of your digital smart card to the DVLA. This must be done within seven days. (In Northern Ireland, report to DVA.) You can apply for a replacement card by phone if no details have changed on the card. You can make payment Visa, Mastercard, Maestro or Delta.

Replacement cards can be collected from a DVLA local office or VOSA testing station, once you've been advised that the card is ready. In Northern Ireland, the replacement card must be collected and signed for by you in person at a local vehicle licensing office or DVA test centre, and you must state the most convenient location for card collection.

If your card is lost, stolen or faulty, you must take a print at the start and end of the day, showing start and end times. On both prints you need to list manual

entries showing periods of driving, rest, breaks, other work and availability. You also need to add your

• name

• licence number or driver card number

• signature.

You can do this for a maximum of 15 calendar days. If you don't have a replacement card by then, you must cease driving vehicles equipped with digital tachographs.

Company cards

These are used as a key by vehicle operators to lock in data recorded when the vehicle is being used by their drivers – doing so enables them to readily identify their own data and prevents unauthorised persons from being able to see or download their data. The card also acts as the key that enables them to download data from the tachograph. Without the company card and suitable equipment and/or access to support services an operator won't be able to properly manage data.

Workshop cards

A workshop card is issued only to qualified fitters who have successfully completed a training course that has been approved by VOSA. It should be used in the same way as a driver card, during digital tachograph-related road tests, to enable this to be recorded together with the calibration or check. This will then form a complete record of the activities relating to a vehicle, which can be downloaded at a later time.

The loss or malfunction of a card, because of the security implications, must be notified immediately to VOSA, and a replacement card will be issued through a VOSA office. A workshop card mustn't be used as a company card and, as this would be recorded by the VU, any such abuse or any other illegal use would probably lead to the card being withdrawn. Workshop cards will be issued to the holders of company cards only under the strictest conditions, with the consequences of illegal use fully explained.

Control cards

These are used by VOSA (DVA in NI) enforcement officers or the police. An enforcement officer or examiner can use this card to download information from a digital tachograph. You must stop when requested to do so by such officers. Any person who fails to comply with, or obstructs, a vehicle examiner during the course of their duties, can be fined up to a maximum of £5000.

Tampering

Drivers who are convicted of forging, using or altering in any way, the seal of the tachograph with intent to deceive, can be fined up to the statutory maximum of £5000, or be imprisoned for a term not exceeding two years. The penalty for tampering with tachographs/data, or falsifying records sheets/driver cards, is two years imprisonment or the statutory maximum fine (currently £5000), or it can be both.

EC drivers' hours

'Driving' means being at the controls of a vehicle for the purposes of controlling its movement, whether it's moving or stationary with the engine running.

Drivers' hours regulations

An EU regulation on drivers' hours (Regulation (EC) No 561/2006) was introduced on 11 April 2007. It aims to simplify and clarify the rules and update the exemptions and national deviations. For more information about drivers' hours regulations, visit **www.gov.uk**

Daily driving

A day is defined as any period of 24 hours beginning when you start other work or driving after the last daily or weekly rest period. The maximum daily hours you may drive is nine. This can be increased to 10 hours twice a week.

daily rest period | 4.5 hours driving | 45 mins break | 4.5 hours driving | 45 mins break | 1 hr driving | daily rest period

The daily driving period must be between two daily rest periods, or a daily rest period and a weekly rest period.

Unforeseen events

Providing road safety isn't compromised, a departure from the rules may be permitted. This is only to enable a driver to reach a suitable stopping place. The stopping place should be chosen to ensure the immediate safety of persons, the vehicle or its passengers.

Drivers must ensure that tachographs are annotated accordingly (on the back of an analogue tachograph chart or on a printout or temporary sheet if using a digital tachograph). The reasons for exceeding driving hours **MUST** be recorded while at this suitable stopping place. Repeated and regular occurrences could indicate that employers aren't scheduling work correctly. Examples of the reasons for such events are

- delays caused by severe weather
- road traffic incidents
- mechanical breakdowns
- interruption of ferry services
- any event likely to cause, or which is already causing, danger to people or animals.

This concession is only to enable drivers to reach a suitable stopping place – not necessarily to complete their planned journey. Drivers and operators would be expected to reschedule any disrupted work to remain in compliance with EU rules. To avoid exceeding drivers' hours when

experiencing traffic delays on a motorway, exit at the next junction and find a suitable place to take a break.

During a journey on which the vehicle has been driven on a public road, any driving off the public roads now counts as driving time and should be recorded as such. However, if no driving has been carried out on a public road then it counts as other duty and should be recorded as other work.

Breaks

You must ensure that you take an uninterrupted break of 45 minutes after four and a half hours of driving.

daily rest period	4.5 hours driving	45 mins break	4.5 hours driving	daily rest period

This break may be replaced by a break of at least 15 minutes followed by a break of at least 30 minutes, each distributed over the period. A break **MUST** be at least 15 minutes to be a qualifying break and the second break **MUST** be at least 30 minutes to comply with EU rules. A 45-minute break (or split breaks totalling 45 minutes) is required before getting back behind the wheel. During a break you mustn't drive or undertake any other work. For example

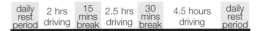

daily rest period	2 hrs driving	15 mins break	2.5 hrs driving	30 mins break	4.5 hours driving	daily rest period

Employers must schedule work to enable drivers to comply with EC rules on drivers' hours. However, providing road safety isn't jeopardised, and to ensure the safety of persons, vehicle or load, a driver may depart

111

from the rules in order to reach a suitable stopping place. Reasons for doing so must be recorded on the back of the tachograph record sheet. This shouldn't be a regular or repeated occurrence, as it would indicate that work wasn't being correctly scheduled.

Planned breaches of the driver's hours aren't permitted. If you're using a digital tachograph you must take a print of your activities and note the reasons on the back of the print. If the authorities find that any scheduled breaks have been missed, immediate prohibition and possible prosecution could result.

Daily rest periods

A regular daily rest period means any period of rest of at least 11 hours.

Alternatively this may be taken in two periods, the first of which must be an uninterrupted period of at least three hours and the second an uninterrupted period of at least nine hours.

Mon 06:00 — work + driving — rest 3 hrs — work + driving — rest 9 hrs — Tues 06:00

A reduced daily rest period is any period of rest of at least nine hours but less than 11 hours. This reduced daily rest period

cannot be taken more than three times between any two weekly rest periods.

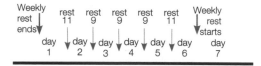

If you're taking your rest period when accompanying a vehicle on a ferry or train, a regular daily rest period may be interrupted not more than twice by other activities not exceeding one hour in total. However, the driver must have access to a bunk or couchette during that rest period.

Weekly driving

A week means the period of time from 00:00 hours on Monday to 24:00 hours on the following Sunday.

Mon 00:00	day 1	day 2	day 3	day 4	day 5	day 6	Sun 24:00
	9 hrs	10 hrs	9 hrs	10 hrs	9 hrs	9 hrs	

There's a weekly driving limit of 56 hours and you mustn't exceed 90 hours in any two consecutive weeks.

Weekly rest periods

A regular weekly rest period is any period of rest of at least 45 hours. In any two consecutive weeks you must take either two regular weekly rest periods or one regular weekly rest period and one reduced weekly rest period of at least 24 hours.

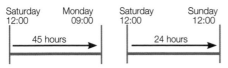

If you take a reduced rest you must add the period of time by which it was reduced to a daily or weekly rest period of at least nine hours before the end of the third week following the week in question.

A weekly rest period that begins in one week and ends in another week may be counted in either week but not both.

Any period of compensatory rest taken away from base can be taken in a stationary vehicle as long as it has suitable sleeping facilities for each driver.

Compensation of 12 hours must be paid back by 24:00 on Sunday of the third week following the week of reduced rest.

Catching up on reduced rest

If you've reduced your weekly rest period the compensatory rest must be added to another rest of at least nine hours. You can request to take this at either your base or where your vehicle is based. Rest taken as compensation for the reduction of a weekly rest period must be taken in one continuous block.

Two or more drivers (multi-manning)

If the vehicle is used by two drivers (multi-manning) each driver should ensure their card is inserted into the correct slot. The driver needs to insert their card into slot 1 and the second person's card goes into slot 2. The system records availability and time for the driver in the passenger seat who isn't currently driving. When the drivers change then the cards are swapped over. By selecting the 'crew' option the system will recognise that the vehicle is being used in a multi-manning capacity.

Multi-manning means that drivers' duties can be spread over 21 hours so that the duty time of the drivers can be extended. During each period of 30 hours, each driver must have a rest period of not less than nine consecutive hours. There must always be two or more drivers travelling with the vehicle for this rule to apply. A driver may take a break while another driver is driving, but not a daily rest period.

The internal clock of a digital tachograph is set to Universal Time Coordinated (UTC). The time display can be set to display any time the driver chooses; however, all data recorded to the VU or card will be in UTC.

UTC is effectively the same as Greenwich Mean Time (GMT) so it must be remembered that, during British Summer Time (BST), UTC time will be one hour behind BST. Any manual inputs for activities not recorded on a driver card must take account of the one hour time difference during BST.

In the interest of road safety all rules regarding drivers' hours should always be followed. However, there might be an emergency situation where you have to depart from the drivers' rules to ensure the safety of people, the load or the vehicle. In these unusual situations you should note the reasons on the back of the tachograph chart.

Regular services

A regular service on a route of over 50 km is subject to EC rules and a tachograph is now required to be used on such a journey.

A regular service on a route of up to 50 km is free from the EC rules but will, in most cases, be subject to the domestic drivers' hours rules.

Vehicles operating services under the 'permit' scheme may not require tachographs or be subject to the EC rules. The requirements will be explained when the permit is issued and will depend on the use made of the vehicle.

Domestic drivers' hours

The domestic rules apply to those vehicles on journeys within the UK that are specifically exempted from the EC rules. No written records are required under these rules.

Driving limit

You mustn't drive for more than 10 hours in any one day. This limit applies to the time actually spent driving. Off-road driving counts as duty rather than driving time.

Breaks

When a driver has been driving for five and a half hours and, during that period, they haven't had a 30-minute break for rest and refreshment, they must then take such a break unless the end of the five and a half hours marks the end of the working day. However this requirement doesn't apply if, in any continuous period of eight and a half hours a driver doesn't drive for more than a total of seven and three-quarter hours and that, between the driving periods, there are periods totalling at least 45 minutes in which no driving is performed and the last of their driving periods marks either the end of the working day or the start of a 30-minute break.

Duty (working day)

The working day mustn't exceed 16 hours. Between any two successive working days a driver must have a rest period of at least 10 hours but, on three occasions in a working week, the rest may be reduced to 8.5 hours.

Fortnightly rest

In every period of two successive working weeks, a driver must have a period of 24 hours off duty.

Record keeping (passenger vehicles domestic rules)

Under the domestic rules the driver of a PCV isn't required to keep records but, when driving such a vehicle, the driver must carry the record book at all times if he/she also drives goods vehicles.

Exemptions from domestic rules (passenger vehicles)

* *Emergency work* An emergency means an event which causes or is likely to cause such danger to life or health of one or more individuals or a serious interruption in the maintenance of public services for the supply of water, gas, electricity or drainage, or of telecommunications or postal services, or, a serious interruption of the use of roads, or, a serious interruption in private transport or public transport (not being an interruption caused by a trade dispute).

If a driver doesn't drive a commercial passenger vehicle for more than four hours a day in any week, they're exempt from domestic rules that week.

* *Partial hours exemptions* If a driver drives a commercial passenger vehicle for more than four hours for up to two days in any week, they're exempt from domestic rules, but on those two days

all duties must start and finish within a 24-hour period, a 10-hour rest period must be taken immediately before the first duty and immediately after the last duty and the rules on driving times and length of working day must be obeyed.

Mixed EC and domestic rules

You may find yourself working partly under EC rules and partly under UK domestic rules (sometimes even on the same day). In situations where you work mixed hours you must know which set of rules to apply.

Remember the following points.

* When driving under each set of rules you must comply with the requirements of the specific rules being followed.

* Time spent driving or on duty under one set of rules can't count as a break or rest period under the other set of rules.

* Driving and other duties under EC rules count towards the limits on driving and other duties under UK domestic rules.

* Driving and other duties under UK domestic rules (including non-driving work in another employment) count as attendance at work under EC rules.

Additionally, drivers who are members of the Territorial Army or Cadet Corps instructors have limited exemption from daily and weekly rest requirements in certain circumstances. Further details can be obtained from VOSA (see contact details on page 322).

Recording 'mixed' hours

Tachographs aren't required under UK domestic rules, but you'll need to make a manual entry on your tachograph chart, showing periods of domestic driving as 'other work', when driving under EC rules.

If you're using a tachograph when driving under domestic rules you'll have to record, on the back of the record sheet, the start and finish times of the domestic driving as this will automatically be recorded as 'driving' and not 'other work'. If you're using a digital tachograph you must take a print of your activities and note the periods of time on the back of the print.

Unforeseen events and emergencies

Employers must schedule work to enable drivers to comply with the EC rules on drivers' hours. However, providing road safety isn't jeopardised, and to ensure the safety of persons, vehicle or load, a driver may depart from the rules in order to reach a suitable stopping place. Reasons for doing so must be recorded on the back of the tachograph record sheet. If you're using a digital tachograph you must take a print of your activities and note the reasons on the back of the print. This shouldn't be a regular or repeated occurrence, as it would indicate work wasn't being correctly scheduled. Planned breaches of the drivers' hours aren't permitted.

Rules on working time

Drivers subject to the UK domestic drivers' hours rules are affected by four provisions under the Horizontal Amending Directive (HAD) introduced on 1 August 2003. These are

- a requirement to limit hours to no more than an average 48-hour week (although individuals will be allowed to 'opt out' of this requirement if they want to)
- an entitlement to four weeks' paid annual leave
- health checks for night workers
- an entitlement to adequate rest.

The reference period for calculating the 48-hour average working week is normally a rolling 17-week period. However, this reference period can be extended up to 26 weeks, if representatives from both sides of industry can agree to do so.

Self-employed drivers aren't currently subject to HAD, but this may change at some point in the future. However, there are some strict rules about who qualifies as 'self-employed', for example, those who work for just one customer are unlikely to qualify.

Drivers subject to EU drivers' hours and tachograph rules are required to adhere to separate working time provisions under the Road Transport (Working Time) Regulations which came into force in March 2005.

The following are the main provisions of UK's implementing regulations:

Weekly working time Mustn't exceed an average of 48 hours per week (calculated over the reference period of 17 weeks). A maximum working time of 60 hours can be performed in any single week, providing the average 48-hour limit isn't exceeded.

Night work Will be limited to 10 hours' working time in a 24-hour period, where any work is carried out during the night-time period of 1.00 am to 5.00 am. The 10-hour limit may be exceeded if this is permitted under a collective or workforce agreement.

Breaks When driving is being carried out, the break provisions under EU drivers' hours rules (EC/3820/85) take precedence. However, drivers aren't permitted to work for more than six consecutive hours without a break. Where working hours total between six and nine hours a day, a break of at least 30 minutes is required and at least 15 of those minutes must be taken immediately on reaching the six hours. A further 15-minute break is required (45 minutes in total) if total working hours exceed nine hours. Break periods can be divided, but their duration must be at least 15 minutes long.

Rest Same as EU (561/2006) or AETR drivers' hours rules.

Record keeping Records need to be kept for two years after the period in question.

As stated previously, the reference period for calculating the 48-hour week is normally 17 weeks, but it can be extended to 26 weeks if this is permitted under a collective or workforce agreement. There's no 'opt-out' for individuals wishing to work longer than an average 48-hour week, but break periods and 'periods of availability' won't count as working time.

Examples of what might count as a period of availability, the length of which must be known in advance, are

- accompanying a vehicle on a ferry crossing
- waiting while tourists spend time looking round each location (waiting time may only be classed as availability, if the duration of any such periods are known about in advance by the driver)
- for mobile workers driving in a team, it includes time spent sitting next to the driver while the vehicle is in motion.

More information can be found at **www.gov.uk**

117

Other issues

Security

In order to discourage crime and increase passenger confidence you should carry out basic security checks on your vehicle and be aware of security issues at all times.

Much of what's written about security is based on good housekeeping practices such as locking doors, windows, equipment boxes, etc. Suggestions for good practice are given below, but you should also make sure that you follow any security measures given by your operator.

Searching of buses/coaches

Search your vehicle at the end of a route, before starting your return journey, to ensure that nothing has been concealed or left behind. Checks should include underneath seats and any storage areas within the bus.

On a coach you should also check luggage holds, other storage compartments, overhead luggage shelves and toilets. You should follow any instructions given by the operator to deal with any items you find.

Securing of bus/coach

When you're at a stop and leave the vehicle unattended, eg at the start and end of a journey or during a comfort break, where possible make sure that passenger doors and baggage holds are locked and,

if appropriate, windows secured. If any passengers wish to re-board the coach for any reason during a designated stop, they should be accompanied at all times by a member of the coach crew.

Control of passengers boarding and leaving

Buses Carry out a security check before you let passengers board. Then only let passengers board when you're present. Carry out similar checks at the end of the route.

Coaches On a scheduled service where tickets are issued, make sure that all passengers present a valid ticket before they board the coach.

On any coach make sure that no-one is allowed on board without a valid form of authorisation (ticket or pass) for that particular journey. If you make a stop while on route, ask passengers to present their ticket before re-boarding. At the beginning of any journey and after any stops, make sure that the number of passengers on board matches your records for that journey. If you're responsible for loading the luggage, finish doing so before letting any passengers board.

Luggage reconciliation on coaches

Ensure that you, or a member of the coach crew, are responsible for loading and unloading all passenger baggage. It's important to make sure that all baggage is reconciled with passengers using your coach for that particular journey. This is to ensure that a member of the public can't place an item into the baggage hold without boarding the coach.

Remind passengers not to leave bags unattended and to report any unattended or suspect packages.

International travel

With the current level of threat to national security, coaches may be subject to search by a number of authorities at ports or the Channel Tunnel. If those authorities aren't satisfied, from a security aspect, with a coach or its passengers or crew, they may refuse to allow travel.

Documentation

When taking your bus abroad and in order to complete road journeys from the UK that cross international borders, a number of documents are required.

Passports The bus/coach driver or drivers – and all passengers or crew members in the vehicle – must each have a valid passport.

Visas Holders of EU passports don't need visas for entry into other EU member states, but there are many countries where visa requirements are enforced.

Driving licence Drivers must hold a licence appropriate to the vehicle they drive.

Luggage reconciliation

You should therefore try to ensure that you don't fail any security checks. For example, if a coach search is undertaken and any baggage is found that can't be accounted for (including items left from previous journeys), it may result in a significant delay while the baggage is removed and checked, or the coach may be refused travel.

If unaccompanied baggage or hand luggage (ie not belonging to a passenger) is discovered while on route to or from the Channel Tunnel or ports, contact your company immediately and make arrangements for it to be removed at the earliest opportunity.

To prevent the carriage of illegal immigrants

Coach drivers may be liable for penalties if they bring illegal immigrants into the UK in their vehicles. Each individual 'responsible person' (eg the vehicle owner, hirer and driver) may face a penalty of up to £2000 for each illegal immigrant carried.

The legislation requires the operation of an effective system to protect vehicles against the carriage of illegal immigrants. It's only by operating an effective system that penalties can be avoided in the event that illegal immigrants are carried.

An effective system consists of three separate areas – vehicle security, vehicle checking and documentation.

Security and checking All the points regarding security and checking mentioned above should be even more rigorously carried out when travelling abroad, especially if your vehicle has been unattended at any time when parked at a border crossing. For example, when searching the coach, check the interior (including under seats, overhead lockers, toilets, lounge/kitchen areas and crew compartments if accessible to passengers) and baggage compartments.

Before the return crossing, also check the engine bay, the underside of the vehicle and any other space accessible from the outside, including on top of the vehicle.

If you suspect your vehicle has been tampered with, also check for any visual signs, for example that the fuel cap is still in place and door locks are intact.

Documentation You should have a manifest (waybill) detailing the names of all the passengers and, before passing through immigration control, should check that all these persons are accounted for.

In order to show that you're operating an effective system you should, in addition to the manifest, have

- a document detailing the system to be operated to prevent unauthorised entry
- a report detailing the checks that have been carried out.

> **Remember,** it's only by properly operating an effective system that penalties can be avoided if illegal immigrants are found on board.

Lost property If an item is found in your vehicle you should hand it in to the operator within 24 hours. The item must be in the condition in which it was found, together with details of the property and the circumstances in which it was found.

The operator should keep it in safe custody, until it's returned to the owner or otherwise legally disposed of.

If it's not possible to hand the item in within 24 hours, the operator should be given full details as above and informed of where the item is being stored. You may wish to consider asking a suitable witness to check and verify the contents with you.

Driving in Europe

When driving abroad or in other European (or EC) countries you must carry your national driving licence, insurance certificate and vehicle registration document. Other documentation may also be required for some countries.

Public service vehicle operator licensing

A public service vehicle operator's licence is required for any vehicle that carries passengers by road for payment (this is called 'hire or reward'). Hire or reward is any sort of payment that gives a person a right to be carried on a vehicle regardless of whether a profit is made or not. The payment may be made by the actual person, or on their behalf, and may be a direct payment (eg a fare) or an indirect payment (such as membership subscription to a club, payment for a room in a hotel or school fees).

For further information on the requirement to hold a PSV operator's licence, contact your local traffic area office. For contact details, see pages 318–319.

Northern Ireland operations

In Northern Ireland, anyone who carries passengers by road for reward must hold a road service licence, which is granted by the Road Transport Licensing Division of the Driver and Vehicle Agency (DVA).

Your passengers

Various regulations cover how you should deal with passengers and their behaviour. Specific rules relate to

- the conduct of drivers, conductors, couriers and inspectors
- the number of passengers carried
- the carriage of schoolchildren
- the carriage and consumption of alcohol on coaches travelling to football matches, which is prohibited in England and Wales
- smoking
- passengers causing danger or offence by their behaviour or condition
- the carriage or use of dangerous, noxious or illegal substances by passengers.

In addition to the legal obligations and restrictions, most operators require that specific rules must be followed. It's in your own interest to read and comply with them. You may risk dismissal if you don't.

Your health and conduct

Health and safety

In Britain during 2009, around 7800 passengers and drivers became casualties in collisions involving buses and coaches. In the same year, 13 passengers and one driver died and there was an average of 17 incidents a day involving PCVs*. A small, but significant, proportion of these involved a PCV driver breaking the law in some way. Drivers are also prosecuted for offences where no incident has occurred. Don't let this happen to you. You must comply with regulations that affect

- your health and conduct
- your vehicle
- your driving
- your passengers
- health and safety issues.

It's essential that you know and keep up to date with the regulations and the latest official advice.

The total value of prevention of UK road traffic incidents in 2009 was estimated to be £15.8 billion. This includes an estimate of the cost of damage-only incidents but doesn't allow for unreported injury incidents. A number of assumptions have been made to produce a broad illustrative figure which suggests that allowing for incidents not reported to the police could increase the total value of prevention of road traffic incidents to around £30 billion.*

*Figures taken from Road Accidents Great Britain: 2009, The Casualty Report, published by The Stationery Office on behalf of DfT.

It has been estimated that up to a third of all road traffic incidents (RTIs) involved somebody who was at work at the time. This may account for over 20 fatalities and 250 serious injuries every week. Incidents involving buses and coaches account for less than 3% of all deaths and injuries caused by RTIs.

Many incidents happen due to inattention and distraction as well as failure to observe the rules of the road. These are published in an easy-to-understand format in The Highway Code. The DSA publication *Driving – the essential skills* also gives very useful information about best driving practice. This is in addition to the specialist advice available for bus and coach drivers given in this book.

Companies can suffer substantial downtime and staff may need time to recover, which leads to more vehicles off the road and lost business. Road safety is of paramount importance and it's the responsibility of all drivers to try to reduce the numbers of incidents on the road.

Health issues

Even apparently simple illnesses can affect your reactions. You should be on your guard against the effects of

- flu symptoms
- hay fever
- a common cold
- tiredness.

Fatigue and mental ability

Much research into the effects of fatigue and sleep-related vehicle incidents (SRVIs) has been undertaken on behalf of the Department for Transport. This research has shown that about 40% of SRVIs are probably work-related, as they involve commercial vehicles. These incidents are more likely to result in serious injury than the average road incident because they often involve running off the road or into the back of another vehicle, and are worsened by the high speed of impact (ie no braking beforehand).

There's a particular risk when driving between 2.00 am and 7.00 am because this is when the body clock is in a daily trough. There's another, smaller trough between about 2.00 pm and 4.00 pm. It has been shown that SRVIs are more evident in male drivers up to 30 years of age who often deny or ignore that they're suffering the effects of sleep loss or sleepiness.

It has been shown that sleepy drivers are normally aware of their sleepiness. However, there's always the possibility that drivers who are already mildly sleepy, because of previous sleep disturbance or insufficient sleep, are more vulnerable to any additional sleep loss and perhaps may not easily perceive an **increase** in sleepiness.

If you begin to feel sleepy, stop in a safe place before you get to the stage of fighting sleep. Sleep can ensue more rapidly than you would imagine.

The most effective countermeasures to sleepiness are caffeine and a short nap or doze (about 15 minutes). The combination of caffeine (in the form of a caffeinated drink; for example, two cups of caffeinated coffee) followed by a nap is particularly effective. This is because caffeine takes 20–30 minutes to be absorbed and act on the brain, hence the opportunity for a nap. However, this should be considered as a temporary measure only.

Fatigue can lead to reduced concentration and can also impair your reaction time. To avoid fatigue, it's important to take proper rest before starting duty and to take adequate rest breaks during driving and between duty periods. Always take planned rest breaks and, if necessary, take more rest than is required by law.

Stress

Driving in heavy traffic and trying to stick to a timetable can cause stress. Stress affects people in different ways. It can build up over time and cause various mental and physical symptoms. Mental symptoms include

- anger
- depression
- anxiety
- changes in behaviour
- food cravings
- lack of appetite
- frequent crying
- feeling tired
- difficulty in concentrating.

Physical symptoms include

- chest pains
- constipation or diarrhoea
- cramps or muscle spasms
- dizziness
- fainting spells
- nail-biting
- nervous twitches
- pins and needles
- feeling restless
- increased sweating
- breathlessness
- muscular aches
- difficulty with sleeping.

Becoming over-stressed may cause you to make poor and potentially dangerous decisions while driving. In the longer term stress can also result in the development of more serious medical problems including high blood pressure, heart attack and stroke.

Falling asleep

Falling asleep while driving accounts for a significant proportion of vehicle incidents, particularly under monotonous driving conditions. Incidents where vehicles have

- left the road
- collided with broken-down vehicles, police patrol officers or other people on the hard shoulder of motorways

have now been attributed to the problem of drivers falling asleep at the wheel.

Be on your guard against boredom on comparatively empty roads or motorways, especially at night. Always

- take planned rest breaks
- keep fresh air circulating around the driving area
- avoid allowing the driving area to become too warm
- avoid driving if you aren't 100% fit
- avoid driving after a heavy meal.

Stop at the next lay-by or pull off the motorway (or slip road) into a service station if there's one available, if you start to feel tired. As a professional driver you must make sure you're always fit and able to concentrate for the whole of your shift. A relief driver should be used at any time if you feel unwell.

Modern vehicles with air suspension, power-assisted steering and automatic transmission are less demanding to drive, but road and traffic conditions require full concentration at all times.

Alcohol

It's an offence to drive with

- a breath alcohol level in excess of 35 µg per 100 ml
- a blood alcohol level in excess of 80 mg per 100 ml.

Be aware that alcohol may remain in the body for around 24–48 hours. Your ability to react quickly may be reduced, and the effects will still be evident the next morning so you could still fail a breath test.

Your body tissues actually need up to 48 hours to recover, although your breath/blood alcohol levels may appear normal after 24 hours. The only safe limit, ever, is a zero limit.

The police can ask you to perform a breath test if they suspect you've been drinking. This includes if your driving seems erratic or if you've been involved in a collision. Failure to give a breath sample is an offence. Drink-driving offences will result in mandatory disqualification from driving. If you're convicted of a drink-driving offence while driving an ordinary motor vehicle, a driving ban will result in you losing your PCV entitlement.

> **Remember,** don't drink if you're going to drive.

If you're disqualified and you're found to be two and a half times over the legal limit, you'll then have to satisfy DVLA's medical branch that you don't have an alcohol problem before your licence can be returned.

Drugs

Some operators, concerned about drug abuse among staff, have introduced random drug-testing for their drivers. Drivers who fail such tests face instant dismissal.

You mustn't take any of the following drugs, classified as banned substances, while driving

- amphetamines (eg diet pills)
- barbiturates (sleeping pills)

- benzodiazepine (tranquilizers)
- cannabis
- cocaine
- heroin
- methaqualone (sleeping pills)
- methylamphetamines (MDMA)
- morphine/codeine
- phencyclidine ('angel dust')
- propoxyphene.

Check whether any medication will cause drowsiness.

Unlike alcohol (the effects of which last for about 24–48 hours), many of the effects of drugs will remain in the body for up to 72 hours.

Off-the-shelf remedies, even everyday cold or flu remedies, can cause drowsiness. Read the label of any medicines carefully. If in doubt, consult either your doctor or pharmacist. If still in doubt, **don't drive**.

If you're being prescribed any medication by your doctor, make sure you tell them that you intend to drive and that you're a professional driver.

125

Smoking in work vehicles

Legislation was introduced in 2006/2007 in England, Scotland and Wales concerning smoking in certain vehicles and this particularly affects professional LGV and PCV drivers. You **MUST NOT** smoke in public transport vehicles or in vehicles used for work purposes under certain prescribed circumstances. Separate regulations apply to England, Scotland and Wales. You **MUST** ensure that you're aware of, and adhere to, all the legal restrictions (and any others that may also be introduced by your company) relating to whatever vehicle you drive.

Further information can be found at
clearingtheairscotland.com
smokefree.nhs.uk
smokingbanwales.com

Other safety issues

A wide range of activities are covered by the health and safety regulations. These include

- limits on the weight of objects that should be lifted manually (for example, loading suitcases)
- requirements for protective clothing when handling oils and other maintenance materials, and when disposing of waste (emptying toilet tanks, etc)
- safe operating procedures in the event of emergencies or breakdowns
- safe working practices in garages, bus depots and bus stations.

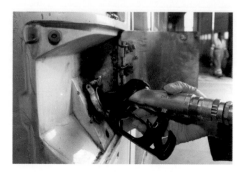

Safe working practices

Every year someone in the bus and coach industry is killed or badly injured in an incident involving moving vehicles in confined spaces. When parking close to a wall or another vehicle make sure that

- you leave room for other vehicles
- you're not trapping or crushing anyone.

The bodies of those vehicles fitted with air suspension may move a considerable amount when parked or when started, as air is exhausted or injected into the air bags. Parking one of these vehicles too close to a pillar, wall or another vehicle may cause damage or injury.

Vehicle maintenance and repair work isn't normally your responsibility. However, drivers are responsible for the condition of their vehicles when in use on the road. You should be able to recognise faults with your vehicle and fill in defect reports correctly, or inform the person responsible for recording faults. You may have to carry out minor emergency repairs on the road, when conditions dictate, but don't attempt anything beyond that. You shouldn't do any work on engines or any other vehicle components unless you're fully trained or supervised.

In workshops and garages, keep to the designated walkways and be careful of

- asbestos dust
- paint spray
- solvents
- exhaust fumes
- degreasing agents
- inspection pits
- moving and reversing vehicles
- vehicle batteries
- vehicle chair lifts or 'kneeling' mechanisms
- bus washers
- trailing cables or air lines
- spills of oil or fuel.

If you don't have to be in the workshop or garage, keep out.

The professional driving standards described in this book should also apply to drivers employed as shunters or mechanics who drive buses and coaches as part of their job.

You should always take care and do all you can to avoid incidents at work. Companies can experience substantial downtime because staff need time off to recover. This results in more vehicles off the road, and lost business.

Personal protection

Even if the activities involved in your job have no requirement for such things as ear protection or safety glasses, the two most important and essential safety items are

- a fluorescent and reflective high-visibility jacket or vest to maximise your visibility
- protective footwear to guard feet against drop or crush injuries.

Differing types of protective footwear can also guard against things like corrosive substances, oil or heat. It's important to ensure you have the ones most relevant to your job. High-visibility clothing is especially important when loading or unloading – there could be other vehicles reversing in the area around you, or fork-lift trucks in operation.

You should also make sure you're clearly visible during rest stops or breakdowns where you may be outside your vehicle adjacent to moving traffic. Drivers of passenger vehicles should also wear high-visibility clothing when making vehicle checks or when loading or unloading luggage. Make sure you carefully follow any instructions or procedures provided by your operator, who should provide you with advice on what protective equipment they feel is necessary.

Under the Personal Protective Equipment at Work (PPEW) Regulations (1992), every employer is required to ensure that suitable personal protective equipment (PPE) is provided to their employees who may be exposed to a risk to their health or safety at work, except where such a risk is being controlled by other means. Such equipment includes

- safety helmets
- gloves
- eye protection
- high-visibility clothing
- safety footwear
- safety harnesses.

The regulations also require employers to maintain, replace and clean any PPE to make sure that it's in a good state and working order. Employers also have to ensure that requisite safety equipment is at hand and their management must ensure that operators use it. Employees have specific duties under these regulations and must immediately report any defect in, or loss of, equipment to their employer.

Personal safety awareness

Consider your personal safety throughout any journey. Be aware of what's going on around you (especially if you have a regular known route) during breaks, walk-round checks, or when locking and unlocking your vehicle, etc. Proceed with caution – watch for anything unusual such as people who seem to be loitering or taking an interest in your activities. Follow any instructions given by your operator, stay aware and stay safe.

Diffusing an awkward situation

You must always ensure your own safety. Conductors should try to alert the driver as soon as possible if an awkward situation seems to be developing. Don't refuse help from customers but don't try to force their involvement.

Drivers should stay in their cabs, unless there's no alternative, as this gives some physical protection and control of the vehicle. You're also within easy reach of the emergency radio and/or vehicle alarm button. Activating the alarm could make any potential assailant back off or leave the scene.

If you're already out of your vehicle when a situation develops, and physical violence seems like a possibility, your body language can be important both to protect you and to help calm things down. You could benefit by

- standing at a 45-degree angle to the aggressor. This presents less target area which helps protect you; you also appear physically smaller and less threatening
- keeping your hands raised and open towards the aggressor. This helps signal non-aggression but also allows you to deflect a blow
- tilting your head slightly back and to one side, which lessens the effect of any impact
- keeping your body weight on the back foot, which increases the distance between you.

If you're confronted by an angry passenger, take nothing that's said personally. Accept that people do get angry on occasions and, as a company representative, you'll be the focus of this anger. They don't have the right to vent that anger at you, but you still need to be able to handle the situation correctly.

Don't aggravate any situation by losing your temper in return. You need to appear calm while being assertive in a positive and very specific way, using three main steps. The order in which these occur can be important in resolving a situation successfully. You should be

Calming Focus on what the other person is saying. Listen and encourage them to keep talking. Often all they want is to be heard. Avoid prolonged eye contact, finger-pointing or standing too close, all of which can seem intimidating.

Assuring Once calm, the aggressor needs to feel you've listened. Repeat the main points of their argument back to them to confirm this. Show some understanding of their situation. Avoid any body contact as this can be misinterpreted.

Controlling This is partly about offering a solution or a way out which is mutually acceptable. But think about what you're saying and how you say it. A raised voice could change the message you're trying to give from polite to threatening. Avoid sarcasm, or hot phrases such as 'So what?', 'I don't care', 'Whatever', as these can instantly give the wrong message.

Once the atmosphere has calmed down, try to explain the current situation, perhaps apologise for a gap in service provided or confusion over fares. Suggest they write to your company's public relations office (have a phone number or address available). This will normally help, as it lets the aggressor know you've listened and provided an alternative course of action they can pursue.

Your vehicle

The law relating to vehicles is extensive. Manufacturers, operators and drivers must all obey specific regulations.

The manufacturer is responsible for ensuring that the vehicle is built to comply with the Construction and Use Regulations.

The operator is responsible for making sure that a vehicle

- continues to comply with those regulations
- meets all current requirements and new regulations as they're introduced
- is tested as required
- displays all required markings, signs, discs and certificates
- is in a serviceable condition, including equipment, fittings and fixtures.

In addition, the operator must operate a system whereby drivers of the vehicle can report defects and have them solved effectively. The operator shouldn't cause or permit a vehicle to be operated in any way other than the law allows.

The driver has a legal responsibility for

- taking all reasonable precautions to ensure that legal requirements are met before driving any vehicle
- checking that the vehicle is fully roadworthy and free from significant defects before driving it
- ensuring that any equipment, fittings or fixtures required are present and serviceable, including a height restriction plate in the cab which should be visible to the driver
- not driving the vehicle if any fault develops that would make it illegal to be driven
- ensuring that all actions taken while in charge of the vehicle are lawful.

You should consider whether it would be illegal to drive the vehicle if anything that should by law be fitted to or carried on the vehicle isn't in place or in a serviceable condition.

Similarly, if something is fitted to the vehicle which isn't required by law but is

- unserviceable
- in a dangerous condition
- not fitted so as to comply with the regulations

you should consider its legal status. For example, your vehicle isn't required by law to have spot or front fog lights. However, if they're fitted they must be positioned no less than 0.6 m (2 feet) from the ground.

If a vehicle has to be taken off the road this can result in loss of revenue. The operator may not have a replacement vehicle to run a service and passengers may need to find other means of transport. This could have long-term effects on the number of passengers choosing to travel by bus or coach.

Daily walk-round check

A daily walk-round check (including items that need to be checked from inside the vehicle) must be undertaken and should cover

- brakes
- lights and indicators
- bodywork
- tyres

- windscreen wipers and washers
- horn
- fuel tanks/caps
- mirrors
- speedometer
- tachograph
- number plates
- reflectors and reflective plates
- exhaust system
- any coupling gear
- speed limiter
- seat belts (if fitted).

Any defects must be reported. Make sure you know the defect reporting procedure.

Remember, this list isn't exhaustive. There may be other checks you need to make, depending on the type of vehicle and trailer you're driving.

Your instructor or operator is the best person to advise you on the necessary checks your vehicle requires.

You should also make sure your vehicle is washed and cleaned regularly, both inside and out, particularly in winter, to ensure that windows, lights and mirrors are clean. This improves road safety and also presents an enhanced company image. Additionally, it will make it easier to identify defects during the daily walk-round checks and at scheduled safety inspections.

Roadside checks

VOSA (DVA in Northern Ireland) and the police both carry out frequent spot checks of vehicle condition. Where serious defects are found, the vehicle is prohibited from further use until the defects are rectified. Details of the prohibition are notified to the traffic commissioner.

VOSA/DVA officers may be accompanied by staff from other departments or agencies. For example, staff from a local authority environmental health department, who would check the vehicle and its exhaust emissions. They have the power to prosecute the driver and/or the operator if excess emissions are found.

Staff from a trading standards department would make checks on vehicle weights, and have the power to prohibit a non-compliant vehicle and/or prosecute the driver and/or operator. Department for Work and Pensions staff would be checking for benefit fraud.

HM Revenue and Customs staff can carry out a variety of checks during a roadside stop, which include checking for the correct type of fuel being used, and the type and legality of any load being carried.

Officers should be carrying identification. If you're asked to leave your vehicle by an official who isn't in uniform, you should ask to see a warrant card. The officer is likely to be a police or enforcement officer but, in the interests of safety and security, you shouldn't assume this.

Prohibitions A VOSA examiner can prohibit any goods or passenger-carrying vehicle that's being used illegally in respect of Construction and Use Regulations, including overloading, or if the vehicle is being used in contravention of the drivers' hours and record-keeping regulations.

A vehicle examiner issues a prohibition in respect of the vehicle when an offence or a defect relating either to the vehicle or to the driver is found at an inspection. This could take place either at the roadside or where the vehicle is parked. Most prohibitions come into force immediately but some, issued in respect of less serious roadworthiness defects, are delayed so that they may come into force up to 10 days from the date of the offence being found. The length of the delay will be decided on the road safety risk of the defect.

In all cases the fault or defect has to be rectified before the prohibition is lifted, therefore a prohibition issued in respect of a construction and use offence (including overloading) will only be lifted following an inspection of the vehicle. In many cases relating to more serious roadworthiness offences, that will mean a full inspection of the vehicle at a VOSA goods vehicle testing station. In the case of overloading the vehicle must be reweighed and found to be at or below the legal weight limits before the prohibition is lifted.

Some prohibitions issued in respect of drivers' hours regulations are for a specific period (eg 24 hours) after which time the driver can continue on the journey without having to be released by the traffic examiner.

Cockpit drill

Make these checks for the safety of yourself, your passengers and other road users. Every time you get into your vehicle, check that

- the driving seat and head restraint are correctly adjusted for position, height and back support, so that you can sit with the correct posture, reach all the controls comfortably and take effective observations
- all interior and exterior mirrors are clean and correctly adjusted
- lenses and screens of rear-view video equipment are clean and clear
- gauges and warning systems are working correctly (never start a journey with a defective warning device or when a warning light is showing)

- the parking brake is applied
- the gear selector is in neutral (or in 'Park' if driving an automatic vehicle)
- you have sufficient fuel for your journey
- your mobile phone is switched off
- the doors are working correctly and are closed before moving off.

Before starting your journey, make sure you know and understand the

- controls: where they are and how they work
- vehicle size: its width and height, and its weight
- handling: the vehicle's characteristics
- brakes: whether ABS brakes are fitted.

Other safety issues

Many buses have a separate door on the offside for the driver. Before opening this door to leave the bus, you should always check the mirrors and look around for any overtaking vehicles. Make sure that the parking brake is applied and the engine switched off before leaving the vehicle. Finally, in the interests of health and safety, climb down while facing the bus and using all the footholds.

Road speed limiters

PCVs requiring speed limiters are those

- with a maximum authorised mass (MAM) over 7.5 tonnes and capable of speeds over 100 km/h (62 mph) if first used on or after 1 January 1988
- with more than eight passenger seats (irrespective of weight), first used on or after 1 January 2005. However if they're used only for national transport operations and have a MAM not exceeding 5 tonnes, they didn't have to be fitted with limiters until January 2008.

For diesel-engined vehicles, limiters also had to be fitted retrospectively to vehicles first used between 1 October 2001 and 1 January 2005. This had to be done by 1 January 2006, apart from those used only for national transport operations which had to be fitted by 1 January 2007.

The speed at which the limiter is set must be shown on a plate displayed in a conspicuous position in the driver's cab.

Your vehicle may be fitted with a speed limiter. Lorries will be set at 56 mph (approx 90 km/h), buses at 62 mph (approx 100 km/h). Be aware that national speed limits allowed for these vehicles may also change to reflect this.

Your driving

When driving, it's your responsibility to follow all the relevant regulations. You must keep up to date with the road traffic rules and apply them.

This book covers the approach that you should take as a professional PCV driver. It doesn't include general driving principles – that is, everything that you should know and apply when driving **any** vehicle.

You may wish to refer to other DSA publications, such as *The Official DSA Guide to Learning to Drive* and *The Official DSA Guide to Driving – the essential skills*. You should also refer to The Highway Code to keep up to date with revisions in traffic rules and any new road signs that may be introduced. Books by other publishers also cover general driving rules and regulations.

Keep in mind that ignorance of the law is no defence. It's reasonable to expect that you, as a professional driver, will be knowledgeable.

Your driving licence
You need your PCV licence in order to earn your living driving buses, coaches and minibuses. To keep it you'll want to drive to a high professional standard.

When you drive any other vehicle – your own car, for example – it's essential that your driving continues to be to the same high standard.

Your PCV licence will be at risk if you accumulate penalty points from offences committed while driving **any** vehicle.

Speed limits
Your vehicle will probably be fitted with a speed limiter, which will generally prevent you from exceeding motorway speed limits. However, it won't stop you exceeding lower speed limits. Observing speed limits is part of your responsibility.

The speed limit for buses and coaches not exceeding 12 metres in overall length is
- 70 mph (112 km/h) on motorways
- 60 mph (96 km/h) on dual carriageways
- 50 mph (80 km/h) on any other road unless another, lower, speed limit applies.

The speed limit for buses and coaches over 12 metres in length and for PCVs with a trailer is
- 60 mph (96 km/h) on motorways and dual carriageways
- 50 mph (80 km/h) on any other road unless another, lower, speed limit applies.

Buses and coaches with two or more trailers are limited to
- 40 mph (64 km/h) on motorways
- 20 mph (32 km/h) on any other road unless another, lower, speed limit applies.

Speeding offences

Many police forces and local authorities now use up-to-date technology to persuade drivers to obey speed limits, and to catch and prosecute those who don't.

Sophisticated detection equipment can 'lock on' to individual vehicles in busy traffic flows. Cameras can photograph vehicles exceeding the speed limit. At some motorway sites, roadside detection equipment displays the registration number and speed of vehicles to 'show up' the drivers concerned.

Speeding drivers who've been prosecuted find that the penalties are often linked to how much the legal speed limit was exceeded. But remember, the aim is to improve driving standards, not to increase prosecutions.

Red light cameras

Cameras are increasingly being installed at light-controlled junctions to record drivers who don't comply with the signals. These cameras are also intended to act as a deterrent and to improve safety in general for road users.

Any photograph produced as evidence will be difficult to dispute if it shows the

- time
- date
- speed
- vehicle registration number
- length of time a red signal had been showing.

Red Routes

On many roads in London, yellow lines have been replaced with red lines. A network of priority Red Routes for London was approved by Parliament in June 1992 as a means of addressing traffic congestion problems and widespread disregard of parking restrictions in the capital. Red Route measures currently apply to 580 kilometres of London's roads.

Yellow-line exemptions **don't** apply on Red Routes. During the day, loading is only allowed in marked boxes. Overnight and on Sundays most controls are relaxed to allow unrestricted stopping. It's important to check signs carefully as the hours of operation for Red Routes vary from area to area.

Red Route controls are enforced by Metropolitan Police traffic police community support officers (PCSOs). There's a fixed fine for illegal stopping on a Red Route, with no discounts for early payment.

The traffic PCSOs are able to provide limited dispensations for the rare occasions when loading provisions aren't adequate. These will be available from the local police station.

There are five main types of Red Route markings.

Double red lines These ban all stopping 24 hours a day, seven days a week. You're not allowed to stop for

- loading
- dropping off passengers
- visiting shops.

Single red lines These ban all stopping during the daytime, such as 7.00 am to 7.00 pm Monday to Saturday. Outside these hours unrestricted stopping is allowed.

Parking boxes Allow vehicles free short-term parking and can be used for loading.

- **Red** Allow parking or loading outside rush hours, eg 10.00 am and 4.00 pm for periods of 20 minutes to one hour.
- **White** Allow parking or loading at any time but a stay may be restricted to 20 minutes or an hour during the day.

At other times, such as 7.00 pm to 7.00 am and on Sundays, unrestricted stopping is allowed in either type of parking box.

Loading boxes These mark the areas where only loading is allowed.

- **Red** Allow loading outside rush hours, such as between 10.00 am and 4.00 pm, for a maximum of 20 minutes.
- **White** Allow loading at **any** time, but during the day the length of stay is restricted to a maximum of 20 minutes.

At other times, such as between 7.00 pm and 7.00 am and on Sundays, unrestricted stopping is allowed in either type of loading box.

Loading is defined as when a vehicle stops briefly to load or unload bulky or heavy goods. These goods must be so heavy or bulky that they can't be carried any distance and may involve more than one trip. If possible your vehicle should be parked legally and the goods carried to the premises. Picking up items that can be carried, like shopping, doesn't constitute loading.

Clearways These are major roads where there's no need to stop. There will be no red lines, but Red Route clearway signs will indicate that stopping isn't allowed at any time.

For more information on Red Routes visit **tfl.gov.uk/roadusers** or call Transport for London Customer Services on **0843 222 1234.**

Congestion charging

A congestion charging scheme has been introduced in central London to help reduce traffic and make journeys and delivery times more reliable. The congestion charge applies from 7.00 am to 6.30 pm Monday to Friday, excluding public holidays. Failure to pay the charge will lead to a fine.

Exemptions Those who are exempt from the charge include

- disabled drivers
- residents who live within the congestion charging zone
- alternative fuel vehicles
- vehicles with nine or more seats
- roadside recovery vehicles
- all two-wheeled vehicles
- London licensed taxis and minicabs.

Drivers in some categories of exemption need to register with Transport for London (see congestion charging contact details given below).

Discounts Businesses and other organisations operating a fleet of 25 or more vehicles are entitled to a discount when they register with a dedicated fleet scheme.

For more information, to register or to make a payment, call the Congestion Charge Line on **0845 900 1234** or visit the website **cclondon.com**

Congestion charging is gradually being introduced in other towns and cities.

Bus lanes

Bus lanes are marked on busy roads to assist the flow of public transport. As a local service bus driver, you can use the bus lane at any time. Traffic signs will indicate if coaches are permitted to use the lane. Use them sensibly and don't be tempted to speed just because the lane is clear ahead. You may be driving along the inside of stationary or slow-moving traffic where pedestrians could be tempted to cross the road. They may not be prepared for you moving faster along the bus lane.

Where the lane has been obstructed, try not to get annoyed. It achieves nothing except to distract you from your driving.

Indicate in good time when you're ready to move out and then wait patiently for an opportunity to proceed.

Be prepared for the end of the lane, where other traffic may be changing position.

Bus stops

Bus stops are sometimes blocked by other vehicles. If this happens, make sure you check for traffic on your left, and check your mirrors, before opening your doors. Even if passengers are waiting to get off the bus, don't open your doors until your vehicle has stopped safely and you're sure there's no danger from other traffic. Put the safety of your passengers first.

Parking restrictions

Whenever you're driving, whether on stage carriage, on a private hire contract, on tour work, or while not in service, maintain your professionalism. Don't stop in places where

- loading and unloading aren't allowed
- you'll cause an obstruction
- you'll inconvenience other road users.

Similarly, don't park

- where parking is prohibited
- where there's a risk of theft or vandalism
- less than 10 metres (33 feet) from any junction, wherever possible, unless there's an authorised parking space.

Route planning

Plan your route carefully. It's never advisable to take short cuts through residential or narrow streets to avoid traffic congestion; you may get stuck. In some towns, weight, size and other vehicle restrictions prohibit you from leaving the main through-routes and ring roads, except for access. You could refer to a satellite navigation system but don't rely on it exclusively as it may have out-of-date or incomplete information at any given time, even if it's one that's specifically designed for large vehicles.

The Metropolitan Police operates an advisory service for coach operators. The telephone number is given on page 321.

Anti-theft measures

There are many anti-theft systems on the market, some of which manufacturers are fitting as original equipment to vehicles.

This book isn't intended to provide a detailed description of the precautions that you can take to avoid having your vehicle stolen or broken into, except in general terms. To provide this information would only alert criminals to the ways in which they can be overcome.

Unless you're handing a vehicle over to another driver, or parking it on an operator's premises where it's safe to do so, don't

- leave a vehicle unlocked or unattended
- allow passengers to leave personal effects on board, except in locked luggage compartments
- forget to set any fitted anti-theft devices.

Remember, there have been numerous incidents when considerable damage has been done by buses or coaches which were driven away by unauthorised persons. Not only has there been damage to the stolen vehicle, but also to vehicles belonging to innocent parties.

The basic rules are simple:

- avoid carelessness
- assess the risks of theft or damage
- set all devices fitted
- park in a safe place.

There may be situations where your passengers will have access to the bus while parked, for example on a day trip or excursion to the coast. If this is the case, you should ensure that the cab area is shut off securely, and that there's a responsible person available who can remain on board to ensure everyone's safety.

YOU DRIVE FOR A LIVING BUT YOU'D KILL FOR SOME SLEEP?

Tiredness Kills. Make time for a break.
think.direct.gov.uk

section **four**
DRIVER SKILLS

This section covers
- Professional driving
- Driving at night
- Motorway driving
- All-weather driving
- Avoiding and dealing with congestion
- Green issues – helping the environment
- Breakdowns
- Road traffic incidents
- First aid

Professional driving

Essential skills

Professional drivers adopt a positive approach to driving. This means

- looking after yourself, your vehicle and your passengers
- planning well ahead
- practising good observation
- keeping in control
- anticipating events.

Professional driving also means making allowances. You must always consider the safety and comfort of passengers. Sometimes you'll have to allow for the ignorance of other road users. In most cases, they'll have very little idea of the problems a bus or coach driver faces when driving such a large vehicle.

Control

It's essential that your vehicle is under control at all times. You must drive it skilfully and plan ahead, so that your bus is always travelling at the correct speed and ready for your next manoeuvre. You should never have to do anything at the last minute.

If you get caught out, you've got it wrong.

Awareness

You need to develop your awareness, to know what's going on around you at all times. This can be achieved through

- planning ahead
- anticipating – experience will soon tell you what other road users are probably going to do next
- being in control. Plan your actions don't be forced into situations by others
- understanding what might happen
- remembering similar situations.

You must always drive

- responsibly
- carefully
- considerately
- courteously.

At all times, show that your standards are high and that you can drive a PCV with skill and safety.

Consideration

It's also important to consider the effects of your vehicle on pedestrians, especially if they're standing on or very near the kerb. When pulling into a stop, watch for anyone who may suddenly step off the pavement. Also take care to ensure that your nearside mirror doesn't strike a person's head.

Anticipation

There aren't many excuses for being taken by surprise when you're driving; almost every event is predictable to some extent.

You must consider and prepare for all possibilities in all situations, especially when you can never be completely sure of what other road users will do. Remember, you won't be able to brake or swerve like lighter, smaller vehicles can.

Put yourself in other people's shoes. Make allowances for

- children
- cyclists and motorcyclists
- horse riders (on the road or grass verge)
- older pedestrians
- obviously less able drivers
- learner drivers.

Problems arise particularly when you aren't sure what vulnerable road users intend to do. Try to prepare yourself for all possibilities.

Avoiding aggression

Your passengers trust you; their safety is in your hands once they board your bus. Don't betray that trust. When you're driving

- accept that mistakes can be made
- expect others to make mistakes
- don't rise to aggression.

People who drive aggressively often see their driving as a competition. It's preferable to let them go on their way. Refuse to be involved in their bad driving behaviour – and their road traffic incident.

Your driving should always be a good example to others. By driving patiently and being prepared for the unexpected you'll avoid

- giving offence to others
- creating hostility
- provoking others to drive dangerously.

Safe procedure

It may seem to other road users that coach drivers are racing when one coach overtakes another. This is usually because of a coach's load or its speed limiter, and tends to be more obvious on hills.

Sometimes the bus being overtaken may be more powerful and the overtaking vehicle must drop back. If another coach has started to overtake you but appears to be unable to pass, be prepared to adjust your own speed if you think that it would be safer for the other driver to move back to the left. Don't signal to the overtaking driver – let them decide when it's safe to pull in.

For this reason you mustn't drive in close convoy. If you're driving with other vehicles from the same company, don't drive nose-to-tail or look as though you're vying for position with each other along the road.

Competing with other drivers will eventually lead to you risking your own safety or that of your passengers and other road users.

Effective observation

As a PCV driver, you'll often have a better view from your driving position than most other road users. You can take advantage of this, for example, when approaching a blind bend, by using your added height to see over hedgerows or other obstructions; you can then scan ahead for potential hazards. However, because of your vehicle's size and design, it will have more blind spots than many smaller vehicles.

You must use the mirrors effectively and act upon what you see in them. Just looking isn't enough. You need to know what road users around you're doing, or might do next. Check frequently down the sides of your vehicle. Your mirrors must be clean and properly adjusted for maximum view at all times. See cockpit drill on page 133.

Check the offside

- for overtaking traffic coming up behind, or already alongside
- before signalling
- before changing lanes, overtaking, moving or turning to the right.

Check the nearside

- for cyclists or motorcyclists filtering up the nearside and for pedestrians who may be standing very close to the kerb
- for traffic on your left when moving in two or more lanes
- when you've passed another road user, parked vehicle or pedestrians before moving back to the left
- to see where your wheels are in relation to the kerb or gutter
- before changing lanes, after overtaking, before turning left or moving further to the left, before leaving roundabouts.

You should use your mirrors frequently so that you're constantly aware of what's happening around you.

With a high seating position you must also be aware of pedestrians, cyclists or motorcyclists. They may be out of sight below the windscreen line, directly in front of your vehicle. Check for them

- before moving off
- at pedestrian crossings
- in slow-moving, heavy traffic
- when manoeuvring to park.

Remember, just a simple glance isn't enough. You need to check carefully.

Blind spots
Large vehicles have many blind spots resulting in very limited vision when reversing. When parking, it's preferable to choose a parking place that you can drive into forwards, and where you can also drive out forwards, without having to use reverse gear. If this isn't possible then it's better to reverse in and drive out forwards. In addition, inside some coaches – particularly those with high side windows – it's difficult to see to either side. When you want to move off you should open the window and look down and round to the right to ensure that it's clear before you pull away.

Many modern vehicles are fitted with additional mirrors on the left-hand side, positioned so that the driver can observe the nearside front wheel in relation to the kerb. Use them whenever you're pulling in to park alongside the kerb, in addition to checking the vehicle's position when you have to move close to the left in normal driving.

Hitting the kerb or wandering onto a verge can seriously deflect the steering or damage the tyre, which could result in a blow-out later.

Observation at junctions

Despite your higher seating position there will still be some junctions where you can't see past parked vehicles or even road signs. If possible, try to look through the windows of other vehicles, or watch for other vehicles' reflections in shop windows, which can give you some valuable information.

If you still can't see properly you'll have to ease forward until you can do so, without emerging too far out into the path of approaching traffic. Remember, some road users are more difficult to see than others, particularly cyclists and motorcyclists. Remember LADEN

- **L**ook
- **A**ssess
- **D**ecide before you
- **E**merge or enter, then
- **N**egotiate the junction.

At junctions, check for everything that you would normally look for whenever you move off from a standstill position. For example, it can be difficult to predict what pedestrians might do at junctions. Sometimes they might run out into the road, or other times they might just step out without having seen you. If a vehicle is approaching from the right and indicating to turn into the junction where you're waiting, don't pull out until they've started to turn in, just to be sure.

Never decide to go after just one quick glance. Take in the whole scene before you commit yourself to moving out.

Don't block access or exit from a side road when in stationary traffic, especially in busy or built-up areas. This is inconsiderate to other road users. Stay aware of side junctions when you're slowing down or stopping.

Think once

Think twice

Think bike.

Zones of vision

As a PCV licence holder your eyesight must be of a high standard. A skilful driver will constantly scan the road ahead to see what's happening. You need to anticipate what might happen next.

Because you use the scanning technique you'll know what's behind and next to you. Note what's happening at the edges of your vision and check what changes there are out of the corner of your eye. You need to act on **all** your observations, and be ready to slow down or stop if necessary. Check for

• vehicles about to come out of junctions

• children running out

• cycles and motorcycles

• pedestrians stepping out.

Remember, if you don't know, don't go.

Look for clues. If you see a cyclist ahead glance round to the right, they're probably going to try to turn right into the next road. Be ready for it. Similarly, watch the actions of pedestrians as they approach kerbs and cross the road. Older people sometimes become confused and change direction suddenly, or even turn back.

Keep a good look out for horse riders. If the animal starts to behave nervously allow the rider time and space to control it. The noise from an exhaust system or air brakes can disturb even a normally calm horse. Similarly, headlights or flashing lights can also startle horses. Take care even if the horse and rider are on the grass verge; you should still slow down and allow them the same courtesies.

Safe distances

Never drive at such a speed that you can't stop in the distance that you can see is clear ahead. You need to keep a safe distance regardless of the weather, the road and whether you're carrying passengers or not. This is one rule of safe driving that must never be broken.

- Always keep a safe separation distance between your vehicle and the one in front.
- In good weather conditions, leave at least 1 metre (about 3 feet 3 inches) per mph of your speed, or a two-second time gap.
- On wet roads you'll need to leave at least a four-second time gap.

The two-second rule

You can check the time gap easily. Watch the vehicle in front pass a stationary object such as a bridge, pole or sign and then say to yourself:

Only a fool breaks the two-second rule.

You should have finished saying this by the time you reach the object. If you haven't, you're too close.

On some motorways this rule is drawn to drivers' attention by chevron markings painted on the road surface. The instruction 'Keep at least two chevrons from the vehicle ahead' also appears on a sign at these locations.

In heavy, slow-moving traffic you may not need to leave as much space, but you must still leave enough distance to be able to stop safely.

Tailgating

If you find another vehicle is tailgating, that is, driving too close behind you, gradually reduce your speed to increase the gap between you and any vehicle ahead. You'll then be able to brake more gently and remove the likelihood of the close-following vehicle running into you from behind.

If another vehicle pulls into the safe separation gap you're leaving, ease off your speed to extend the gap again.

Never drive, at speed, within a few feet of the vehicle in front. It isn't only car drivers in motorway right-hand lanes who commit this offence. Lorry and bus drivers can sometimes be seen driving much too close behind another vehicle – often at normal motorway speeds. If anything unexpected happens, a road traffic incident could follow.

You mustn't rely on someone else to plan ahead for you. They may not possess the same skills as you. Always keep your distance.

Being aware of others

Look well ahead for 'stop' lights. On a road with the national speed limit in force or on the motorway, watch for hazard warning lights flashing. These show that traffic ahead is slowing down quickly. If you notice vehicles in front of you flashing hazard warning lights, or you see traffic ahead slowing down, then briefly flash your own hazard warning lights to warn traffic behind you of the hazard.

When you plan well ahead, less effort is needed to drive a bus. You should be able to keep your vehicle moving by anticipating traffic speeds. Your fuel economy should improve and this could help your company to stay competitive.

Before you change direction or speed you must decide how any change will affect other road users. It's important to know what's happening behind you as well as what's going on in front of you. Fast-moving cars or motorcycles can catch up with you surprisingly quickly.

Bus or coach drivers can't usually see much by looking round, which is why you must always be aware of vehicles just behind you and to either your left- or right-hand side as they come into your blind spot position.

A quick sideways glance is often helpful, especially

- before changing lanes on a motorway or dual carriageway
- where traffic joins from the right or the left
- prior to merging from a motorway slip road.

Don't take your attention off the road ahead for any longer than is absolutely necessary.

Other road users

Others on the road might make mistakes. You have to accept that other road users aren't always aware of the extra room or time you need, due to the size of your vehicle.

Young children

Young children are particularly unpredictable and might run out into the road suddenly. If you're passing pedestrians who are walking on the pavement but close to the kerb, you must be aware that the size of your vehicle could cause a draught. This could unsteady a small child or, indeed, an adult. Always check your nearside mirror as you pass.

When in school areas, you may see a pole with two flashing amber lights, one above the other. This means children will be crossing the road to or from school. Slow down and watch out for them.

Older people

Some older pedestrians may have poor eyesight or hearing difficulties. This might make them indecisive and they may sometimes become confused. They also might take longer to cross the road. You need to understand this and allow them more time.

Older drivers might be hesitant or become confused at major junctions or gyratory systems. Don't intimidate them by driving up too close or revving the engine.

Learner drivers

Learner drivers who aren't used to all driving situations and other types of road user might be affected by a close-following bus or coach. They might be driving at an excessively low speed or be hesitant. Be patient and give them room.

Cyclists

You need to allow cyclists as much room as you would cars. They might swerve to avoid a drain cover or a steep camber in the road. If they're approaching a junction or roundabout, you must be aware that they might turn right from the left-hand lane, crossing the path of traffic. It's essential that you're aware of the presence of cyclists **all around** you. Use your nearside mirror as you pass a cyclist to ensure that you've done so safely.

When you're waiting at a junction, be aware that cyclists might move up along either side. If they're positioned in front of your nearside mirror, between the kerb and your front nearside wheel, they may be difficult to see. You should be aware of this situation as it develops and allow them to move away before you move off.

Motorcyclists

Much of what has been said about cyclists also applies to motorcyclists. They're very vulnerable because, like cyclists, they're much smaller than other vehicles, with a narrow profile, so they're difficult to see. However, they also travel much faster than cyclists, so any situation develops much more quickly.

Many incidents occur because drivers fail to notice motorcyclists, so look out for them when

- emerging at junctions – the motorcyclist may be travelling along the major road and may be hidden behind other traffic. They can be completely hidden from you in the blind spots caused by the vehicle's door pillars, mirrors etc. They may also be hidden by signs, trees, or street furniture.

- turning into a road on your right – the motorcyclist may be following, overtaking or meeting you. Oncoming motorcyclists may be particularly difficult to see if they're following a larger vehicle

- straddling lanes, eg to turn left or to negotiate a roundabout

- changing lanes or moving out to overtake slower-moving or parked vehicles. Motorcyclists will often ride between slower-moving traffic in queues to make progress (commonly known as filtering), particularly in urban areas. When you're in heavy, slow-moving traffic, always ensure it's safe before you change direction.

When a motorcyclist is intending to turn right, they'll look over their right shoulder to check their blind area, just before turning. This is called the 'lifesaver' look. Watch out for this and be aware that they'll be changing direction shortly.

When roads are wet during or after rain, pay particular attention to the path a motorcyclist might take, particularly on bends. There could be drain covers or white lines which the motorcyclist might need to avoid, to prevent the motorcycle skidding. Give them time and space to do so.

Pay special attention to motorcycles and mopeds displaying L plates (or D plates in Wales). The riders of these machines may be riding on the road with very little experience, so they're particularly vulnerable.

Horses and other animals

Horses are easily frightened by

- noise
- headlights or flashing lights
- vehicles passing too close.

If you see horse riders ahead, either on the road or on the grass verge, plan your approach carefully. Slow down safely and don't rev the engine. You should allow for the fact that some of the riders might be learners and may not have full control if the animal is startled or frightened. Novice riders may sometimes be on a leading rein and have someone walking with them. When you pass them, do so slowly and leave plenty of room.

Always check your mirrors to ensure that you've safely completed the manoeuvre. Don't flash your headlights unnecessarily, and **do not** release air brakes behind animals, particularly horses as this could cause them to shy or bolt. If someone in charge of animals signals you to stop, do so and switch off your engine.

Guide dogs

A guide dog usually has a distinctive loop-type of harness. Remember the dog is trained to wait if there's a vehicle nearby.

The presence of a guide dog doesn't necessarily indicate only a visual impairment. When a person is both deaf and blind, they may carry a white stick with a red band and their dog may have a red and white checked harness. This could also mean they may neither see nor hear your signals.

Mirrors

You must use the mirrors well before you signal or make any manoeuvre, such as before

- moving away
- changing direction
- turning left or right
- overtaking
- changing lanes
- slowing or stopping
- speeding up
- opening any offside door.

Mirrors must be

- clean
- properly adjusted
- free from defects

Whenever you use the mirrors you must act sensibly on what you see. Take note of the traffic behind you and what it's doing.

Remember to check the nearside mirror for any vehicles moving up on the left. This is particularly important on motorways where it can take some distance to overtake safely because of the limits on your vehicle.

Remember, just looking isn't enough.

Traffic lights

At many busy road junctions the road is covered in skid marks. This shows that vehicles have come up to the junction too fast and have had to brake hard.

Approaching traffic lights

Lights on green Ask yourself the following

- How long has green been showing?
- Can I stop safely at this speed if the lights change?
- If I do have to brake hard, will the traffic behind be able to stop safely?
- Are there any vehicles waiting to turn left or right?
- How will weather conditions affect my braking?

Lights on red You must, of course, stop at red traffic lights. However, you may be able to time your approach so that you keep your vehicle moving as they change. Timing your approach to avoid stopping and moving off again may make your driving easier and your passengers more comfortable.

Lights not working If you come up to traffic lights that aren't working, or there's a sign to show that they're out of order, treat the junction like an unmarked junction and proceed with great care. Practise good, all-round observation and be prepared to stop if others assume priority.

Lights stuck on red By law you **MUST NOT** go through a red traffic light, unless a police officer tells you to do so. Occasionally, the signals may go out of phase and the red light shows for longer than it should. Remember, if you drive on and there's a collision, you'll have broken the law.

Never attempt to beat any traffic lights. Don't

- speed up to try to beat the signals. Remember what might happen to your passengers if you have to brake suddenly
- leave it until the last moment to brake. Heavy braking may well end up in loss of control.

A vehicle coming across your path may anticipate the lights changing and accelerate forward while the lights are still on the red-and-amber phase. Don't take any risks.

Remember, a green light doesn't give you right of way; it means 'go on if the way is clear'. Check the junction to make sure other traffic using the junction stops at their red lights. Don't emerge at a green light if it will cause you to block the junction.

Giving signals

You should signal to

- warn others about what you're going to do, especially if this involves a manoeuvre
- help other road users.

Road users you need to consider include

- drivers of oncoming vehicles
- drivers of vehicles behind
- motorcyclists
- cyclists
- crossing supervisors
- police directing traffic
- pedestrians
- horse riders.

Give all signals clearly and in good time. Also, use only those signals that are shown in The Highway Code.

You should avoid giving any signals that could confuse, especially when you're going to pull up just past a road on the left. Another road user might misunderstand the meaning of the signal.

Avoid giving unauthorised signals, no matter how widely you assume they're understood. This applies to headlight codes and alternating indicator signals. Remember, any signal that doesn't appear in The Highway

Code is unauthorised and could be misunderstood by another road user.

Avoid unnecessary signals. Always consider the effect your signal will have on all other road users.

Remember, see and be seen.

Using the horn
There are few instances when you'll need to use the horn. Using it doesn't

- give you any right of way
- relieve you of the responsibility of driving safely.

You should only sound the horn if you

- think that another road user may not have seen you
- need to warn other road users of your presence – at blind bends or on a hump bridge, for example

Don't use the horn

- to rebuke another road user
- simply to attract attention (unless to avoid an incident)
- when stationary (unless a moving vehicle presents a danger)
- at night between 11.30 pm and 7.00 am in a built-up area, unless there's danger from a moving vehicle.

Avoid long blasts on the horn, which can alarm pedestrians. If they don't react, they may be deaf.

Mobile phones

You **MUST** exercise proper control of your vehicle at all times. It's illegal to use a hand-held mobile phone or similar device when driving. You should also never use a hand-held microphone while driving. Even using hands-free equipment is likely to distract your attention from the road. Find a safe place to stop before using all such equipment. Driving a PCV demands your full attention all of the time (see section 1 of this book, on responsibility).

Driving through tunnels

On approaching and while in a tunnel

- switch on your dipped headlights
- don't wear sunglasses
- observe the road signs and signals
- keep an appropriate distance from the vehicle in front
- switch on your radio and tune it to the indicated frequency.

If the tunnel is congested

- switch on your hazard warning lights when you're stationary
- keep your distance, even if you're moving slowly or stationary
- listen out for messages on the radio
- leave at least a five-metre gap between you and the vehicle in front if you have to stop
- follow instructions given by tunnel officials or variable message signs.

Many tunnels have radio transmitters to give drivers information and advance warning of any incidents, congestion or roadworks. Some European tunnels can be many miles long.

When entering a tunnel in a large vehicle, you should slow down gradually, and increase the gap between your vehicle and the one in front to at least four seconds, to allow more time to brake if necessary. In some tunnels a legally enforceable minimum separation distance is specified.

Marker lights (usually blue) may also be located in the tunnel to help drivers maintain a safe separation distance.

When driving a large vehicle through a tunnel, other vehicles may become harder to see, particularly in mirrors, owing to lower light levels. This might increase drivers' response times.

Remember that larger vehicles may also block the view of following road users if they in turn don't increase their separation distances, to improve their ability to see and plan ahead.

If you break down or have a collision in a tunnel, remember that the passengers on board your vehicle are your priority. Circumstances will dictate your actions, but in general

- switch on your warning lights
- switch off the engine
- if the vehicle is parked in a dangerous position then remove the passengers, keep them together and take them to the nearest exit point
- give first aid to any injured people, if you're able
- call for help from an emergency point.

If your vehicle is on fire, and you can drive it out of the tunnel, do so. If not

- pull over to the side and switch off the engine
- remove the passengers, keep them together and take them to the nearest exit point
- when the passengers are in a safe place, and without putting yourself in any danger, try to put out the fire using the vehicle's extinguisher or the one available in the tunnel. **Do not** open the engine compartment. You may be able to insert the extinguisher nozzle through the small gap available when the release catch is operated, but **don't** take risks.
- move without delay to an emergency exit if you can't put out the fire
- call for help from the nearest emergency point.

If the vehicle in front is on fire, switch on your warning lights, then follow the above procedure, giving first aid to anyone who's injured if possible.

Emergency diversion routes

In an emergency, when it's necessary to close a section of motorway or other main road to traffic, a temporary sign may advise drivers to follow a diversion route. This route guides traffic around the closed section, bringing it back onto the same road further along its length.

To help drivers navigate the route, black symbols on yellow patches may be permanently displayed on existing direction signs, including motorway signs. A trigger sign will initially alert road users to the closure, then the symbol is shown alongside the route that drivers should follow.

A number of different symbols may be used, as in some places there may be more than one diversion operating. The range of symbols used is shown below.

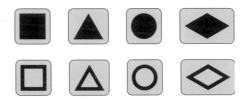

Drivers and riders should follow signs bearing the appropriate symbol. These may be displayed on separate signs or included on direction signs, giving the number of the road to follow.

If you're driving a double-deck vehicle, in the interests of safety you may need to check a map, satellite navigation equipment or other route information before proceeding, for any low bridges that may be present along the diversion route.

Driving at night

Problems encountered

You need extra skills to drive a bus, long distances. There are also additional responsibilities for the driver.

The problems related to driving in the dark are

- much less advance information
- limited lighting (street lights or vehicle lights only)
- dazzle from the headlights of oncoming vehicles
- shadows created by patchy street lighting
- poor lighting on other vehicles, pedal cycles, etc

- dangers created by the onset of tiredness. Fatal road traffic incidents have happened because the driver of a large vehicle either fell asleep briefly or didn't see an unlit broken-down truck or car until it was too late.

You need to plan long journeys at night carefully, particularly on motorways where there's little to ease the boredom. You should also make sure that you get proper rest and refreshment stops.

Above all, you must drive at a speed that allows you to stop safely in the distance that you can see to be clear ahead. In many cases, that's within the distance illuminated by your headlights or by street lights.

Tiredness

The smallest lapse of concentration at the wheel can result in loss of control. Many fatal incidents have been attributed to the driver becoming over-tired and falling asleep at the wheel. Remember

- don't begin your journey if you're tired
- don't drive without proper rest periods
- keep plenty of cool, fresh air circulating through the driving area
- don't allow the air around you to become too warm
- avoid eating a heavy meal before or during a journey
- pull up at the next safe, convenient place if you feel your concentration slipping

- listen to the radio or a CD if you can do so without disturbing your passengers (but don't change CDs while driving)
- walk around in the fresh air before setting off again after a rest stop.

Night vision

Have your eyesight tested regularly and make sure that your night vision is up to the standard required. If in doubt, have it checked. Don't

- wear tinted glasses
- use windscreen or window tinting sprays.

Lighting-up time

Regardless of the official lighting-up times (when you must turn your lights on; see The Highway Code), you should be ready to switch on any lights that you may need. If the weather conditions are poor or it becomes overcast, don't be afraid to be the first driver to switch on.

Unlit vehicles

Only vehicles under 1525 kg are allowed to park in 30 mph zones without lights at night. Be on the alert when driving in built-up areas, especially when the street lighting is patchy.

Although builders' skips must be lit and show reflective plates to oncoming traffic, these items are often either forgotten or vandalised, so be on the lookout for skips.

Remember, see and be seen.

Adjusting to darkness

When you step out from a brightly lit area into darkness, such as when leaving a motorway service area, your eyes will take a short while to adjust to the dark conditions. Use this time to check and clean lights, reflectors, lenses and mirrors.

At dawn

Other drivers may have been driving through the night and may also be less alert. Leave your lights on until you're satisfied that other road users will see you.

Remember, it's harder to judge speed and distance correctly in the half-light at dusk and dawn. The colour of some vehicles makes them harder to see in half-light conditions. By switching your lights on you could prevent another road user stepping, riding or driving out into your path because they hadn't realised how close you were or how fast your vehicle was travelling.

Vehicle lighting

It's essential that all lights are clean and that the bulbs and light units work properly. As well as being able to see ahead properly, other road users must be able to recognise the size of your vehicle and which way it's going.

In general, white lights indicate that the vehicle is

- moving towards you
- stationary, facing you
- reversing towards you (or is about to do so).

Red lights mean that the vehicle is

- moving away from you
- ahead of you and braking
- stationary, facing away from you.

Amber lights that aren't flashing mark the side of a vehicle.

Auxiliary lighting

High-intensity rear fog lights and additional front fog lights must only be used when visibility is less than 100 metres (about 330 feet). Remember to switch them off when conditions improve.

Interior lights

You should also turn on the interior lights if it's gloomy during the day, as well as at night. It helps passengers to move about the bus more easily and safely.

Coaches may have special lighting for night use. Never leave the interior of your coach in darkness when you have passengers aboard.

If your bus or coach is completely empty of passengers, you can travel with the interior lights off. However, interior lights have another role in road safety. Newer buses may have marker lights along the side to help make them more visible as they emerge from junctions, etc. Remember, a well-lit bus interior is even easier to see.

Exterior lights

Buses and coaches which exceed 2.1 metres wide and were first used on or after 1 April 1991 must be fitted with end-outline marker lights to indicate the presence of a wide vehicle. The requirement is two white lights to the front and two red lights to the rear. Some newer buses have marker lights along their sides. These help ensure they're visible as they emerge from roundabouts and junctions, as well as in other situations.

Parked vehicles

All buses and coaches and most minibuses – depending on their weight – must have lights on when parked on the road at night.

A lay-by is generally very close to the carriageway, and you must still have your lights on when parked in one. Unless your vehicle is parked off-road, such as in a coach park, by law it must be clearly lit.

You must park on the left-hand side of the road unless you're on a one-way street and it's safe to park on the right-hand side of the road.

Vehicles with air suspension can sometimes move a fair amount on start-up, as the air bags are injected with gas. Don't park too close to another vehicle or obstruction, to avoid any collision damage.

Driving in built-up areas

Always use dipped headlights in built-up areas in the dark. It helps others to see you and also aids your visibility if the street lighting changes or isn't working properly.

Watch out for

- pedestrians in dark clothing
- joggers
- cyclists (often without lights).

Take extra care when approaching pedestrian crossings. Drive at such a speed that you can stop safely if necessary.

Make sure that you still obey the speed limits even if the roads appear to be empty.

Maintenance work

Remember that essential maintenance work is often carried out at night. Street cleansing in the larger cities often takes place at night, so be on the lookout for slow-moving vehicles.

Be on the alert for diversion signs, obstructions, coned-off sections of road, etc, which may be difficult to see at night.

Driving in rural areas

If there's no oncoming traffic you should use full beam headlights to see as far ahead as possible. Dip your lights as soon as you see the lights of traffic coming towards you. This will avoid dazzling the oncoming driver or rider.

If there's no footpath, watch out for any pedestrians on the nearside of the road. The Highway Code advises pedestrians to walk facing oncoming traffic in these situations, but not all pedestrians follow this advice.

The Highway Code advises large groups of people on organised walks to walk on the left, carrying appropriate lights and wearing fluorescent clothing.

Also, be prepared to find temporary traffic lights on rural roads.

Fog at night

If fog is forecast at night don't drive. You'll be a serious hazard to other traffic if the fog becomes so thick that you're unable to go any further safely. Because of the difficulties of getting a bus or coach off the road in thick fog it's better not to start out in the first place.

If you start your journey when there's fog about and you're delayed, you'll be committing an offence if you drive for more than your permitted hours. After all, the delay was foreseeable.

Unfortunately, seriously reduced visibility has resulted in a number of major incidents involving multiple collisions. If conditions become severe enough, scheduled journeys may have to be cancelled. There's ample justification for putting caution before inconvenience.

Overtaking at night

Because PCVs can take longer to overtake other vehicles, you must only attempt to overtake when you can see well ahead that it's safe to do so.

This means that, unless you're driving on a dual carriageway or motorway, you'll have few opportunities to overtake. Unless there's street lighting, you might not be able to see properly if there are bends, junctions, hills, dips in the road, etc, which may prevent you from seeing an oncoming vehicle.

If you do decide to overtake, make sure that you can do so without cutting in on the vehicle you're overtaking, or causing oncoming vehicles to brake or swerve. Never close on the vehicle ahead before you attempt to overtake it, as this will restrict your view ahead.

When overtaking, switch to main beam headlights when you're past the point where you would dazzle the driver in their external mirrors. Using headlights will improve your vision ahead, but don't dazzle approaching traffic (on a dual carriageway, for instance).

Separation distance

Avoid driving so close to the vehicle in front that your lights dazzle the other driver. Make sure that your lights are on dipped beam.

If another vehicle overtakes you, dip your headlights as soon as the vehicle starts to pass you. Your headlight beam should fall short of the vehicle in front.

Remember, react in good time.

Motorway driving

Accident records show that, statistically, motorways are the safest roads in the UK. However, motorway incidents often involve several fast-moving vehicles and consequently result in more serious injuries and damage than collisions on other roads.

Because of the high numbers of large vehicles using motorways, many of these collisions involve lorries and, occasionally, coaches and minibuses. But if everyone who used the motorway drove to the same high standard as PCV drivers, it's arguable that many of these incidents could be avoided.

There's often little room for error when driving fast on a motorway. The generally higher speeds and the volume of traffic mean that conditions can change much more quickly on motorways than on other roads. Because of this you need to be

- totally alert
- physically fit
- concentrating fully
- assessing well ahead.

If you aren't, you may fail to react quickly enough to any sudden change in traffic conditions.

Fitness

Don't drive if you're

- tired
- feeling ill
- taking medicines that could affect your driving
- unable to concentrate for any reason.

Any of these factors could affect your reactions, especially in an emergency.

Rest periods

You must take the compulsory rest periods in your driving schedule. On long journeys, try to plan them to coincide with a stop at a motorway service area. This is especially important at night, when a long journey can make you more tired than usual.

If you eat a large meal immediately before driving, the combined effects of a warm coach, the constant drone of the engine and long, boring stretches of road, especially at night, can soon cause the onset of drowsiness. Falling asleep at the wheel can happen so easily; don't let it happen to you.

Unless it's an emergency, it's against the law to stop anywhere on the motorway, including the hard shoulder and slip roads, for a rest. Tiredness is foreseeable and isn't considered to be an emergency.

If you start to feel even slightly tired, open the windows, turn the heating down and get off the motorway at the next junction. Even if you aren't scheduled to stop, it's preferable to falling asleep at the wheel.

When you reach a service area have a hot drink, wash your face (to refresh yourself) and walk round in the fresh air before driving on.

Regulations

You must follow the special motorway rules and regulations. Study the sections in The Highway Code that relate to motorways. Know, understand and obey any warning signs and signals.

Vehicle checks

Before driving on the motorway you should ensure that you carry out routine checks on your vehicle, especially considering the long distances and prolonged higher speeds involved.

For fuller details on vehicle maintenance, see page 70.

Tyres

All tyres should be checked regularly, especially if you're going to drive on the motorway. Tyres can become hot and may disintegrate under sustained high-speed running (for tyre care and maintenance see pages 78–81).

Mirrors

Ensure that all mirrors are properly adjusted to give the best possible view to the rear. Also, make sure that they're clean.

In winter, make full use of any demisting heating elements fitted to your mirrors.

Keep the lenses and screens of any rear-view video equipment clean and clear.

Windscreen

All glass must be

- clean
- clear
- free from defects.

Keep all windscreen washer reservoirs topped up and the jets clear. Make sure that all wiper blades are in good condition.

Don't hang mascots or put stickers where they could restrict your view or distract you.

Windscreens can be either laminated or toughened. Toughened screens might shatter, laminated ones will crack. If you notice a crack or chip during a walk-round check, report it immediately. A small crack can quickly become larger if the screen flexes during a journey, particularly if the road is uneven or potholed.

Spray-suppression equipment

A spray-suppression system is designed to reduce the amount of water thrown upwards by the tyres of a vehicle in motion. It can consist of mudguards, rain flaps, wheel skirts, etc. Air is allowed to pass through normally but the amount of water and spray thrown up is reduced.

It's essential that you check all spray-suppression equipment fitted to the vehicle before setting out, especially if bad weather is expected. If wheel arches have sections of anti-spray fitments missing, report it as a defect.

Instruments

Check all gauges, especially any warning lights such as air, oil pressure and coolant.

Lights and indicators

By law, all lights must be in working order, even in daylight. Make sure that all bulbs, headlight units, lenses and reflectors are fitted, clean and working properly.

High-intensity rear fog lights and marker lights (if fitted) must also work correctly. Indicator lights must flash between 60 and 120 times per minute. Reversing lights must either work automatically when reverse gear is chosen or be switched on from the cab, with a warning light to show when they're on.

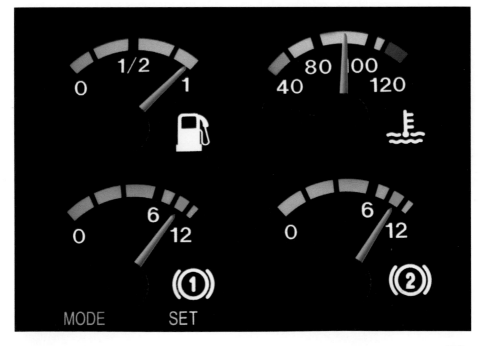

Fuel

Make sure that you either have enough fuel on board to complete the journey or have the facility (eg cash or agency card) to refuel at a service area.

Oil and coolant

The engine operates at sustained high speeds on a motorway so it's vital to check all oil levels before setting out. Running low can result in costly damage to the engine and could cause a breakdown at a dangerous location. Similarly, it's essential to check the levels of coolant in the system.

Audio and video equipment

Don't allow the use of audio and video equipment to distract you from driving carefully and safely. You shouldn't use microphones or headphones of any kind, or be distracted by tuning the radio while driving. Even if your vehicle is fitted with a hands-free radio communication or telephone system these can still distract you. Don't use them while driving; select a safe and suitable place to stop.

Any video or television screen fitted to your coach for passenger use mustn't be visible to you while you're driving.

Joining a motorway

There are three ways in which traffic can join a motorway. All these entrances will be clearly signed.

At a roundabout

The motorway exit from a roundabout will be signposted to prevent traffic that doesn't want to use the motorway from driving onto it unintentionally.

Main trunk road becoming a motorway

There will be prominent advance warning signs so that prohibited traffic can leave the road before the motorway regulations come into force.

Via a slip road

Slip roads leading directly onto the motorway will be clearly signed to prevent prohibited traffic entering the motorway. In many cases the slip road begins as an exit from a roundabout.

Effective observation

Before joining the motorway from a slip road, try to assess the traffic conditions on the motorway itself. You may be able to do this as you approach from a distance or if, before joining it, you have to cross the motorway by means of a fly-over.

Get as much advance information as you can to help you to plan your speed on the slip road before reaching the acceleration lane. You must give way to traffic already on the main carriageway. Plan your approach so that you don't have to stop at the end of the acceleration lane. Never use the size or speed of your vehicle to force your way onto the motorway.

Use the MSM/PSL routine. A quick sideways glance may be necessary to ensure that you correctly assess the speed of any traffic approaching in the nearside lane.

Remember to

- look for approaching traffic
- assess the speed of approaching vehicles
- decide when you can build up speed
- emerge safely onto the main carriageway
- negotiate the hazard – adjust to the speed of traffic already on the motorway.

Don't

- pull out into the path of traffic in the nearside lane if this would cause it to slow down or swerve
- drive along the hard shoulder to filter into the left-hand lane.

At a small number of locations, traffic merges onto the motorway from the right. Take extra care in this situation.

Making progress

Approaching access points

After passing a motorway exit there will usually be an entrance onto the motorway. Look well ahead and, if there are several vehicles joining the motorway

- don't try to race them while they're in the acceleration lane
- be prepared to adjust your speed
- move to the next lane, if it's safe to do so, to allow joining traffic to merge.

Lane discipline

Keep to the left-hand lane unless you're overtaking slower vehicles.

PCVs that are required to be fitted with a speed limiter aren't allowed in the extreme right-hand lane on a three-lane or multi-lane motorway, unless there are roadworks or signs that indicate otherwise. Details of which vehicles are required to be fitted with

speed limiters, and are therefore prohibited, are shown on page 134. This restriction doesn't apply to 'A' class roads with three lanes. On two-lane motorways, all vehicles may use the right-hand lane for overtaking.

If a bus or coach is fitted with a speed limiter it will be set to a maximum speed of 100 km/h (62 mph), so consider this before attempting any overtaking. Watch out for signs showing a crawler/climber lane for LGVs. This will suggest a long, gradual gradient ahead.

Use the MSM/PSL routine well before you signal to move out. Don't start to pull out before signalling, or signal at the same time as you begin the manoeuvre. Other drivers need time to react.

Before pulling back in after overtaking, be sure to check your left mirror even if the driver flashes their headlights at you. Don't rely on this signal. As the driver of a long vehicle, it's important that **you** check the position of the road user you've overtaken to ensure you've passed safely before returning to the left. Take extra care with motorcycles as they're more vulnerable and may be affected by buffeting from your vehicle.

On a three- or four-lane motorway make sure that you check for any vehicles in the right-hand lane or lanes that might be about to move back to the left. Most of the traffic coming up from behind will be travelling at a higher speed. Look well ahead to plan any overtaking manoeuvre, especially given the effect a speed limiter will have on the power available to you.

If a very large slow-moving vehicle is being escorted, watch for any signal by the police officers in the escort vehicle at the rear. You might need to move into the right-hand lane to pass it.

On some roads, crawler lanes may be provided. These are separate lanes which can be used by heavy and slow vehicles to help them make progress on a long, gradual uphill gradient.

If a motorway lane merges from the right (this only happens in a few places), you should move over to the left as soon as it's safe to do so. You must use the MSM/PSL routine, make careful checks in the left-hand mirror and constantly be aware of vehicles in your blind spots.

Separation distance

When driving at motorway speeds you must allow more time for everything that you do. Allow

- greater safety margins than on normal roads
- a safe separation distance.

This means that in good conditions you'll need at least

- 1 metre (about 3 feet 3 inches) for every mile per hour
- a two-second time gap.

In poor conditions you'll need at least

- double the distance
- a four-second time gap.

In snow or icy conditions the stopping distances can be up to 10 times those needed in normal dry conditions.

If you're following a working snow plough, don't overtake, as there may be deep snow ahead.

Seeing and being seen

Make sure that you start out with a clean windscreen, mirrors and windows. Use the washers, wipers and demisters to keep the screen clear. In poor conditions use dipped headlights.

Keep reassessing traffic conditions around you. Watch out for brake lights or hazard warning lights that show the traffic ahead is either stationary or slowing down. (Hazard warning lights may be used on moving vehicles to alert traffic to danger ahead.)

High-intensity rear fog lights must only be used when visibility falls below less than 100 metres (about 330 feet). They should be switched off when visibility improves, unless fog is patchy and danger still exists.

Motorway signs and signals

Motorway signs are larger than most normal road signs. They can be read from further away and can help you to plan ahead.

Know your intended route. Be prepared in good time for the exit you require.

Where there are major roadworks there may be diversions for large vehicles. Look for the yellow

- square
- diamond
- circle
- triangle

symbols and follow the symbol on the route signs.

Remember, react in good time.

Signals

Warning lights show when there are dangers ahead such as

- accidents
- fog
- icy roads.

Look out for variable-message warning signs, which will warn you about

- lane closures
- speed limits
- hazards
- traffic stopped ahead.

Red light signals

If the red 'X' signals show on the gantries above your lane, don't go any further in that lane.

- Be ready to change lanes.
- Be ready to leave the motorway.
- Watch out for brake lights and hazard warning lights showing that traffic has stopped or is moving very slowly ahead.

If the matrix sign indicating 'Stop: all lanes ahead closed' shows over every lane, stop and wait. You may not be able to see the reason for the signals and other drivers may be ignoring them. Remember, you're a professional driver who should know what the signals mean and can demonstrate to other drivers what they should do.

Weather conditions

Because of the higher speeds used on motorways, it's important to remember the effects that the weather can have on driving conditions.

In windy conditions, be alert for places where the road is shielded, ie by hedges or banks. When there's a break in this shielding, the sudden effect of high winds may mean your steering could become more difficult, and your vehicle might be blown off course.

Crosswinds

Be aware of the effects of strong crosswinds on other road users.

In particular, watch out for these effects

- after passing motorway bridges
- on high, exposed sections of road
- when passing vehicles towing caravans, horse boxes, etc.

If you're driving a high-sided vehicle, such as a double-deck or a high-floor coach, take notice of the warnings for drivers of such vehicles. The vehicle's extra height means you'll feel the effects of wind to a greater degree. Avoid known problem areas such as viaducts and high suspension bridges, if possible. Be aware that some may be closed to certain vehicles under high wind conditions. On high bridges, one lane is sometimes kept free of other traffic. This is known as a buffer lane and is used to prevent vehicles being blown into the path of other road users in the next lane.

If you must travel under conditions of high winds, it may be useful to plan an alternative route before you set off, just in case. Motorcyclists are especially vulnerable to severe crosswinds on motorways. Watch out for them. Allow plenty of room when overtaking, and check the left-hand mirror after you've overtaken them.

Hot weather

Vehicles can be very stifling and uncomfortable in very hot weather, especially when there are many passengers. However, you must never leave the doors open to allow fresh air in. Passengers may decide to get on or off at inappropriate moments, which could be very dangerous. Also, many buses have air-operated doors that close automatically on release of the clutch. You mustn't override this set up. Passenger safety must come first.

Rain

The spray thrown up by large, fast-moving vehicles can make it very difficult to see ahead. Higher speeds also cause more spray.

- Use headlights so that other drivers can see you.

- If overtaking another large vehicle that's throwing up spray, move out earlier than normal.

- Reduce speed when the road surface is wet. You need to be able to stop in the distance that you can see is clear.

- Leave a greater separation gap. Remember the four-second rule as a minimum.

- Make sure that all spray-suppression equipment fitted to your vehicle is undamaged.

Take extra care when the surface is still wet after rain. Roads can still be slippery even if the sun's out.

In wet conditions, especially where there are puddles at the side of the road, try to avoid splashing pedestrians near the edge of the kerb or passengers waiting at bus stops. Slow down and avoid driving through the puddle if possible – your consideration will be much appreciated.

Ice or frost

In cold weather, especially at night when temperatures can drop suddenly, watch out for any feeling of 'lightness' in the steering (not always obvious with power-assisted steering). This may suggest frost or ice on the road. Watch for signs of frost along the hard shoulder. Remember, a warm coach interior can isolate you from the real conditions outside.

Motorways that appear wet may in fact be frozen. There are devices that fix onto an outside mirror to show when the temperature drops below freezing point. Also, some manufacturers fit ice-alert warning lights on the instrument panel.

Allow up to 10 times the normal distance for braking in these conditions. Remember, any braking must be gentle.

Fog

If there's fog on the motorway you must slow down so that you can stop in the distance that you can see is clear.

You should

- use dipped headlights
- use the rear high-intensity fog lights if visibility is less than 100 metres (about 330 feet)
- stay back
- check your speedometer.

Don't

- speed up again if the fog is patchy; you could quickly run into dense fog again
- hang onto the rear lights of the vehicle in front.

Fog affects your judgement of speed and distance. You may be travelling faster than you think.

Slow down.

Remember, don't use high-intensity rear fog lights unless visibility is less than 100 metres (330 feet).

Multiple collisions on motorways don't just happen – they're caused by drivers who

- travel too fast
- drive too close
- assume nothing has stopped ahead
- ignore signals.

Remember, you can't see well ahead in fog – so always slow down.

Watch out for any signals that tell you to leave the motorway. Also, look for incidents ahead and for emergency or incident support vehicles coming up behind (possibly on the hard shoulder). Police cars or traffic officer vehicles may be parked on the hard shoulder with their lights flashing. This might mean that traffic has stopped on the carriageway ahead.

'Motorway madness' is the term used to describe the behaviour of reckless drivers who drive too fast for the conditions. The police prosecute drivers after serious multiple collisions. This is to get the message across to all drivers that they **must** slow down in fog.

Breakdowns on the motorway

If your vehicle develops a problem, leave the motorway at the next exit or go to a service area. If you can't do this, pull onto the hard shoulder and stop as far to the left as possible.

- Switch on the hazard warning lights.
- Make sure that the vehicle lights are on at night, unless there's an electrical problem.
- When passengers are alighting from the bus, ensure they keep away from the carriageway and hard shoulder, and that children are kept under control.
- If removing passengers from the bus isn't immediately feasible, move passengers as far forward in the vehicle as possible. This should help to limit injuries if another vehicle runs into the back of it.
- Don't try to carry out even minor repairs on the motorway.

You mustn't place a warning triangle or any other warning device on the carriageway, hard shoulder or slip road.

Some motorways have emergency refuge areas at the side of the hard shoulder, usually about 500 metres apart. Try to use this area if you do break down. Take care when rejoining the carriageway, especially if the hard shoulder is being used as a running lane within an active traffic management area.

Emergency telephones

Motorway emergency telephones are free of charge to use and easily located. You'll be connected to a Highways Agency regional control centre. The operator will then get in touch with a recovery company for you, or reroute your call to the police if it's a criminal matter.

In most cases the emergency telephones are 1.6 km (about 1 mile) apart. The direction of the nearest phone will be shown by the arrow on the marker posts along the edge of the hard shoulder. Don't cross the carriageway or any slip road to get to a telephone. Face the oncoming traffic while using the telephone.

If your vehicle has its own telephone, make sure that whoever you contact also informs the police or the Highways Agency control centre, or telephone them yourself.

If you use a mobile phone, identify your location from the marker posts on the hard shoulder before you phone.

If anything falls from either your vehicle or another vehicle

- use the nearest emergency telephone
- don't attempt to recover it yourself
- don't stand on the carriageway to warn oncoming traffic.

Leaving the motorway

Progressive signs will show upcoming exits. At one mile you'll see the

- junction number
- road number
- one-mile indicator.

Half a mile from the exit you'll see signs for the

- main town or city served by the exit
- junction number
- road number
- half-mile indicator.

Finally, from 300 yards (270 metres) before the exit there will be three countdown markers, one every 100 yards (90 metres).

Remember, the driver of a vehicle travelling at 60 mph (95 km/h) has 60 seconds from the one-mile sign to the exit. Even at a speed of 50 mph (80 km/h) there's still only 80 seconds from the one-mile sign to the exit.

Plan well ahead in order to be in the left-hand lane in good time. Large vehicles in the left-hand lane may prevent a driver in the second lane from seeing the one-mile sign, leaving very little time to move to the left safely.

You must use the MSM/PSL routine in good time before changing lanes or signalling. Assess the speed of traffic well ahead.

Avoid the situation where you try to overtake but then have to pull back in quickly in order to slow down to leave the motorway at the next exit. Don't

- pull across the carriageway at the last moment
- drive over the white chevrons that divide the slip road from the main carriageway.

If you miss the exit that you wanted to take, drive on to the next one.

Occasionally there are several exits close together or a service area close to an exit. Look well ahead and plan your exit in good time. Watch out for other drivers' mistakes, especially those who leave it too late to exit from the motorway safely.

Traffic queuing

In some places traffic can be held up on the slip road. Look well ahead and be prepared for this. Don't queue on the hard shoulder.

Illuminated signs have been introduced at a number of these sites to give advance warning of traffic queuing on the slip road or in the first lane. Watch out for indicators and hazard warning lights when traffic is held up ahead.

Use the MSM/PSL routine in good time and move to the second lane if you aren't leaving at such an exit.

End of the motorway

There are 'End of motorway regulations' signs

- at the end of slip roads
- where the road becomes a normal main road.

These remind you that different rules apply to the road that you're joining. Watch out for signs advising you of

- speed limits
- dual carriageways
- two-way traffic
- clearways
- motorway link roads
- part-time traffic signals.

Reduce speed

After driving on the motorway for some time it's easy to become accustomed to the speed. When you first leave the motorway, 40 mph (64 km/h) seems more like 20 mph (32 km/h). You should

- adjust your driving to the new conditions as soon as possible
- check the speedometer to see your actual speed.

Start reducing speed when you're clear of the main carriageway. Remember, motorway slip or link roads often have sharp curves that need to be taken at lower speeds.

Look well ahead for traffic queuing at a roundabout or traffic signals. Be prepared for the change in traffic at the end of the motorway. Watch out for pedestrians, cyclists, etc.

Contraflows and roadworks

Essential roadworks involving two-way traffic on one carriageway of the motorway are called contraflow systems. The object is to let traffic carry on moving while repairs or resurfacing take place on the other carriageway or lanes.

Red and white marker posts are used to separate opposite streams of traffic. The normal white lane-marking reflective studs are replaced by temporary yellow/green fluorescent studs.

Signs

Take notice of advance warning signs, gantry signs or flashing signals (often starting five miles before the roadworks). Get into the correct lane in good time and don't force your way in at the last moment as this can greatly increase the chance of mistakes and incidents.

A 50 mph (80 km/h) compulsory speed limit is usually in force in contraflow systems. However, in the event of a head-on collision, the closing speed will **still** be about 100 mph (approx 160 km/h). You **MUST** obey all speed limits, they've been imposed for a reason. Roadworks are complicated environments and you'll need more time to spot hazards, for your own safety and the safety of road workers.

Travelling through roadworks

When you drop your speed to travel through roadworks, it may seem as if you're travelling more slowly than you really are. It's important to observe the speed limit and not just slow down to the speed that feels safe to you. When you're approaching or driving through roadworks or contraflow areas, you should

- concentrate on what's happening ahead
- keep a safe separation distance from the vehicle in front – you'll need time to brake if that vehicle stops suddenly
- look out for road workers who are placing or removing signs
- look well ahead to avoid having to brake hard
- obey advance warning signs that tell you which lanes mustn't be used by large vehicles
- avoid sudden steering movements or any need to brake sharply
- be aware that lanes may be narrower than normal. You must take care not to let your vehicle 'wander' out of such lanes.

Don't

- let the activity on the closed section distract you
- change lanes if signs tell you to stay in your lane
- let your concentration wander – road workers can appear in unexpected places and can be difficult to spot in cluttered environments

- exceed the speed limit
- speed up until the end of the roadworks when normal motorway speed limits apply again.

If all drivers observe the speed limits when travelling through these areas, this will help to keep traffic moving and not 'bunching up'. This is good for journey time as well as the environment.

Exiting roadworks

Stay within the speed limits even when you're leaving the coned areas. There may be road worker vehicles leaving the roadworks at this point. Don't speed up until you're clear of the roadworks.

Incidents

Serious incidents can occur when vehicles cross into the path of the other traffic stream in a contraflow. You must

- keep your speed down
- keep your distance
- stay alert.

Breakdowns

If your vehicle breaks down in the roadworks section, stay with it. These sections of motorway are usually under television monitoring, so a recovery vehicle (free of charge within the roadworks section) will be with you as soon as possible.

Watch out for broken-down vehicles blocking the road ahead.

All-weather driving

Passengers want to be able to travel 24 hours a day, 365 days a year. Whatever the weather, you'll need to drive safely so that you, your passengers and your vehicle arrive safely at your destination, with as few hold-ups as possible.

It's essential that you take notice of warnings of severe weather such as

- high winds
- floods
- fog
- snow and blizzards.

If a bus or coach becomes stranded the road may become blocked for essential rescue and medical services. In the case of fog it could result in other vehicles colliding with the stranded vehicle.

Training and preparation are vital. Don't venture out in severe conditions without being properly prepared. If the weather is very bad, cancel or postpone your journey.

Your vehicle

Your vehicle must be in good condition at all times. This means making regular safety checks and observing maintenance schedules strictly. Far too many cases brought before a traffic commissioner result from incidents caused by vehicles that weren't looked after properly. Make sure that the vehicle you drive is fully roadworthy. For fuller details on vehicle maintenance, see page 70.

Tyres

Check the tread depth and pattern.
Examine tyres for cuts, damage or signs of
cord visible at the side walls.

Brakes

It's essential that the brakes are operating
correctly. This is especially important on
wet, icy or snow-covered roads. Any
imbalance could cause a skid if the brakes
are applied on a slippery surface.

Oil and fuel

Use the correct grades of fuel and oil in very
hot or very cold weather.

Long periods of hot weather will make the
oil in engines and turbo-chargers work
harder. You should always allow engines
with turbos fitted to idle for about a minute
before increasing engine revs above
tick-over speed (when starting) or before
stopping the engine. This prevents the
bearings from being starved of oil.

In extremes of cold you'll have to use
either diesel fuel anti-waxing additives or
a suitable grade of diesel fuel with these
properties to stop fuel lines freezing up.

Use of the correct coolant when topping up
prevents dilution of the rust inhibitors and
anti-freeze components of the liquid. Also,
remember that allowing a cooling system to
freeze will wreck components and possibly
crack the engine block or cylinder heads.

Icy weather

Ensure that the whole of the windscreen
is clear before you drive away in frosty
conditions. Make full use of all heaters and
demisters fitted.

If you're driving at night, remember that
falling temperatures may lead to icy conditions.
This will cause ungritted roads to become
very slippery. If the steering feels light you're
probably driving on ice. Ease your speed as
soon as you can. Braking must be gentle and
over much longer distances.

Leave more time for the journey, because
you'll need to drive more slowly than usual.
On slippery surfaces, keep a safe separation
distance from any vehicle in front. Allow
10 times the normal stopping distance.

Drive sensibly, and be careful of other
road users getting into difficulties. Don't
accelerate, brake or steer suddenly. No
risks are ever justified. **If conditions are
really bad, don't drive**.

Heavy rain

You must make sure that you can see clearly ahead at all times. Don't drive if a windscreen wiper is faulty, even though many PCVs have more than one pair of wipers. In addition, the windscreen must be demisted fully and the windscreen washer bottle(s) topped up with the correct washing fluid. This is particularly important in winter. It's against the law to drive with frozen or ineffective windscreen washers.

Allow more space for braking – at least twice as much as in dry conditions. If possible, brake only when the vehicle is stable (and preferably when travelling in a straight line). Also, avoid sudden or hard braking.

Obey advisory speed limit signs on motorways.

Take great care when overtaking on motorways in very wet weather. Your tyres may lose grip because of build-up of a water layer between the road surface and the tyres (known as aquaplaning). If your steering suddenly feels light, ease your foot off the accelerator and slow down gently without braking. When the tyres regain their grip, the steering should feel normal again.

When driving through deep water such as a ford, drive slowly in low gear with the engine speed high to prevent water entering the engine through the exhaust system.

Other road users will have more difficulty seeing when there's heavy rain and spray so make sure that all spray-suppression equipment on your vehicle is secure and working correctly.

Other vehicles could be temporarily blinded by spray from your vehicle so take care when you need to change lanes. When overtaking cyclists in heavy rain, take care that spray from your vehicle doesn't affect their control. Leave plenty of room when passing them and check your left-hand mirror to see whether they're still in control.

Don't use rear fog lights unless visibility is less than 100 metres (330 feet). Fog lights reflect and dazzle following drivers.

Remember, no risk is worth taking.

Mud

Take care when driving on off-road sites, such as at rallies, showgrounds, festivals, etc. If you get stuck there's very limited scope to rock your PCV out of ruts (as you might with a car). Clearance underneath is often so limited that the exhaust could be ripped off, even if the vehicle has sunk as little as four or five inches. Seek assistance before this happens.

You may be able to recover the situation without damage by using a winch or a bar from another vehicle on hard standing. Once the vehicle has sunk in, however, only the use of heavy-duty jacks and steel sheeting will get you out without further problems.

If the surface is hard but slippery, drive at a crawling pace in the highest possible gear and with the minimum revs. Try to select a course that avoids you having to turn.

It's against the law to deposit mud on the road to the extent that it could endanger other road users.

Snow

Falling snow can reduce visibility quite seriously. Use dipped headlights and slow down. Leave a much greater stopping and separation distance – up to 10 times the stopping distance on dry roads. When driving on snow, and particularly if it's also windy, the best way to control your vehicle is to drive slowly in as high a gear as possible.

Road markings and traffic signs can be covered by snow. Take extra care at junctions.

High-level or exposed roads are sometimes closed by deep snow. Listen to any weather warnings. Don't try to use such roads if

- warning signs indicate that the road is closed to large vehicles or other traffic
- severe weather is forecast.

Some country roads in exposed places have marker posts at the side of the road, which tell drivers how deep the snow is.

Remember, if a bus gets stuck it could

- stop snow ploughs from clearing the road
- delay emergency vehicles
- cause other road users to become stuck
- put passengers at risk.

If your vehicle is fitted with a manually selected retarder system, engage it before going down a hill covered with snow.

Another technique for freeing a vehicle stuck in snow is to use the highest gear possible to try to get out. Alternating between the reverse and forward gears,

if possible, is a good way of getting moving again when the snow is soft.

Don't keep revving in a low gear; you'll only make the driving wheels dig in even further.

It's often helpful to keep a couple of strong sacks in your vehicle to put under the drive wheels if you get stuck, but remember that your vehicle undercarriage can also be an issue. Hardened snow can cause considerable damage. A shovel is often handy if you must go through areas where snow is a problem during the winter.

Make sure that your vehicle is properly prepared for any journey. This is especially important in the winter. In some countries you must carry snow chains at certain times of the year, and they must be used in bad weather.

Ultimately, ask yourself whether you should drive through an area where such conditions are likely.

Ploughs and vehicles spreading sand or other de-icers

Don't try to overtake a snow plough or vehicle spreading sand or other de-icers. You may find yourself running into deep snow or skidding on an untreated stretch of road, which these maintenance vehicles could have treated had you followed on behind them.

Keep well back from these vehicles. Their presence could mean that the weather is already bad or that it's expected to be.

Fog

Don't drive in dense fog if you can postpone your journey and avoid driving at all at night if there's fog.

Don't start a journey that might need to be abandoned because it becomes too dangerous to drive any further.

If you must drive in fog, **slow down**.

Also, keep a safe separation distance from any vehicle in front. If you can see the rear lights of a vehicle in front you're probably too close to stop in an emergency.

A large vehicle ahead of you may temporarily displace some of the fog, making it seem thinner than it really is. Overtaking at that point could quickly lead to a problem. Stay back.

Then again, in a larger vehicle you may be able to see ahead over low-lying fog. Don't speed up in case there are smaller vehicles in front that may be hidden from view.

Only overtake if you're sure that the road ahead is clear – and then only on a multi-lane road.

Slow down

- Don't speed up if the fog appears to thin. It could be patchy and you may run into it again.

- Keep checking the speedometer to see your true speed. Fog can make it difficult to judge speed and distance.

Stay back

- Keep a safe separation distance from any vehicle ahead.

- Don't speed up if a vehicle appears to be close behind.

- Only overtake if you can be sure the road ahead is clear.

Don't take risks.

There aren't many places where you can park a bus safely in thick fog. You mustn't leave a bus on or near a road where it could be a danger to other road users; and your passengers won't be pleased with the prospect of spending the night in a lay-by. Certainly don't park a bus anywhere in fog without lights.

Lights

Use dipped headlights whenever you find it difficult to see. You need to see clearly and be seen at all times.

Use high-intensity rear fog lights and front fog lights (if fitted) when visibility is less than 100 metres (330 feet). Rear fog lights must only be capable of operating with dipped headlights or front fog lights. Switch off front and rear fog lights when you can see further than 100 metres (330 feet), but beware of patchy fog.

Keep all lights and reflectors clean and make sure that they're working correctly at all times, particularly in bad weather.

Remember, you can't afford to take risks. Slow down and stay back.

Reflective studs

Reflective studs are provided on dual carriageways and motorways to help drivers to see in poor visibility. The colours of reflective studs are

- **red** On the left-hand edge of the carriageway
- **white** To indicate lane markings
- **amber** Between the right-hand edge of the carriageway and the central reservation
- **green** At slip roads and lay-bys
- **yellow/green fluorescent** At roadworks contraflow systems.

On some country roads there are black and white marker posts with red reflectors on the left-hand side and white reflectors on the right-hand side of the road.

All these reflective devices are designed to help you know where you are on the road.

In fog don't

- drive too close to the centre of the road
- confuse centre lines with lane markings
- drive without using headlights
- use full beam, especially when following another vehicle. You'll make it more difficult for the other driver to see by casting shadows and causing glare in the mirror.

High winds

In bad weather it's a good idea to listen to, watch or read the weather forecast if you're going to drive

- a double-deck bus or coach
- a high-floor coach
- a light or empty bus, coach or minibus.

Listen to advance weather warnings if you have to drive on roads that often have strong winds, such as

- high bridges
- high-level roads
- exposed viaducts
- exposed stretches of motorway.

Ferry crossings will also be affected by very strong winds. There could be delays or cancellations, so it's a good idea to check before setting off.

Watch out for signs warning of high winds, and beware of fallen trees or damaged branches that could fall on your vehicle. Take notice of signs and warnings and remember that

- roads may be closed to certain large vehicles
- there may be delays due to lanes being closed. This is done on high bridges to create empty buffer lanes in the event of any large vehicles being blown off course
- you may need to use another route.

If you ignore any signs or warnings you could put your passengers, your vehicle and yourself at risk. If there's an incident your passengers could be injured and you could be prosecuted.

Other road users

In very windy weather, other road users are likely to be affected when

- they overtake you
- you overtake them.

Those road users who can be particularly affected include motorcyclists, double-deck buses, horse boxes, high-sided lorries and vehicles towing caravans or trailers.

Although cars are the most stable vehicle under high winds, buffeting can still affect them to some extent. Check your mirrors as you overtake to see that they still have control of their vehicle. Also, watch out for vehicles or motorcycles wandering into your lane. Don't ignore warnings of severe winds.

Avoiding and dealing with congestion

The increasing number of vehicles on the roads has caused a level of congestion that can lead to frustration and increases in journey times. This affects urban areas, higher-speed roads and motorways. However, there's an opportunity for all drivers to help alleviate this problem to some extent, by changing their driving habits. Detailed below are ways to do this.

Journey planning

Time of day

If possible, try to plan journeys to avoid the busy times of day. Much congestion is generated by work/school-related travel, causing delays in the early morning and late afternoon/early evening. If you're not on a scheduled route and you don't have to travel at these times, try to avoid them.

This will help ease the congestion caused by traffic that's governed by work/school schedules. This will also allow you an easier, more pleasant journey that's less likely to be delayed.

Route planning

Make sure you know where you're going by planning beforehand. If possible, include alternatives in your plan in case you find your original route blocked, especially if the route is unknown to you. You could

- use a map – you may need to use different scale maps depending on how far and where you're travelling
- refer to a satellite navigation system (but don't rely on it exclusively)
- consult a motoring organisation or use one of the route planners available on the internet
- print out or write down the route, using place names and road numbers to avoid problems if a certain place isn't adequately signed.

For an online journey planner, smartphone traffic apps and live traffic updates from the Highways Agency, visit **highways.gov.uk**

Be aware of the size of your vehicle in relation to the width of certain accesses or narrow town roads – it can be very difficult or impossible to manoeuvre a large vehicle if, for example, a one-way street or sharp turn is found to be too narrow, or where weight or height restrictions apply. If you drive a double-deck vehicle you also need to be aware of low bridges.

Satellite navigation systems are a useful tool when in transit but you should never rely upon them exclusively. Most are designed only for cars and smaller vehicles, so they won't filter out inappropriate items, such as narrow lanes, weight-restricted areas or low bridges, all of which physically restrict or prohibit the passage of larger vehicles. Only those systems specifically designed for use in large goods vehicles, buses, coaches and mobile homes will have the facility to identify and filter out areas through which it would be difficult, unsafe or impossible for such a vehicle to manoeuvre.

Be aware also that, because situations can change very quickly on roads, it's possible there may be sudden delays or diversions which a global positioning system (GPS) can't detect. It's also best to identify narrow roads, height restrictions, tight turnings or overhanging buildings (eg in town areas) for yourself, by manually planning your route before starting your journey. When in transit, your vehicle radio may pick up and broadcast local warnings of any sudden emergencies, delays or diversions in your vicinity. This extra warning information will help you make any urgent or necessary adjustments to your route plan.

Remember that any in-vehicle navigation system can reduce your concentration on the road and your level of control of the vehicle, so it's advisable to restrict any visual or manual interaction with a system to an absolute minimum (see Rule 150 in The Highway Code). In the interests of safety, you should find a safe and legal place to stop before making adjustments.

Your journey

Leave plenty of time, especially if you're connecting with other forms of transport. Concern about reaching your destination in time can lead to frustration and the increased tendency to take risks, which in turn could lead to an incident. Timetables and schedules need to allow for this so that you aren't forced into taking unnecessary risks to stay on time. Carry your map or directions with you so you can check positions or identify alternative routes if you're delayed or diverted, but don't attempt to look at a map or read directions while driving. A GPS will help identify your route for you.

Mobile phones

A mobile phone can be useful in case of delays or breakdowns. However, remember that it's illegal to use a hand-held mobile phone while driving, and this includes while you're waiting in a queue of traffic. Find a safe place to stop before making a call. If you're driving alone on a motorway, you must leave the motorway before using the phone. (Also see section 1, on responsibility.)

Hazard perception

Looking well ahead to see what other road users in front of you are doing will enable you to plan your driving. If you see any changes that could cause you to slow down or alter course, ease off the accelerator and gradually slow down rather than leaving it late and having to brake harshly. By slowing down early the traffic situation ahead will often have cleared by the time you get there.

Constant speed

When you can see well ahead and the road conditions are good, you should try to drive at a constant speed – this is the time to use cruise control if it's fitted to your vehicle.

Whether or not you have cruise control, choose a speed which is within the speed limit and one which you and your vehicle can handle safely. Make sure you also keep a safe distance from the vehicle in front. Remember to increase the gap on wet or icy roads. Also remember that, in foggy conditions, you'll have to slow down to the distance you can see to be clear.

At busy times, there are some stretches of motorway that have variable speed limits shown above the lanes. The maximum speed limits shown on these signals are mandatory and appear on the gantries above the lanes to which they apply.

These speed limits are in place to make traffic proceed at a constant speed as this has been shown to reduce bunching, and consequently, over a longer distance, congestion eases. Your overall journey time normally improves by keeping to the constant speed, even though at times it may appear that you could have travelled faster for shorter periods.

Lane discipline

You should drive in the left-hand lane of a dual carriageway or motorway if the road ahead is clear.

If you're overtaking a number of slower-moving vehicles it may be safer to remain in the centre lane until the manoeuvre is completed rather than continually changing lanes. Return to the left-hand lane once you've overtaken all the vehicles or if you're delaying traffic behind you, but don't hog the middle lane.

You mustn't normally drive on the hard shoulder, but at roadworks and certain places where signs direct, the hard shoulder may become the left-hand lane.

Using sign information

Look well ahead for signals or signs, especially on a motorway. Signals situated on the central reservation apply to all lanes.

On very busy stretches, there may be overhead gantries with messages about congestion ahead, and a separate signal for each lane. The messages may also give an alternative route which you should use if at all possible. If you're not sure whether to use the alternative route (for example, can you reach your destination if you use the route suggested), take the next exit, pull over at the first available safe area (lay-by or service area) and look at a map.

Remember, on a motorway, once you've passed an exit and encounter congestion, there may not be another opportunity to leave and you could be stuck in slow-moving or stationary traffic for some time. Take the opportunity to leave the motorway when it arises; you can always rejoin it if you feel that this is the best course of action, once you've had time to consider the options.

If you need to change lanes to leave the motorway, do so in good time. At some junctions a lane may lead directly off the motorway. Only get in that lane if you wish to go in the direction indicated on the overhead signs.

Motorway signals can be used to warn you of a danger ahead. For example, there may be a road traffic incident, fog, or a spillage, which you may not immediately be able to see.

Amber flashing lights warn of a hazard ahead. The signal may show a temporary maximum speed limit, lanes that are closed or a message such as 'Fog' or 'Queue'. Adjust your speed and look out for the danger. Don't increase your speed until you pass a signal which isn't flashing or one that gives the 'All clear' sign and you're sure it's safe to increase your speed.

Active traffic management

Active traffic management (ATM) is a project to try to reduce congestion and make journey times more reliable. Also known as 'managed motorways', ATM features many benefits including

- closed-circuit television (CCTV) monitoring on every section of this stretch
- high-visibility driver information panels
- new lighting to improve visibility at night and in poor light
- new emergency roadside telephones for use in an emergency or breakdown
- emergency refuge areas for vehicles to use in an emergency or breakdown
- use of the hard shoulder as an additional running lane under controlled conditions to manage traffic in peak congestion or during an incident
- Highways Agency traffic officer patrols monitoring the motorway (see page 202).

Gantries

The gantries have been built about 500 metres apart on this stretch of motorway. They feature a large message sign board and signal boxes above each of the lanes and the hard shoulder.

The signs on the gantries show the mandatory speed limit across the carriageway, displayed in a red circle and enforced by law.

Variable speed limits help to keep traffic moving when the route is congested. The speed and availability of lanes is controlled so that traffic is able to flow more smoothly.

The signals can also be used to control and divert traffic around road traffic incidents, or in order to close a lane for roadworks. This provides additional protection for road workers and more advance notice to road users of what's happening ahead.

Emergency refuge areas

These are 100 metres long, wider than the hard shoulder and are located about every 500 metres. They're designed to be used in cases of emergency or breakdown. Features include

- sensors to alert the control centre that a vehicle has entered

- CCTV enabling the control centre to monitor the vehicles and send assistance as necessary

- new-generation emergency roadside telephones containing additional multilingual and hard-of-hearing support, and the ability to pinpoint your location

- additional distance from the main carriageway.

Driving in actively managed areas

As on any motorway, you must obey the signals displayed on the overhead gantries.

In addition to the normal signals that are used on any motorway (see page 178–179), there will also be a single red 'X' without flashing beacons which is applicable to the hard shoulder only. When you see this sign, don't use this lane, except in an emergency or breakdown.

There are three driving scenarios, as explained below. These are

- normal motorway driving conditions
- actively managed mode
- hard shoulder running mode.

Normal motorway conditions

- There's no congestion or incident.
- There are no speed limits shown on signals.
- National speed limits apply.
- The hard shoulder is for emergency and breakdown use only.
- Use emergency refuge areas in an emergency for added safety and increased distance from the carriageway.
- Use emergency roadside telephone for assistance.

Actively managed mode

- There may be an incident or congestion ahead.
- All speed limit signals are set and must be obeyed.
- Driver information panels will provide information for road users.

- A red 'X' over the hard shoulder means 'do not use this lane', except in an emergency or breakdown.
- Use the emergency refuge areas in an emergency or breakdown for added safety and increased distance from the carriageway.
- Use the emergency roadside telephone if you need assistance.

Hard shoulder running mode

This is similar to the actively managed mode, except that the hard shoulder may be used as a running lane between junctions, during periods of congestion. This increases the motorway's capacity, keeping traffic moving more smoothly.

In this mode, the red 'X' above the hard shoulder is replaced by the appropriate speed limit.

Highways Agency traffic officers

Working in partnership with the police, Highways Agency traffic officers are extra eyes and ears on the motorways. They're a highly trained and highly visible service patrolling the motorway to help keep traffic moving and make your journey as safe and reliable as possible.

Traffic officers wear a full uniform, including a high-visibility orange and yellow jacket, and drive a high-visibility vehicle with yellow and black chequered markings.

Every traffic officer will also have a unique identification number and photographic identity card. They'll normally patrol in pairs.

The vehicles contain a variety of equipment for use on the motorway, including temporary road signs, lights, cones, debris removal tools and a first aid kit.

Role of traffic officers

Traffic officers

- help broken-down motorists to arrange recovery
- offer safety advice to motorists
- clear debris from the carriageway
- undertake patrols in clearly identifiable vehicles
- support the police and emergency services during incidents
- provide mobile or temporary road closures
- manage diversion routes caused by an incident.

If you have an emergency or breakdown on the motorway the best action to take is to use an emergency roadside telephone and follow the advice given on page 183.

In some areas, emergency roadside telephones are answered by Highways Agency control centre operators located in a regional control centre.

Control centre operators are able to monitor any stranded motorists on close circuit television screens and despatch the nearest available traffic officer patrol to assist.

Powers of traffic officers

Unlike the police, traffic officers don't have any enforcement powers; however, they're able to stop and direct anyone travelling on the motorway.

It's an offence not to comply with the directions given by a traffic officer. Refer to The Highway Code, Rules 107 and 108.

Extent of scheme

There are seven regional control centres in England, managed by the Highways Agency, able to despatch traffic officers to any English motorway.

Urban congestion

Congestion in urban areas leads to

- longer journey times
- frustration
- pollution through standing and slow-moving traffic.

London suffers the worst traffic congestion in the UK and among the worst in Europe. It has been estimated that

- drivers in central London used to spend 50% of their time in queues
- London lost £2–4 million every week in terms of wasted time caused by congestion.

Various measures have been introduced to try to reduce and alleviate the congestion and make traffic flow more freely. Red Routes and congestion charging are two of the schemes initiated in the London area. These are also being introduced into other congested towns and cities.

Red Routes

Red Routes keep traffic moving and reduce the pollution that comes from vehicle emissions. Stopping and parking is allowed only within marked boxes.

There's a fixed penalty for an offence and illegally parked vehicles may be towed away.

There are five main types of Red Route markings.

Double red lines Stopping isn't allowed at any time, for any reason. They're normally placed at road junctions or where parking or loading would be dangerous, or cause serious congestion.

Single red lines Parking, loading or picking up passengers isn't allowed during the day (generally 7.00 am to 7.00 pm). Stopping is allowed outside these hours and on Sundays.

Red boxes Indicate parking or loading is permitted during the day at off-peak times, normally 10.00 am to 4.00 pm. Some allow loading and some allow parking; the rules in each case are clearly shown on a sign beside the box.

White boxes Indicate that parking or loading may be allowed at any time, restrictions being clearly shown on the sign beside the box.

Red Route clearway There are no road markings but clearway signs indicate that stopping isn't allowed except in marked lay-bys.

For more details about Red Routes see page 137.

Green issues – helping the environment

The effects of pollution

If you follow the principles of ecosafe driving set out in the following pages, you'll become a more environmentally friendly driver. Your journeys will be more comfortable and you could considerably reduce both your fuel bills and those emissions that cause damage to the atmosphere. As a professional driver, you can set an example to other road users in helping to keep the environment green. Fossil fuels are a finite resource which must be used wisely; use the advice contained in this book to become an ecosafe driver.

Developing your planning, perception and anticipation skills will obviously help to make you a safer driver. However, although it's beneficial to save fuel, you mustn't compromise your safety or that of other road users when attempting to do so. Road safety is more important. At all times you should be prepared to adapt to changing conditions and it may be that you'll have to sacrifice fuel-saving for safety.

It's vital that professional operators monitor and manage the fuel used by their vehicles. This can be done by implementing a fuel management programme, which can help reduce fuel consumption across the fleet by at least 5%, as well as providing cost savings. As part of this management process, use of safe and fuel-efficient driving techniques will contribute to this fuel saving.

Reducing fuel consumption by 1000 litres per year will

- save 2.6 tonnes of carbon dioxide emissions per year
- save £1000 per year for the operator (assuming a price of £1.00 per litre excluding VAT).

Using fuel more efficiently means

- improved profit margins
- lower emissions
- lower costs
- improved environmental performance.

What you can do to help

Driving in a more fuel-efficient way is known to save on costs. It's better for the environment and can also improve the image of a company and the transport industry as a whole, by showing that they're making an effort to reduce their carbon footprint. Try to drive in an eco-friendly manner at all times, whether you're driving for business or pleasure. Fuel, like all forms of power, costs money as well as having an impact on the environment. Minimising the fuel or power you use is always important, both for the planet and for your pocket.

It's still possible to drive a bus or coach in a manner that's more beneficial to the environment by applying a little care and thought to how, and when, you drive. Here are some suggestions on what you can do.

Becoming an ecosafe driver

Ecosafe driving is a recognised and proven style of driving that contributes to road safety, while reducing fuel consumption and emissions.

One of the main factors in increasing road safety is the emphasis on planning ahead so that you're prepared in advance for potential hazards. By increasing your hazard perception and planning skills you can make maximum use of your vehicle's momentum and engine braking. By doing this, you can help reduce damage to the environment. Momentum allows the engine to run more efficiently, with less strain on components. Keeping your vehicle moving at a slow walking pace, instead of moving it from a standstill, will use less fuel.

The speed gathered when climbing a hill can be used to descend without touching the accelerator. The vehicle uses little or no fuel in these circumstances and won't do so until the accelerator is needed again when descent is complete and momentum begins to slow.

Hazard awareness and planning

You should be constantly scanning all around as you drive. Check into the far distance, midground and foreground. Also check behind and to the sides by using all mirrors frequently.

Early recognition of potential hazards is important, but just looking isn't enough; you need to act correctly on what you've seen. This will mean you're able to

• anticipate problems

• take appropriate action in good time to ensure that you're travelling at the correct speed when dealing with a hazard.

By doing this you'll avoid late braking and harsh acceleration, both of which lead to higher fuel consumption. Whenever you drop down a gear, fuel consumption increases. Forward planning helps to eliminate excessive gear changes, such as when approaching junctions or roundabouts.

It isn't always necessary to use every gear. Reducing the number of gear changes not only improves fuel consumption but also means you save time and physical energy, which in turn can mean less fatigue.

Keep a safe distance from the vehicle in front as this will help you to plan your driving. Try to leave yourself sufficient room so you don't always have to brake immediately or harshly when traffic in front of you slows down. By simply taking your foot off the accelerator, your vehicle will slow down and fuel consumption will be reduced. However, you may wish to use your brakes to advise vehicles behind that you're slowing down.

If you plan early for hazards you'll avoid causing other road users to bunch, traffic will flow more smoothly and you'll use less fuel.

Starting up

If your vehicle is fitted with an excess fuel device and you need to use it to start the engine when it's cold, push it in as soon as the engine will run smoothly without it.

Driving away

Avoid over-revving your engine when you start your vehicle and try to pull away smoothly.

Choosing your speed

Always drive sensibly and keep within the speed limit. Exceeding a speed limit by only a few miles per hour will mean that you use more fuel but, more importantly, you're breaking the law and increasing the risk of serious injury if you're involved in a collision.

Cruise control

Use cruise control, when appropriate, if it's fitted. Using cruise control keeps a steady setting on the accelerator so not varying the intake of fuel. Use of constant speeds on motorways and dual carriageways enables full use of cruise control, which helps to optimise the engine management system's ability to precisely measure and deliver the appropriate amount of fuel for any given situation. This not only gives more economic fuel use but also reduces engine wear.

Use of cruise control, combined with effective route planning and keeping the rev counter in the green band, can all help to minimise the amount of fuel used.

If your vehicle has a fuel consumption readout display on the instrument panel, use it to monitor the fuel used during the journey. Cruise control can also help to maintain your speed within the speed limit. But remember, it shouldn't be used as a substitute for concentration – you must exercise proper control of your vehicle at all times.

The accelerator

Try to use the accelerator smoothly and progressively. When appropriate, take your foot off the pedal and allow the momentum of the vehicle to take you forward. Taking your foot off the accelerator when going downhill can save a considerable amount of fuel without any loss of vehicle control. Rather than use your brakes for a long period, with the risk of brake fade, you should control downhill speed by use of lower gears.

Whenever possible, avoid rapid acceleration or heavy braking as this leads to greater fuel consumption and more pollution. Driving smoothly can reduce fuel consumption by about 15% as well as reducing wear and tear on your vehicle.

Selecting gears

It isn't always necessary to change up or down through each gear – it's possible to miss out intermediate gears. This helps to reduce the amount of time you spend accelerating, and as this is when fuel consumption is at its highest, you can save fuel by skipping some gears. As soon as conditions allow, use the highest gear possible without making the engine struggle, and don't use the accelerator fiercely.

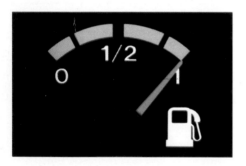

Fuel consumption

Check your fuel consumption regularly. To make sure you're getting the most from your vehicle, simply record the amount of fuel you put in against miles travelled. This will help you check whether you're using fuel efficiently.

If you haven't changed your driving method, or the conditions in which you're driving, an increase in the average fuel consumption can mean the vehicle needs servicing. An eco-friendly driver is constantly aware of how much fuel their vehicle uses. If a trip computer is fitted, this can help you check fuel consumption.

Overfull fuel tanks can cause fuel to leak through the breather vent. Fuel expands when hot, so leaks can happen once expansion occurs if the tank is filled to the brim. This can waste fuel and make the road surface dangerous for other road users. Always leave a little room for expansion in the interests of safety. Remember spilt fuel can make the road surface very slippery.

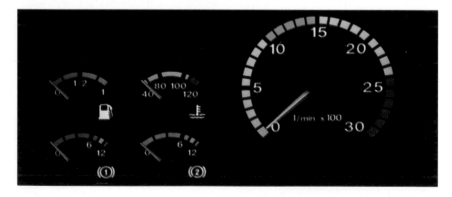

Braking

Smooth and progressive braking will save fuel and reduce stress on the vehicle, driver and passengers. When using the footbrake, the lost road speed has to be made up by accelerating, which burns fuel. If it's necessary to change down a gear or half gear, even more fuel is used.

Harsh braking uses more fuel and increases the number of gear changes required to regain speed. It's possible that the safety and comfort of passengers being carried is more likely to be compromised under heavy or sharp braking. By using smooth, progressive braking, the amount of road speed lost can be minimised.

Engine braking

With your foot fully off the accelerator the engine needs very little fuel, so take advantage of engine braking wherever possible. Use lower gears rather than extended use of the brakes to avoid brake fade.

Engine power

Modern vehicles are designed to deliver power even when engine revs are quite low. You'll find that you can make use of the higher gears at low speeds.

Planning unscheduled routes

Whenever possible, plan your route to avoid known hold-ups, roadworks, busy times and congestion.

- Try to avoid town centres, use bypasses where possible.

- If you use a satellite navigation system, don't rely on it exclusively as it may have out-of-date or incomplete information at any given time, even if the system you're using is specifically designed for large vehicles.
- Always know where you're going – you'll use more fuel by getting lost.
- If you're likely to be making a prolonged stop, say for more than two minutes at a level crossing or roadworks, you may consider it best to stop the engine.
- Try to use uncongested routes.
- Make sure you know of any narrow roads or areas where it may be difficult to pass through or manoeuvre a very large vehicle, or where there may be weight, width or height restrictions.
- Try to plan for the easiest way to access your destination.
- If you're required to travel on an unfamiliar or new route always ask your supervisor for scheduled and detailed route information.

Continuous research has resulted in new methods of helping the environment by easing traffic flow (see page 196 for advice on avoiding congestion).

Select for economy and low emissions

There are advantages and disadvantages in all types of fuel; however, most large buses and coaches are now diesel powered.

These engines are very fuel efficient and produce less carbon dioxide (a global warming gas) than any other road transport fuel. They also emit less carbon monoxide and fewer hydrocarbons than petrol-engined vehicles, but they do produce more emissions of oxides of nitrogen (NOx) and particulates, which are bad for local air quality.

Fitting a particulate trap to a vehicle can help to reduce harmful emissions by filtering hydrocarbons, carbon monoxide and particulate matter.

Newer vehicles have to meet strict new emissions standards aimed at reducing these pollutants, and all diesel vehicles can now use ultra-low sulphur diesel fuel to reduce exhaust pollution.

When you obtain a new vehicle, the vehicle's handbook will be helpful in advising how to drive it in the most fuel-efficient way. Some advantages of driving in a fuel-efficient way are

- reduced emissions
- improved operating costs.

Low Emission Zone

The Low Emission Zone (LEZ) is a specified area in Greater London within which the most polluting diesel-engined vehicles are required to meet specific emissions standards. If they don't, they'll need to pay a daily charge.

The Greater London Low Emission Zone started on 4 February 2008. In this area, the most polluting diesel-engined vehicles must meet specific standards relating to their emissions. Not meeting these standards will incur a daily charge.

The zone initially applied to diesel-engined lorries over 12 tonnes in weight but, from July 2008, also applied to all lorries over 3.5 tonnes as well as to all buses and coaches. From 3 January 2012, minibuses, larger vans, motor caravans and other specialist vehicles will also be affected.

Further information on this subject can be found at **tfl.gov.uk/roadusers/lez**

Keep your vehicle well maintained

You should make sure that your vehicle is serviced and maintained regularly.

- Make sure the engine is tuned correctly. Badly tuned vehicles use more fuel and emit more exhaust fumes. MOT tests now include a strict exhaust emission test to ensure correct tuning, so vehicles operate more efficiently and cause less air pollution.

- Have your vehicle serviced as recommended by the manufacturer. The cost of a service may well be lower than the cost of running a badly maintained vehicle – for example, even slight brake drag can increase fuel consumption.

- If you do your own maintenance, make sure that you send oil, old batteries and used tyres to a garage or local authority site for recycling or safe disposal. Don't pour oil down the drain; it's illegal, harmful to the environment and could lead to prosecution.

- Use good quality engine oil – if you use synthetic engine oils rather than the cheaper mineral oil, you can save fuel.

- Make sure your tyres are properly inflated. Incorrect tyre pressure results in shorter tyre life and may create a danger as it can affect stability and braking capacity. In addition, under-inflation can increase fuel consumption and emissions.

When refuelling your vehicle, you should aim to fill it up to the bottom of the filler neck and no further. If you fill the tank to the brim, when the fuel becomes hot and expands, its only way of escape is via the breather vent. If, at any time, you notice that your fuel filler cap is missing you **MUST** get it replaced before continuing.

Also, knowing your particular vehicle's average miles or kilometres per litre (mpl or km/l) can help early identification of problems. If the ratio drops, this may indicate a problem with the vehicle. Drivers are usually the first to notice problems, such as dragging brakes, so here's a check list of signs that may indicate that a commercial vehicle needs workshop attention to stop it wasting fuel. Include this list in your regular vehicle examination.

Check for

- any fuel or oil leaks including missing or broken fuel caps
- missing seal in fuel tank cap or signs of fuel spills around filler neck
- low tyre pressure
- tyre wear suggesting faulty steering or axle alignment
- missing tyre valve caps
- traces of black smoke in exhaust
- any body damage
- missing or damaged air management equipment
- excessive engine oil consumption (no leaks) suggestive of internal wear
- maintenance records showing rapid wear of clutch or brake friction material.

Improving fuel economy

E very time you move off, do so smoothly – avoid harsh acceleration.

C hange down to the appropriate gear, but wait for your speed to decrease.

O n acceleration, try to skip gears where you can.

N ever leave it to chance – maintain your vehicle in good condition.

O bserve and keep within the rev counter green zone.

M inimise brake use – plan ahead and keep monitoring road conditions.

Y our top speed should remain constant – think 'Gear high–rev low'.

Breakdowns

If your vehicle breaks down, try to stop as far to the left as possible. If you can, get off the main carriageway without causing danger or inconvenience to other road users, especially pedestrians.

Move your passengers as far forward in the vehicle as you can. This should help to limit injuries if another vehicle runs into the back of yours.

Some form of warning is vital if an electrical problem has put the rear lights out of action. Place a warning cone, pyramid or reflective triangle at least 45 metres (147 feet) behind the vehicle on normal roads. However, don't attempt to place any type of warning device on a motorway, carriageway, hard shoulder or slip road.

Some foreign-built buses and coaches have outside fuse and relay boxes on the right-hand side of the vehicle. Don't attempt to work on the right-hand side of the vehicle unless protected by a recovery vehicle with flashing amber beacons. Even then, take great care on roads carrying fast-moving traffic. Many road traffic incidents happen at breakdowns. Protect yourself, your passengers and your vehicle.

Assessing the dangers

If your vehicle is creating an obstruction or is a potential danger to other road users, tell the police as soon as possible. This is particularly important if your vehicle is carrying passengers, especially schoolchildren. Their safety must come first.

If you think that there's a serious risk of collision, escort your passengers off the bus. Ensure that they wait somewhere well away from the traffic. Explain carefully what you're doing and ask someone to go for help if necessary.

Make sure that you

* know where all your passengers are
* know what they're doing
* keep them informed.

If you break down on a motorway, pull onto the hard shoulder and move your passengers to the front of the bus before contacting the emergency services. If you and your passengers have to leave the bus, eg if there's a fire, keep everyone together in a safe area. There's usually a grassed area or bank on the left of the motorway beyond, and well away from, the hard shoulder. Never use the central reservation. Don't leave them, unless absolutely necessary.

Recovery agencies

If you're driving long distances or on overnight services you must know what to do if you break down and require

- a replacement vehicle for your passengers
- the attendance of a breakdown vehicle and/or recovery.

If you're an operator, you must be prepared for anything that might happen, even if you only have one vehicle. Under no circumstances must passengers be left stranded.

Vehicles that break down on the motorway must be removed promptly for safety reasons.

Don't ignore danger signals

If you suspect that there's something wrong with your vehicle don't be tempted to carry on driving. You could end up causing traffic jams if your bus eventually breaks down in an awkward place.

A minor problem could turn out to have major effects. For example, a broken injector pipe dripping fuel onto a hot exhaust manifold may only seem to be a slight engine hesitation to the driver. However, this problem has been known to cause fires in which the vehicle was completely destroyed.

Blow-outs

Many PCV breakdowns involve a tyre bursting, commonly known as a blow-out. These are dangerous because they make a bus difficult to control. They also leave debris on the road, which causes danger to other road users.

Front wheel blow-outs

A front wheel blow-out can mean that you won't be able to steer the bus properly. If this happens you should

- keep a tight hold on the steering wheel
- always be aware of anything on the left-hand side of your bus
- signal left
- try to steer to the left-hand side of the road (or to the hard shoulder on the motorway)

- slow down gradually – don't brake hard
- try to stop your bus under control as far to the left as you can
- put a warning triangle, cones, or another permitted device behind the vehicle if you need to (but **not** if you're on a motorway)
- switch on the hazard warning lights if your vehicle is blocking part of the road.

If you can avoid braking hard or swerving you should be able to stop the bus without skidding.

Rear wheel blow-outs

If a rear tyre bursts you might not notice that it's happened. This is because most large vehicles have twin rear wheels. If you carry on driving, the second tyre on that side of the axle could also burst, as it's not designed to run on its own.

Although a rear wheel blow-out usually has less effect on the steering than a front wheel blow-out, the ride will become bumpy. Always try to find out what's causing odd handling.

Follow the same procedure for a front tyre blow-out, and pull off the road as safely as possible.

Safety checks

It's essential to make sure that all wheel nuts are tightened with the approved calibrated torque wrench. The wheel nuts should be checked every day before starting your journey.

Further information is given in the British Standard Code of Practice for the selection and care of tyres and wheels for commercial vehicles. This has been developed with the support and involvement of the major transport operators' associations. The relevant reference number is BS AU 50: Part 2: Section 7a: 1995, and can be obtained from

British Standards Institution
389 Chiswick High Road
London
W4 4AL

Tel **020 8996 9000**
Website **bsi-global.com**

Road traffic incidents

You should drive at all times with anticipation and awareness. By driving defensively you lessen the risk of being involved in a road traffic incident.

If, however, you're involved in or have to stop at an incident, you should act decisively and with care to prevent any further damage or injury. Ultimately, your own safety and that of your passengers and others must be your first concern.

Always stay alert and try to anticipate the actions of other road users. You need to understand how your vehicle will affect other road users, especially

- cyclists
- pedestrians
- motorcyclists.

Pedestrians standing on the edge of a kerb and cyclists are more vulnerable to being hit by your mirrors or being drawn under your wheels.

Assess every risk and try to eliminate it. You can remove most of the incident risk from your own driving by

- concentrating
- driving safely and sensibly
- staying alert
- being fully fit
- planning well ahead
- observing the changes in traffic conditions
- driving at a safe speed to suit the road, traffic and weather conditions
- keeping your vehicle in good overall condition
- making sure that passengers don't distract you
- not rushing
- avoiding the need to act hurriedly.

If you're involved in a road traffic incident you **MUST** stop. It's an offence not to do so.

At an incident scene

If you're one of the first to arrive at an incident scene, your actions could be vital. Find a safe place to stop, so that you don't endanger yourself, your passengers or other road users. You must ensure that either you or others

- warn other traffic by using hazard warning lights, beacons, cones, advance warning triangles, etc
- check that there are no naked lights, or take the correct action if there are
- telephone 999, giving full details of what has happened
- check that all hazard flashers can be seen. If other road users confuse your signals it could make things worse
- switch off all engines
- stop anyone from smoking.

If it's your vehicle that's involved in a collision, you should also check your passengers for signs of injury.

Dealing with injuries

It's best to avoid moving injured people until the emergency services arrive. You should be extremely careful about moving casualties – it could prove fatal. Casualties should only normally be moved if

- they're in need of resuscitation (that is, if they aren't breathing)
- they're in immediate danger (from fire, chemicals, fuel spillage, etc).

You should

- move any apparently uninjured people away from the vehicle(s) to a safe place
- give first aid if anyone is unconscious (see pages 225–227)
- check for the effects of shock. A person may appear to be uninjured but might be suffering from shock
- keep casualties warm but don't give them anything to eat or drink
- give the facts (not assumptions, etc) to medical staff when they arrive.

You shouldn't remove a motorcyclist's helmet unless it's essential to do so; for example, if they aren't breathing normally.

Caring for passengers

You must do everything you can to protect your passengers at a breakdown or scene of an incident. Decide if there's any further danger and how best to reduce the risk. Tell passengers what's happening

- without upsetting them further
- by only giving them accurate information that they need to know.

You'll need to decide whether it's appropriate for passengers to

- stay where they are
- move to a safer position in the bus, if they're able (eg to the front if another vehicle could run into the back)
- get off the bus carefully and wait in a safe place, which you must select.

If you're unable to supervise the movement of your passengers, ask someone responsible to do it for you. You mustn't allow people to wander around. They could put themselves at risk or get in the way of the emergency services.

You should ask for anyone with medical qualifications to come forward and help.

On the motorway

Because of the higher speeds on motorways there's more danger of a minor incident turning into a serious one. You must inform the motorway police and emergency services as quickly as you can.

- Use the nearest emergency telephone, that's connected directly to the police.
- If you use a mobile phone, identify your location from marker posts on the hard shoulder first.
- Don't cross the carriageway to get to an emergency telephone.
- Try to warn oncoming traffic, but don't endanger yourself.
- Move any uninjured people well away from the main carriageway to a safe place such as an embankment.
- Watch out for emergency vehicles coming along the hard shoulder.

Emergency vehicles

Be aware that emergency vehicles may approach at any time while you're on the road. You should look and listen for flashing blue, red or green lights, headlights or sirens being used by ambulances, fire engines, police or other emergency vehicles. When one approaches don't panic; consider the route it's taking and take appropriate action to let it pass. If necessary, pull to the side of the road and stop, but make sure you're aware of other road users and that you don't endanger them in any way.

If you see or hear emergency vehicles in the distance, be aware that there may be an incident ahead and that other emergency vehicles may be approaching.

In addition to the usual emergency vehicles you would expect to see using blue flashing lights (fire service, police, ambulance), there are others which are perhaps not so common. These include the bomb disposal team and blood transfusion vehicles. A green flashing light means a doctor on call.

Dangerous goods

If an incident involves a vehicle displaying either a hazard warning information plate or a plain orange rectangle

- give the emergency services as much information as possible about the labels and any other markings
- contact the emergency telephone number on the plate of a vehicle involved in any spillage, if one is given
- keep well away from such a vehicle. In attempting to rescue a casualty you may become one
- beware of any liquids, dusts or vapours – no matter how small the amount may appear to be. People have been seriously injured from just a fine spray of corrosive fluid leaking from a pinhole puncture in a tanker
- don't use a mobile phone close to a vehicle carrying flammable loads.

Documents and information

If your vehicle is involved in an incident you **MUST** stop. It's against the law not to do so. Also, you must

- inform the police as soon as possible, or in any case within 24 hours, if
  - anybody is injured
  - damage is caused to another vehicle or property and the owner isn't present or can't be found
  - the incident involves any of the animals specified in law
- produce your insurance documents and driving licence, and give your name and address to any police officer who may require it
- give your own and the vehicle owner's name and address, and the registration number of the vehicle, to anyone having reasonable grounds for requiring them.

If you can't show your documents at the time, regardless of whether anyone is injured or not, report the incident to the police as soon as you can, or in any case within 24 hours (in Northern Ireland you must report the incident to the police immediately).

You must inform the police as soon as possible, and in any case within 24 hours, (you must do this immediately in Northern Ireland), if

- there's injury to any person not in your vehicle

- damage is caused to another vehicle or property and the owner is either not present or can't be found easily
- the incident involves any of the animals specified by law.

The police may ask you to take your documents to a police station of your choice within seven days, or as soon as is reasonably possible if you're already on a journey that takes you out of the country.

At the incident scene you must

- exchange details with any other driver or road user involved in the incident
- obtain names and addresses of any witnesses who saw the incident.

Incident reporting

It's likely that, regardless of the operator or insurer, the information required when completing any incident report form will be very similar, with only slight variations. It's a good idea, therefore, to familiarise yourself with your operator's particular reporting requirements, to make sure you collect all the necessary details at the time of the incident.

Your operator may have a company procedure for completing incident reports and you may already have some forms in your vehicle.

Take notes at the scene so that you have the information when you need it. Make a note of

- the time
- the place
- street names
- vehicle registration numbers
- weather conditions
- lighting (if applicable)
- any road signs or road markings
- road conditions
- damage to vehicles or property (see pages 93–95 for the procedure for railway bridge collisions)
- traffic lights (colour at the time)
- any indicator signals or warning (horn)
- any statements made by other people involved
- any skid marks, debris, etc.

Reaction in the event of aggression

Be aware that others involved in an incident may initially behave in an agitated or aggressive manner. This can often be a symptom of shock so try to be as reasonable and gently spoken as possible when asking for personal details or insurance information. The fact that you appear calm and in control may be all that's needed to diffuse a situation.

Fire

Fire can occur on PCVs in a number of locations

- engine
- passenger areas
- kitchens and serveries
- toilets
- crew sleeping accommodation
- luggage lockers
- transmission
- tyres
- fuel system
- electrical circuits.

It's vital that any outbreak is tackled without delay. A vehicle can be destroyed by fire within an alarmingly short period of time. During your walk-round, you should already have made a check of the tyres and electrical equipment, and examined the fuel tank/cap for any leaks.

It's also advisable to be aware of any flammable items which passengers may be bringing onto your vehicle so that, if a fire occurs in the passenger area, the appropriate type of extinguisher can be used, or the emergency services can be advised of any particular hazard.

If a fire is suspected or discovered, in order to avoid danger to others, it's essential to

- stop as quickly and safely as possible (on the hard shoulder if on a motorway)
- get everyone off the PCV as quickly as possible and lead them to stand in a safe place
- either telephone 999 or get someone else to do it immediately
- tackle the source with a suitable fire extinguisher, **if you can do so safely. Do not endanger your own life.**

If a fire is suspected inside the engine compartment, **do not** lift the bonnet. You may be able to insert an extinguisher nozzle in the small gap available when the catch is released but **do not** take risks.

If the fire is in an adjacent vehicle that's carrying dangerous goods

- the driver must have been given training to deal with such an emergency. Follow their advice
- the vehicle should carry special fire extinguishers
- keep the public and other traffic well away from the fire
- isolate the vehicle, if you can, to reduce danger to the surrounding area
- make sure that someone calls, immediately, the emergency telephone number given on the hazard warning plate or the load documents
- warn oncoming traffic.

Remember, stay calm and react promptly.

Fire extinguishers

All PCVs must have at least one fire extinguisher. You must know where they're located and how to get them out and use them.

Regulations specify the type and size of fire extinguisher that must be carried on a bus or coach. You should be able to recognise the various types of fire extinguisher and know which fires they're intended to tackle. For example, it's dangerous to tackle a fuel fire with a water or carbon dioxide fire extinguisher, since this may only spread the fire further. Each extinguisher will have a coloured label or badge relevant to its content.

Most extinguishers are intended to smother the source of the fire by either the action of an inert gas or a dry powder. Try to isolate the source of the fire. If at all possible

- disconnect electrical leads
- cut off the fuel supply.

The location of fire extinguishers and the fuel cut-off switch (if fitted) **MUST** be clearly labelled on buses.

Don't open an engine housing wide if you can direct the extinguisher through a small gap. Also, avoid operating a fire extinguisher in a confined space.

Vehicles carrying dangerous goods and other materials that may pose a hazard are subject to detailed emergency procedures which must be followed. Never put yourself in danger when tackling a fire. Always call the fire service as quickly as possible because they're the experts. Make sure any passengers leave the vehicle and go to a place of safety.

Note

Halon fire extinguishers may still be used. However, halon is no longer manufactured in the EU for environmental reasons. Once used, a halon extinguisher can't be refilled and should be replaced with a suitable alternative, such as a dry powder extinguisher.

First aid

Buses and coaches **MUST** carry first aid equipment, the location of which **MUST** be clearly labelled. Although the carriage of such equipment isn't a legal requirement on a vehicle being used to operate a local service, you must know

- where it is
- how to get at it (if it's kept behind glass or in a safety compartment)
- what's in it
- how and when to use it.

As a professional driver, you're encouraged to take some first aid training. It could help save a life. There are courses available from the

- St John Ambulance Association and Brigade
- St Andrew's First Aid
- British Red Cross Society.

The following information may be of general assistance, but there's no substitute for proper training.

First aid on the road

The following information may be of general assistance, but there's no substitute for proper training. Any first aid given at the scene of an incident should be looked on only as a temporary measure until the emergency services arrive. If you haven't had any first aid training, the following points could be helpful.

1. Deal with danger

Further collisions and fire are the main dangers following a crash. Approach any vehicle involved with care. Switch off all engines and, if possible, warn other traffic. Stop anyone from smoking.

2. Get help

Try to get the assistance of bystanders. Get someone to call the appropriate emergency services on 999 or 112 as soon as possible. They'll need to know the exact location of the incident and the number of vehicles involved. Try to give information about the condition of any casualties, eg if anyone is having difficulty breathing, is bleeding heavily or doesn't respond when spoken to.

3. Help those involved

DO NOT move casualties still in vehicles unless there's the threat of further danger. **DO NOT** remove a motorcyclist's helmet unless it's essential. Remember the casualty may be suffering from shock.

DO NOT give them anything to eat or drink. **DO** try to make them warm and as comfortable as you can. Protect them from rain or snow, but avoid unnecessary movement. **DO** give reassurance confidently and try not to leave them alone or let them wander into the path of other traffic.

4. Provide emergency care

Remember the letters **DR A B C**

D – Danger Check that you're not in danger.

R – Response Try to get a response by asking questions and gently shaking their shoulders.

A – Airway If the person isn't talking and the airway may be blocked, then place one hand under the chin and lift the chin up and forward. If they're still having difficulty with breathing then gently tilt the head back.

B – Breathing Normal breathing should be established. Once the airway is open, check breathing for up to 10 seconds.

C – Compressions If they have no signs of life and there's no pulse, then chest compressions should be administered. Place two hands in the centre of the chest and press down hard and fast – 5–6 cm at a rate of 100/minute. You may only need one hand for a child and shouldn't press down as far. For infants, use two fingers in the middle of the chest when delivering compressions and don't press down too far.

Unconscious and breathing

Don't move a casualty unless there's further danger. Movement could add to spinal or neck injury. If breathing stops, treat as recommended under 'DR ABC' above.

Don't attempt to remove a motorcyclist's helmet unless it's essential – for example, if the casualty isn't breathing normally – otherwise serious injury could result.

If an adult or child is unconscious and breathing, place them on their side in the recovery position (as shown below).

The recovery position

- Place the arm nearest you straight out. Move the other arm, palm upwards, against the casualty's cheek.
- With your other hand, grasp the far leg just above the knee and pull it up, keeping the foot flat on the ground.
- Pull the knee towards you, keeping the casualty's hand pressed against their cheek, and position the leg at a right angle. Make sure that the casualty's airway remains open and that you monitor their condition until medical help arrives.

Bleeding

First, check for anything that may be in the wound, such as glass. Taking care not to press on the object, build up padding on either side of the object. If there's nothing embedded, apply firm pressure over the wound to stem the flow of blood. As soon as practical, fasten a pad to the wound with a bandage or length of cloth. Use the cleanest material available. If a limb is bleeding but not broken, raise it above the level of the heart to reduce the flow of blood. Any restriction of blood circulation for more than a short time could cause long-term injuries. It's vital to obtain skilled medical help as soon as possible. Make sure someone dials 999 or 112.

Dealing with shock

The effects of shock may not be immediately obvious. Warning signs to look for include

- rapid pulse
- pale grey skin
- sweating
- rapid, shallow breathing.

Prompt treatment can help to deal with shock.

- Don't give the casualty anything to eat or drink.
- Reassure the casualty confidently and keep checking on them.
- Keep casualties warm and make them as comfortable as you can.
- Talk firmly and quietly to anyone who's hysterical.
- Don't let anyone suffering from shock wander into the path of other traffic.
- Try not to leave any casualty alone.
- Don't move the casualty unless it's necessary.
- If a casualty does need to be moved for their own safety, take care to avoid making their injuries worse.

Burns

Check the casualty for shock, and if possible, try to cool the burn for at least 10 minutes with plenty of clean, cold water or other non-toxic liquid. Don't try to remove anything that's sticking to the burn.

Electric shock

Some accidents involve a vehicle hitting overhead cables or electrical supplies to traffic bollards, traffic lights or street lights. Make a quick check before trying to get someone out of a vehicle in such cases.

Don't touch any person who's obviously in contact with live electricity, unless you can use some non-conducting item, such as a piece of dry wood, plastic or similar – anything wet shouldn't be used. Use it to push away any electrical equipment or loose cables if you can and separate any contact the casualty has with the electricity supply. You mustn't try to give first aid until contact has been broken.

A person can also be electrocuted by simply being too close to a high voltage overhead cable. Contact the provider (a number may be shown on a nearby pole) then follow their advice.

Be prepared

Always carry a first aid kit – you might never need it, but it could save a life.

Learn first aid – you can get first aid training from a qualified organisation such as St John Ambulance and Brigade, St Andrew's First Aid, British Red Cross Society or any suitable qualified body.

section **five**

PREPARING FOR THE DRIVING TEST

This section covers

- Preparing for the driving test
- Applying for the test
- The official syllabus

Preparing for the driving test

The standard required to pass the PCV driving test is high. After all, you'll be carrying passengers who will be relying on you to deliver them safely to their destinations. Also, the vehicles you'll be licensed to drive require extensive knowledge, skill and responsibility to be driven safely.

The PCV driving test has been carefully designed to assess whether you've reached the required standard. To be properly prepared for the driving test you should cover the specific aspects of the officially recommended syllabus (found on page 239 onwards) and combine this with practice on a wide variety of roads in different traffic conditions. You should be able to demonstrate to the examiner that you can deal with any situation that arises – safely, skilfully and without help or advice.

Training organisations

There are a number of training organisations concerned with passenger transport, which have established the highest standards of training for the PCV driver. In addition, several large operators have driver-training divisions.

If you wish to work for one of these operators and are accepted onto their scheme, you'll be trained to drive using company buses. You may have to pay for this training, or agree to work for the company for a certain time.

The company itself will arrange for your PCV driving test when your driving is good enough. Some operators even have examiners of their own who are authorised to conduct tests. Otherwise you'll be tested by a DSA examiner at a PCV driving test centre.

You can find details of a local training group by contacting

- the Confederation of Passenger Transport UK (see page 320)
- your local bus or coach operators
- your local Learning and Skills Council
- advertisers in your local press or in trade directories.

You'll normally be offered an 'assessment drive', lasting an hour or two. The instructor will then suggest the length of course you'll need and the cost.

Contact more than one training organisation and compare schemes. Try to choose an instructor or organisation with an established reputation for the quality of their instruction and proven PCV test results. Ask what arrangements are made, should you need additional training as a result of failing a PCV test. Also, talk to newly qualified PCV drivers about their training.

Training coverage

It's in your own interest to find out how comprehensive a training course will be before you enrol. The opportunity to drive a variety of vehicles will obviously widen your knowledge and understanding of buses and coaches. In addition, your training should cover driving

- on as many different types of road as possible, including motorways
- in all sorts of driving conditions, including darkness
- on dual carriageways, where the upper speed limit for PCVs applies (you'll probably be asked to drive on such roads during the PCV test).

Whether you select operator training, a commercial driver-training school or an individual trainer, with perhaps only one vehicle, it's essential that all aspects of the syllabus set out in this part are covered. You should also have the opportunity to practise the braking and reversing exercises on a suitable off-road site. However, avoid concentrating solely on the off-road exercises.

Your supervising driver

After April 2010 anyone training or supervising (accompanying) must

- hold a full (ie **not** implied rights*) entitlement for the category of vehicle you're driving, and
- have held that entitlement for the relevant period of time – usually three years.

*'Implied' rights means those drivers who passed their car driving test before January 1997. They were granted implied rights to drive buses and coaches (D1 and D1+E), subject to certain restrictions. Those people will still be able to drive a small bus or coach, but can't supervise a learner D1 or D1+E driver.

Causing a nuisance

Creating undue inconvenience for others should be avoided when you practise. Not all road users appreciate the difficulties that a bus driver faces when manoeuvring a large vehicle, especially

- moving off
- stopping
- turning left or right
- in narrow roads.

The nuisance caused to residents and other traffic, or the continuous noise created by

- the hissing of air brakes or revving the engine to build up air pressure
- persistent stopping and starting

can soon become a reason for complaint in residential areas.

If there's a local problem because PCV or LGV training is already taking place, avoid making the situation worse. Your trainer should be aware of any such difficulties and use an alternative area to practise.

About the driving test

When taking the PCV practical test, you should aim for a professional standard. You'll pass if the examiner sees that you can

- drive safely and to a high standard
- show expert handling of all the controls
- carry out the set exercises accurately, under control and with good observation
- demonstrate a thorough understanding of The Highway Code and vehicle safety matters.

Does the standard of the test vary?

No. All examiners are trained to carry out tests to the same high standards nationally. Whether they're DSA or delegated company examiners, all are regularly checked to ensure that your driving will be assessed uniformly. You should have the same result whoever the examiner is and wherever the test takes place. In addition, test routes

- are as similar as possible
- include a wide range of typical road and traffic conditions.

How your driving test is assessed

Your examiner will assess any errors you make. They'll be assessed and recorded depending on their degree of seriousness and marked on the Driving Test Report form (DL25).

You'll fail your test if you commit a serious or dangerous fault. You'll also fail if you accumulate too many driving faults (previously known as minor faults).

The criteria the examiner will use are as follows

Driving fault Less serious but has been assessed as such because of circumstances at that particular time.

Serious fault Recorded when a potentially dangerous incident has occurred or a habitual driving fault indicates a serious weakness in a candidate's driving.

Dangerous fault Recorded when a fault is assessed as having caused actual danger during the test.

At the end of the test, you'll be offered some general guidance to explain your driving test report. Your instructor can be present during this debrief even if they haven't accompanied you on the driving test.

Are examiners supervised?

Yes, they're closely supervised. A senior officer may sit in on your test. Don't worry about this. The supervising officer won't be examining you, but will be checking that the examiner is carrying out the test properly. Just carry on as if they weren't there.

Can anyone accompany me on the test?

Your instructor is allowed to accompany you but can't take any part in the test. Regulations prevent passengers other than those mentioned above from being carried on a test.

What if I need an interpreter?

If you need an interpreter you should arrange for one to come with you. The interpreter must be 16 years or over and can be your instructor or trainer. Time will be spent at the start of your test discussing the best way to give directions or instructions that are clearly understood.

How should I drive during the test?

Drive in the way your instructor has taught you. If you make a mistake, try not to let it worry you. It might be a trivial mistake and may not affect the results of the test.

Your examiner will be looking for a high overall standard. Don't worry about one or two minor mistakes.

What will my examiner want from me?

Your examiner will want you to drive safely to a high standard under various road and traffic conditions. You'll be

- given directions clearly and in good time
- asked to carry out set exercises.

If at any time you're unable to hear or understand the instructions given, ask for them to be repeated, the examiner won't mind. He or she will try to put you at your ease.

What will the test consist of?

The test will last around 90 minutes. Apart from general driving, the test will include

- reversing within a marked area into a restricted opening
- a braking exercise
- moving off on the level, at an angle, uphill and downhill
- demonstrating the uncoupling and recoupling procedure, if you're taking your test with a trailer.

You'll also need to satisfy the examiner that you're capable of preparing to drive safely by carrying out simple safety checks on the vehicle you're using on the test. The safety checks and some of the manoeuvres are carried out at the test centre. These are

- reversing within a marked area into a restricted opening
- a braking exercise

- an uncoupling or recoupling exercise if relevant.

The remainder of the exercises will take place during the road section of the test.

During the reversing exercise your examiner will remain outside the vehicle. Your examiner will join you in the cab before explaining the braking exercise to you. He or she will watch your handling of the controls and observations as you carry out the exercise. This exercise will be carried out before you leave the test centre. If your vehicle doesn't pull up satisfactorily your examiner may decide not to continue with the test, in the interest of safety.

If a delegated company examiner conducts your driving test, all the exercises may be carried out on public roads or at an agreed private site.

The Highway Code

You must know and understand The Highway Code thoroughly and put it into practice during the test. Study the latest edition carefully. Questions on The Highway Code form part of the theory test for drivers of large vehicles. Training materials for the multiple choice part of the test also include *Know Your Traffic Signs* and *The Official DSA Theory Test for Drivers of Large Vehicles* (available either in book or CD-ROM format). The Highway Code is also available as an interactive CD-ROM and in British Sign Language. Many of the resources are also available as a downloadable PDF.

As well as the multiple choice questions, the theory test includes a hazard perception part. To prepare for this, DSA strongly recommends that you study and work through the hazard perception training material. There's a DVD available, entitled *The Official DSA Guide to Hazard Perception,* which will assist you.

You'll need to put into practice what you've learned for your theory test when taking the practical test.

> **Remember,** make sure that you prepare fully for your test.

You can start driver training before you apply for the theory test, but you must pass before you're permitted to apply for the practical PCV driving test. A theory test pass certificate is valid for two years.

Being fully prepared

Driver training for large vehicles is usually intensive, so it may be necessary for either you or your trainer to book your PCV driving test before you've reached the standard required to pass.

Your instructor may offer you a mock test shortly before your real test is due. This will give you an understanding of how the test will be conducted and may alert you to any weaknesses.

Make sure that you understand what you're asked to do and should you need to work on any problem areas, work with your instructor to overcome them.

Having a test date to aim for can be a good incentive. However, drivers acquire skills and understanding at differing rates and it's possible that you may need more time and training than you'd planned. If this happens, postpone your test; it's better to go in for your test feeling confident. Be advised by your trainer.

Don't leave it too late to cancel your test appointment, as a late cancellation may result in you losing your fee for the driving test.

Driving examiners are observers during a driving test – they're not there to advise you on how to drive, so make sure that you feel confident in your own ability.

If your instructor doesn't feel that you have competent, safe control of the vehicle by the time of the test appointment, accept that judgement. You'll be advised about the options for additional training, and an alternative test appointment may be available to you.

Applying for the test

When you reach the standards set in this book – not before – apply for your practical test.

You should be driving

- consistently well
- with confidence
- in complete control
- without assistance and guidance from your instructor.

You'll then be ready for your PCV driving test. Be advised by your instructor and make sure that you have enough practice before you apply.

To apply for the test you must have an entitlement to drive PCVs (either a category D provisional licence or a full licence for a category that includes provisional entitlement for the category on which you wish to be tested). In addition, you'll need a valid theory test pass certificate.

Special circumstances

If you're disabled in any way you'll take the same PCV driving test as other candidates but extra time could be allowed. Your examiner may wish to talk to you about your disability and any adaptions fitted to your vehicle. For this reason it's important to give details of your disability when you apply for your test.

To make sure enough time is allowed for your test, DSA needs to know if

- you're restricted in any way in your movements
- you have a disability that may affect your driving.

If you would like further information, please see the list of useful addresses at the back of this book.

Language difficulties

If you have difficulty speaking or understanding English you can bring an interpreter with you. The interpreter must be 16 years or over and can be your instructor/trainer. Please include this information on your test application form.

How to apply for your test

You must have a provisional entitlement for the category of vehicle that you're going to drive.

Book online or by phone

You can book your theory and practical tests online or by telephone using a credit or debit card. Most major credit and debit cards are accepted. You must be the card holder; if you aren't then the card holder must be present.

For information about fees and to book a test, go to **www.gov.uk** or by phone **0300 200 1122**.

The booking clerk will want to know

- your driver number, shown on your licence
- the type of test you wish to book
- your personal details (name, address, day and evening telephone numbers)
- unacceptable days or periods
- any special circumstances, such as being accompanied by an interpreter
- your credit card number and expiry date (and the issue number if required).

If you're booking your practical test you'll need to provide your theory test certificate number.

If you use either of these services, you'll be offered a date and time for your test immediately. You'll be given a booking number and sent an appointment within a few days.

Book by post

You can obtain an application form (DL26) from a DSA LGV/PCV test centre. Look at the guidance notes (DL26/I) carefully, especially those that refer to vehicle categories. The postal application form can also be downloaded from **www.gov.uk**

Make sure that you give all the particulars required on the application form. If you miss anything out it could delay the date of your test.

Don't forget to send your fee. You may do this by sending a cheque or postal order. Make sure that it's crossed and made payable to **Driving Standards Agency**. If you send a postal order, be sure to keep the counterfoil.

Send your application form to

**DSA
PO Box 280
Newcastle-upon-Tyne
NE99 1FP**

Remember, please don't send cash.

In Northern Ireland

You may book any category of test in person. You'll need to complete an application form and take it with the appropriate fee to the DVA test centre at which you would like the test to be carried out.

The Belfast centre is open for booking from 9.00 am to 4.00 pm, Monday to Friday. All other centres are open from 8.45 am to 12.30 pm and from 1.15 pm to 4.00 pm, Monday to Friday. You can get an application form by contacting any DVA test centre or by phoning **028 9068 1831**. For more information visit **nidirect.gov.uk**

Trainer booking

If you're learning to drive with a training organisation they'll normally book your test for you. An arrangement with the area office allows them to book and pay for test appointments in advance. This enables them to arrange courses to culminate with a test appointment.

If you're a trainer and are interested in this scheme, contact DSA's booking section on **0300 200 1122**.

Visit the website

More information and guidance on all aspects of booking or taking a driving test can be found at **www.gov.uk**

Saturday and evening tests

Saturday and weekday evening tests are available at some PCV driving test centres. The fees for these are higher than for a test during normal working hours on weekdays. You can get details from

• **www.gov.uk**

• PCV driving test centres

• your instructor

• the national booking telephone number **0300 200 1122**.

Your test appointment

DSA will send notification of your appointment, which is the receipt for your fee. Take this with you when you attend your test.

It will include

• the time and place of your test

• the address of the driving test centre

• other important information.

Your confirmation will be sent in the post if you don't have an email address. If you don't receive notification after 21 days, contact the national booking telephone number **0300 200 1122.**

Check your appointment notification as soon as you receive it to make sure that the date and time of the test appointment are suitable.

To change or cancel your test

If you need to change or cancel the appointment, you should notify DSA as soon as possible. You may even be able to switch to an earlier date.

You can do this online at **www.gov.uk** or by phone **0300 200 1122**.

You must give at least three clear working days' notice. That means three whole working days, counting Saturday as a working day, but not counting the day DSA received your notification nor the day of your test. If you don't give enough notice you'll forfeit your fee and will have to reapply with another fee.

Change of address or vehicle

Please telephone the national booking telephone number immediately if you change your address before the day of your appointment. Also, you'll need to inform DSA if you have to bring a different vehicle from the one described on your application form. Otherwise, there could be a delay when you arrive for your test.

Inform the driving examiner at the test centre, either beforehand or as soon as you arrive, if there's any last-minute change of vehicle.

Extended tests

If you're found guilty of certain driving offences the courts may direct you to retake your PCV driving test. For some offences, which involve disqualification from driving for a period of time, you may need to take an extended car driving test. This means that

• it will be necessary to apply to the DVLA for a provisional licence entitlement

• you may only apply for a PCV test after passing an extended category B driving test

• you'll have to pass a normal PCV driving test if you previously held a PCV entitlement and wish to regain it.

There are higher fees for extended car driving tests, but not for the associated PCV driving test.

Remember, if you lose your category B (car) entitlement you'll also lose your PCV entitlement. Your PCV entitlement may be returned on passing the category B test, but this is at the discretion of the Secretary of State for Transport.

The official syllabus

This syllabus lists the skills and knowledge required to be a good bus or coach driver and to pass the PCV practical driving test. Use the syllabus as a check list while training.

Make sure that you understand all the areas covered. Other parts of this book explain in more detail the various topics in the syllabus. Your instructor will be able to answer any queries you have regarding preparation for your test.

During your driving test you won't be tested on all the items listed in the syllabus. However, you do need to understand them all. You need to know about all the aspects of being a safe and professional driver. While you're driving your examiner will want to see that you put your knowledge into practice. Think of passing the test as only one stage in becoming a good driver.

If you drive a PCV for which no special driving test is needed, this syllabus will help you to achieve the high standard of driving required for your own safety and that of your passengers.

Knowledge

You must have a thorough knowledge and understanding of

1. the latest edition of The Highway Code

2. regulations governing drivers' permitted hours (EC 3820/1985)

3. regulations relating to the carriage of passengers (Public Passenger Vehicles Act 1981 and 1990 amendments)*

4. general motoring regulations, especially

   - road traffic offences

   - producing driving licences

   - holding operator's and road fund licences, and displaying discs where applicable

   - holding and displaying community bus permits, where applicable

   - insurance requirements (including 'green cards' or bail bonds that may be needed when abroad)

   - the Temp 100 regulations, if you intend to drive outside the UK

   - the information that must be shown on PCV manufacturers' plates

   - annual testing and the certification requirements for tachographs and speed limiters

   - the importance of regular vehicle maintenance and defect-reporting procedures

5. health and safety legislation, as it applies to PCV duties.

*Note
Certain minibuses, mobile project buses, playbuses, historic vehicles and community buses are subject to a relaxation of the public service and passenger-carrying vehicles regulations. If you drive one of these vehicles you must be aware of any restrictions on its use.

If your vehicle is equipped with a trailer, you must know which legal requirements apply.

You must also have a basic understanding of the function of the component parts of a PCV, including

6. internal combustion engines
   - petrol
   - diesel
   - other fuels
7. power and control units in electrically propelled vehicles, if appropriate
8. ancillary and control systems
9. the body and its equipment.

Legal requirements

To learn to drive a PCV, you must

1. be at least 18 years old*
2. meet the stringent eyesight requirements
3. be medically fit to drive PCVs of any type
4. hold a full car licence (category B or, if issued prior to 1990, group A)
5. hold and comply with the conditions for holding either
   - a provisional PCV category D entitlement, or
   - a full PCV entitlement for another category of vehicle, which confers provisional entitlement for the vehicle you wish to drive

6. be sure that any vehicle driven
   - is legally roadworthy
   - has the required manufacturer's plate
   - has a current test certificate that covers its use
   - is properly licensed and has the correct tax disc displayed (and 'O' licence or permit disc, if required)
   - complies with the requirements of the tachograph and speed limiter legislation and displays the required certificates, if applicable
   - meets minimum vehicle requirements if used for a PCV driving test (see page 326)
7. make sure that the vehicle being driven is properly insured for its use, especially if it's on contract hire
8. display L plates to the front and rear of the vehicle (or D plates, if you wish, when driving in Wales)
9. be accompanied by a supervisor who's over the age of 21 and has held a full licence for three years in the category of vehicle being driven
10. be aware of the legal requirement to notify the DVLA of any medical condition that could affect safe driving.

*Note
See minimum licence restrictions chart and notes on page 324. (To carry passengers, the vehicle must be covered by a public service vehicle operator's licence or a bus or community bus permit.)

11. ensure that all information required on, or in, the vehicle by law (referred to as the legal lettering) is displayed, as applicable
    - seating/standing capacity
    - emergency exit location
    - fuel cut-off switch
    - electrical isolator switch
    - first aid equipment
    - fire extinguisher(s)
    - unladen weight of vehicle
    - height, displayed in the cab if the vehicle is over 3.0 metres (9 feet 10 inches)
    - registered company name and address
    - engine stop button.

You must also avoid

12. using any mobile telephone or radio transmitter while driving the vehicle (except for limited use of Band III radio systems used for route control and emergency purposes). It's illegal to use a hand-held mobile phone or similar device while driving

13. stopping on the hard shoulder of a motorway to use any mobile telephone or radio transmitter (unless in an emergency)

14. using any public address system fitted in the vehicle to give any commentary while driving (except for brief location information which may be given using a 'hands-free' system)

15. driving the vehicle while
    - issuing tickets
    - giving change
    - holding a conversation, other than in an emergency
    - being distracted
    - smoking
    - the passenger doors are open.

In addition, you must know and apply the legal requirements relating to the vehicle and its use, where applicable, in respect of
    - speed limits
    - seating/standing capacity
    - fire extinguishers
    - first aid equipment (location and use)
    - interior lighting during the hours of darkness
    - the carriage and consumption of alcoholic drinks
    - the emptying of toilet waste storage tanks
    - hazardous substances that may be brought on board by passengers.

Vehicle controls, equipment and components

You must

1. understand the function and use of the main controls of the vehicle's
   - accelerator
   - clutch, if applicable
   - gears
   - footbrake
   - parking brake (handbrake)
   - steering, including power-assisted steering

   and be able to use them competently

2. know the effects speed limiters will have on the control of your vehicle, especially when you intend to overtake

3. know the principles of the various systems of retarders that may be fitted to PCVs
   - electric
   - engine-driven
   - exhaust brakes

   and when they should be brought into operation

4. know the function of all other controls and switches on the vehicle and be able to use them competently

5. understand the information given by
   - gauges
   - warning lights or buzzers
   - other displays on the instrument panel

6. be familiar with the operation of tachographs and their charts and any other time, speed or distance recording equipment that may be fitted. You should know what action to take if a fault develops in this equipment

7. know which checks should be made before starting a journey

8. know the safety factors relating to
   - seated and standing passengers
   - loading
   - stability
   - controls of any driver-operated doors
   - stowing luggage when passengers are carried

9. be able to carry out routine safety checks and identify defects, especially with the
   - engine performance
   - fuel systems
   - lubricating systems and oil levels
   - coolant temperature and levels
   - exhaust systems
   - gearbox operation, controls and transmission
   - braking system efficiency and operation
   - steering (including power-assisted systems)
   - suspension
   - tyres, wheel security and mudguards

- heating, air conditioning and ventilation
- air tanks (air pressure)
- electrical systems, including
  - lights
  - direction indicators
  - destination displays
  - wipers and washers
  - bells, buzzers and linked 'bus stopping' displays
  - 'emergency exit insecure' warning devices, if fitted
  - horns
  - fuses, cut-outs and relays
- windscreen
- reflectors
- exterior bodywork, panels, fittings and trim
- service doors
- side and rear-view mirrors
- interior bodywork, seating, fittings and trim
- floor coverings
- emergency exits
- first aid equipment
- fire extinguisher
- vehicle loading

and, where fitted,

- seat belts and grab rails
- equipment for wheelchair access and security
- mechanically, electrically or air-operated doors
- adjustable suspension on 'kneeling' vehicles
- securing devices on emergency doors
- equipment for breaking emergency windows
- staircases.

Road user behaviour

You must know how to limit the risk of being involved in a road traffic incident by understanding

1. the most common causes of incidents
2. which road users are more vulnerable, for example
   - children
   - young riders and drivers
   - older drivers
   - older or infirm pedestrians
   - cyclists and motorcyclists
   - learner drivers
3. the rules, risks and effects of drinking before driving
4. the effects on your performance of
   - illnesses
   - recreational drugs
   - cold remedies
   - other medication
   - tiredness
5. the importance of complying with rest period regulations

6. how to
   - concentrate
   - plan ahead
   - anticipate the actions of other road users.

Vehicle characteristics

You must know

1. the most important principles concerning braking distances under various road, weather and loading conditions

2. the different handling characteristics of vehicles with regard to
   - speed
   - stability
   - braking
   - manoeuvrability
   - turning circles

3. that some other vehicles, such as cycles and motorcycles, are less easily seen than others.

You must also be aware of

4. blind spots that occur on many large vehicles

5. the need to be extra-vigilant when reversing any PCV into or out of a bay at boarding points or in workshops

6. the safe angle of tilt, which mustn't be exceeded when driving high vehicles

7. the risks and difficulties presented when
   - long vehicles negotiate speed reduction humps or hump bridges
   - high vehicles are driven along roads with an adverse camber, thus leading to possible collisions with
     - shop blinds
     - buildings
     - road signs
     - traffic lights
     - telephone poles
     - overhead cables
     - trees
     - lamp standards
     - scaffolding
     - other high vehicles
   - vehicles with large mirrors pass close to pedestrians, street furniture or other vehicles
   - heavy vehicles drive on, or close to, soft or damaged verges
   - the vehicle being driven encounters the minimum clearance needed under bridges

8. the difficulties caused by the characteristics of both your own and other vehicles, and be able to take the appropriate action to reduce any risks that may arise.

Examples of situations requiring special care are when

– long wheel-base coaches, buses and large goods vehicles move to the right before making a sharp left turn

– articulated vehicles take an unusual line before negotiating corners, roundabouts or entrances

– short wheel-base vehicles with front and rear overhang turn left or right, or when at bus stops, lay-bys, pedestrian crossings, etc

– cycles, motorcycles and high-sided vehicles are buffeted in strong winds, especially on exposed sections of road

– turbulence created by coaches, double-deck buses and large goods vehicles travelling at speed affects

• pedestrians

• cyclists

• motorcyclists

• vehicles towing caravans

• smaller vehicles.

Road and weather conditions

You must

1. know about the hazards that can arise when driving on various types of road with differing volumes of traffic, such as

    – country lanes

    – single-track roads

    – one-way streets

    – those with bus lanes

    – contraflow systems

    – those in built-up areas

    – three-lane roads

      dual carriageways with various speed limits

    – trunk roads with two-way traffic

    – motorways

    – roads or reserved areas where light rapid transit vehicles (LRTs or supertrams) operate

    – busways

2. know about the hazards that can arise when driving in various weather conditions, such as

    – strong sunlight

    – rain

    – snow and ice

    – fog

    – wind, especially when driving high vehicles

    and at all times of the day and night

3. know which surfaces will provide better or poorer grip when accelerating and braking

4. drive sensibly and anticipate how the conditions may affect the driving of other road users

5. understand the need to be aware of other road users when pulling up at bus stops, especially near junctions

6. appreciate the need to give correct signals, especially before pulling up at
   - bus stops
   - road junctions
   - pedestrian crossings, etc

7. recognise the special risks when passengers board or alight from your vehicle, such as
   - schoolchildren
   - older people
   - the disabled
   - those with
     - babies
     - toddlers
     - pushchairs
     - luggage

8. be aware of the presence of other road users by making effective use of the mirrors and by looking round before moving off from a standstill. Watch out, in particular, for passengers attempting to board or alight as you move off.

Traffic signs, rules and regulations

You must

1. have a thorough knowledge and understanding of the meanings of traffic signs and road markings, especially those relating to
   - bus lanes, which may also permit cycles and taxis
   - bus priority systems
   - light rapid transit systems

2. be able to recognise and comply with traffic signs* that point out
   - weight limits
   - height limits
   - length limits
   - width limits
   - prohibited entry for motor vehicles
   - no left or right turns
   - loading/unloading restrictions
   - roads designated as Red Routes
   - traffic-calming measures.

*Note

Some signs may exempt buses.

Vehicle control and road procedure

You must have the knowledge and skill to take the following precautions, some of which will require assistance.

1. Before getting into the vehicle check that

    - you have all the required paperwork (especially for foreign trips)
    - all required discs and certificates are displayed
    - there are no obstructions round your vehicle
    - the emergency exit(s) operate correctly and are closed securely
    - all bulbs, lenses and reflectors are fitted, clean and undamaged
    - all lights, including indicators and stop lights, are undamaged and working
    - tyres and wheel nuts are free from obvious defects (visual check)
    - all windows and mirrors are clean and free of traffic grime and cracks
    - all body panels are secure
    - all external lockers and crew compartment doors are secure
    - there are no fluid or air system leaks
    - fuel and electrical isolation switches are clearly marked and turned on
    - all route numbers and destination blinds or displays are correct* (or replaced by information that indicates that the vehicle isn't in service).

*Note
Controls for route and destination displays are usually on board the vehicle. Adjust them as necessary.

2. After entering the vehicle, check

    - the height of the vehicle and stay aware of it at all times
    - the correct operation of any warning device fitted to an emergency exit that isn't visible from the driving position
    - that the entrance and exit doors (if fitted) operate correctly, and that any warning systems work properly
    - the location of the fire extinguisher(s) and first aid equipment
    - that heating, air conditioning or ventilation equipment is working properly and set for the conditions
    - that the bell or buzzer signal and any passenger information system works
    - that all gangways and staircases are clean, clear and free from defects
    - that all grab rails and overhead luggage racks are securely fitted
    - that the floor is clean and in good condition, free from any slip or trip hazards or anything that could cause soil/damage to clothing
    - that all seats are clean, secure and free from defects (include a visual check of the floor anchor points)

247

- that any separately fitted cushions won't detach from seats during braking
- that trim is clean and securely fitted, and that no sharp objects could snag skin or clothes
- that seat belts are securely fitted at anchor points, using a tug check
- that belts are clean and in good condition
- that the interior lighting operates correctly, including the exit/entrance step lights
- that equipment for wheelchair access is operational

where these items are fitted, and that

- any graffiti is removed at the earliest opportunity, especially if it might cause offence
- any luggage or equipment is safely stowed.

3. Before starting the engine, check
   - that the parking brake is applied and the gear selector is in neutral or the 'start' position
   - your seat, if necessary, for
     - height
     - distance from the controls
     - support and comfort
     - maximum vision
   - the mirrors, if necessary, to give a clear view of
     - traffic behind
     - the entrance/exit
     - waiting or adjacent passengers
     - the upper deck, where appropriate
   - the doors (if fitted) are closed
   - seat belts (if fitted) are in use.

4. When you start the engine, but before moving off, check that
   - the vehicle lights are on, if required
   - gauges indicate correct pressures for braking and ancillary systems
   - no warning lights are showing, which indicate it's unsafe to drive the vehicle
   - no warning buzzer is operating
   - all fuel and temperature gauges are operating normally and that there's sufficient fuel for your journey
   - suspension systems* are at the correct height, if appropriate
   - all doors are closed
   - all equipment operates correctly (wipers, washers, indicators, etc.)
   - special access facilities,* such as kneeling suspension, ramps or lifts, are correctly adjusted or stowed
   - it's safe, by looking all round. Before moving off, especially check
     - the blind spots
     - entry/exit door(s) or boarding platform(s)
     - near the wheels.

*Note
Air-operated systems, such as suspension and doors, may come into operation as air pressure builds up. Ensure this happens safely.

5. At the first opportunity, and before carrying passengers, check the brakes and steering for correct and effective operation. Also check that exhaust emissions aren't excessive (when the engine's warm).

6. When driving you must be able to

    – move off safely

      • straight ahead

      • at an angle

      • on the level

      • uphill

      • downhill

    – select the correct road position and appropriate gear at all times

    – take effective observation in all traffic conditions and give appropriate signals, when necessary

    – drive at a speed appropriate to the road, traffic and weather conditions

    – anticipate changes in traffic conditions

    – take the correct action at all times and exercise care in the use of the controls

    – move into the appropriate traffic lane correctly and in good time

    – pass stationary vehicles safely

    – meet, overtake and cross the path of other vehicles safely

    – turn right or left, or drive ahead at junctions, crossroads or roundabouts

– keep a safe separation gap when following other vehicles

– act correctly at all types of pedestrian crossing

– show proper regard for the safety of all other road users, particularly the most vulnerable

– keep up with the flow of traffic where it's safe and appropriate to do so, while observing all speed limits

– comply with

  • traffic regulations

  • traffic signs

  • signals given by authorised persons, police officers, traffic wardens or school crossing patrols

– take the correct action on signals given by other road users

– stop the vehicle safely at all times

– show courtesy and consideration to passengers at all times, particularly those with special needs

– wait until older or disabled passengers are seated

– be aware at all times of the effects that harsh braking, acceleration or steering will have on passengers, especially those

  • standing

  • moving toward exits

  • moving away from entrances

- pay particular attention to the care of
  - older passengers
  - disabled passengers
  - people with babies or toddlers
- safely cross all types of level crossings, such as railway or light rapid or railed transit systems (LRTs or supertrams)
- select safe and suitable places to stop the vehicle as close to the nearside kerb as is practicable, when requested
  - on the level
  - facing uphill
  - facing downhill
  - before reaching a parked vehicle
- leave sufficient room to move away when the platform of the vehicle is close to passenger boarding points at bus stops and when requested on 'hail and ride' services
- stop the vehicle in an emergency
  - safely
  - as quickly as possible
  - under full control
  - within a reasonable distance
- reverse the vehicle
  - under control
  - with effective observation
  - accurately
- enter a restricted opening to the left or right, and stop with the extreme rear of the vehicle where required

(when carrying out a reversing exercise with a delegated examiner)

- follow advertised timetables and, in particular, not depart early from published timing points.

7. You must be able to carry out, as necessary, all these checks and manoeuvres
  - safely and expertly
  - in daylight
  - during the hours of darkness.

Where your actions may affect other road users you must
  - make proper use of the mirrors
  - take effective observation
  - give signals, when necessary
  - act predictably.

For the PCV driving test you'll be asked to carry out specific exercises to demonstrate your ability to stop quickly and to reverse. If the test isn't conducted by a DSA examiner but by a delegated (company) examiner these manoeuvres may be carried out on the public roads.

8. Before leaving the driver's position you must make sure that
  - the vehicle is stopped in a safe, legal and secure place
  - the parking brake is on
  - the gear lever/selector is in neutral or 'park'
  - the engine isn't running
  - the keys have been removed from the starter switch, if applicable

- the electrical system is switched off, unless lights or other systems are required (on some vehicles the switch may not be within reach of the driving position)

- you won't endanger anyone when you open any door.

9. When leaving a vehicle make sure that

   - all windows are closed

   - the passenger door is secure (if fitted)

   - you take all possible precautions to prevent theft of the vehicle

   - any available anti-theft device is used (eg immobiliser/alarm)

   - you've selected a safe place to leave the unattended vehicle

   - the parking place is

     • legal (not a 'no waiting' zone)

     • safe (it won't cause any danger to others)

     • convenient (not blocking any access or exit)

     • suitable (level and firm enough to support the weight of the vehicle).

10. If you'll be leaving the vehicle but the public will still have access (for instance, on playbuses or mobile project vehicles), ensure that

    - the cab area is isolated

    - a responsible person is in attendance.

Additional knowledge

You must know

1. the importance of inspecting all tyres on the vehicle for

   - correct pressure

   - signs of wear

   - evidence of damage

   - safe tread depth

   - objects between twin tyres

   - indications of overheating

2. safe driving principles that will help to prevent skids occurring, and the action to take if they do occur

3. how to drive when the road is

   - icy or snow-covered

   - flooded

   - covered by excess surface water, loose chippings or spillages

4. what to do if you're involved in a road traffic incident

   - that results in either injury, damage or fire

   - where there's a spillage of hazardous material

   - where danger to other road users results from an obstruction caused by an immobilised vehicle

   - on a motorway

5. the action to take if your vehicle breaks down during the day or at night on a

   - bend

   - road with two-way traffic

   - busy dual carriageway

- clearway
- motorway
- railway or LRT crossing

with particular reference to the safety of passengers

6. the correct procedure to adopt if an incident (eg person falling over) occurs that involves a passenger travelling on your vehicle, or boarding or alighting

7. the dimensions of your vehicle, including the correct height (especially that of double-deck vehicles, in respect of dangers presented by low bridges, etc)

8. the weight of your vehicle, in respect of restrictions on weak bridges, etc

9. the correct procedure to adopt if it becomes necessary to reverse the vehicle while carrying passengers

10. the differences between toughened and laminated glass used in windows and windscreens

11. how to use the hammer or similar tool to exit from the vehicle in an emergency

12. basic first aid for use on the road

13. the correct legal procedure (defined in the 1990 amendments to the 1981 PSV regulations) to be adopted by the driver or, where present, a conductor or courier, in respect of any passenger(s) whose behaviour or condition affects the
    - safety of other passengers
    - comfort of other passengers
    - safety of the crew

14. the appropriate action to take when handed or when finding
    - any lost property
    - suspicious packages

15. the correct action to take in the event of a passenger, or intending passenger, attempting to alight from or board a moving vehicle

16. how and when to use fire extinguishers fitted to the vehicle

17. how to evacuate a PCV when necessary

18. how and when to use emergency radio and public address systems, if fitted.

You must appreciate

19. the importance of avoiding any action that could cause offence or provoke physical retaliation

20. the need to keep control of the permitted number of standing passengers – especially at peak travel times

21. the need to use safe driving techniques and to obey all speed limits when attempting to maintain schedules laid down in the operator's timetable

22. the principles of passenger care, including how to
    - communicate effectively
    - assist passengers with special needs
    - help passengers unfamiliar with the service

23. the importance of presenting a positive image of your company and the industry through your appearance and conduct and the condition of your vehicle.

You must be able to

24. make a written report, promptly, detailing any defects or symptoms of defects that could adversely affect the safe operation of vehicles. You should submit it to the designated person (the recommended system requires, where practical, a daily 'nil' return to be made to ensure that checks are made)

25. appreciate when defects are serious enough to require an unroadworthy vehicle to be removed from service

26. judge whether a defect is serious enough to cause a vehicle to be unsafe to be driven at all.

Motorway driving

You must have a thorough practical knowledge of the special

- rules
- regulations
- driving techniques

that apply to motorways. In particular, you should know about

- overtaking
- exercising lane discipline
- lanes that are prohibited to certain PCVs
- when speed limiters affect driving

- where PCV speed limits differ to those applying to other traffic
- where temporary speed limits apply when joining and leaving motorways
- breakdowns and emergencies
- driving in all weather conditions
- the principal causes of incidents on motorways.

Safe working practices

You should

1. know the risks involved in jumping down from cabs (where applicable), and avoid them

2. ensure that all doors are closed before the vehicle is moved

3. follow safety guidelines when operating

   - under

     - raised engine cowlings
     - raised luggage compartment hatches
     - overhead cables
     - any vehicle

   - near

     - inspection pits
     - wheelchair lift controls
     - refuelling points
     - parked vehicles (especially those likely to be moved or with air suspension)

- while
  - carrying out roadside repairs
  - inflating tyres
  - near any vehicle supported on jacks
  - refuelling
  - topping up oil or water
4. wear protective clothing, including gloves, when
   - refuelling
   - topping up oil or water
   - checking battery levels
   - emptying waste systems

5. know where company policy permits the driver to carry out minor repairs, but do so only
   - if you fully understand how to locate the fault and are able to put it right properly
   - if you can do so without endangering yourself or others
   - with the aid of appropriate equipment, if needed
   - if you're sure that any work you do won't invalidate any manufacturer's warranty.

If in doubt, refer to your company or local authority.

section **six**
THE PCV DRIVING TEST

This section covers

- What to expect on the day
- Safety checks
- The reversing exercise
- The braking exercise
- The vehicle controls
- Other controls
- Moving off
- Using the mirrors
- Giving signals
- Acting on signs and signals
- Making progress
- Controlling your speed
- Separation distance
- Awareness and anticipation
- Hazards
- Selecting a safe place to stop
- Uncoupling and recoupling
- Understanding the rules
- The test results

What to expect on the day

Arrive in good time for your test, otherwise it may not go ahead and you'll lose your fee.

The test will last about 90 minutes, so make sure that you won't exceed the number of hours you're allowed to drive by law, and that you have sufficient fuel.

When you meet the examiner you'll be asked to sign a declaration that the vehicle you're using for the test is fully insured for that purpose and that you meet the residency requirements.

Documents

You must have applied for and received a provisional licence for the category in which you wish to take your test. Make sure that you have your provisional driving licence and your theory test pass certificate with you. Photocopies aren't acceptable.

If you have a photocard licence you must bring both parts of the licence (photocard and paper counterpart) to the test.

If your licence doesn't show your photograph you must also bring your passport with you (your passport doesn't have to be British). No other form of identification is acceptable. Other forms of identification may be acceptable in Northern Ireland: please check **dvani.gov.uk**

If you don't bring these documents with you on the day you won't be able to take your test and you'll lose your fee.

Remember, no photo, no licence, no test.

Preparing your vehicle

To avoid wasting your own time and the examiner's, make sure that your test vehicle

- has no passengers
- is in the category in which you wish to hold a licence
- doesn't exceed 18.28 metres (60 feet) in length
- has red L plates visible to the front and rear (D plates, if you wish, in Wales)
- has the relevant 'no smoking' signs in place as required by legislation
- isn't being used on a trade licence or displaying trade registration plates
- has a secure seat for the examiner and for anyone supervising the test, from which they can observe the driver. (From 1 July 2007, these seats had to be fitted with seat belts)
- is fitted with nearside and offside externally mounted mirrors for use by the examiner and anyone supervising the test
- is fully covered by insurance for its present use and for you to drive
- is legally roadworthy
- has enough fuel, not only for the test (at least 20 miles) but also for you to return to base

Other details of minimum test vehicle requirements can be found on pages 326–327.

Make sure that your vehicle is in a thoroughly roadworthy condition, especially

- stop lights
- direction indicators
- lenses/reflectors
- mirrors
- brakes
- tyres
- exhaust/silencer
- windscreen/washer/wipers.

It would be unusual for your vehicle not to meet these requirements, but where vehicles have been adapted for other uses, they may not be suitable for the purposes of the test. If you're in doubt, ask DSA.

Vehicles with accelerator, brake and clutch are classed as manual; vehicles with accelerator and brake are classed as automatic.

Legal requirements

At the start of your test you'll be asked some 'show me/tell me' questions on vehicle safety.

The test route will cover a wide variety of road and traffic conditions. It will take in roads carrying two-way traffic, dual carriageways and, where possible, one-way systems.

You'll be expected to demonstrate that you can move off smoothly and safely, both uphill and downhill, in addition to moving off normally ahead and at an angle.

You'll also need to show that you can safely

- meet other vehicles
- overtake
- cross the path of other vehicles
- keep a safe separation distance
- negotiate various types of roundabouts
- exercise correct lane discipline
- display courtesy and consideration to other road users, especially
  - pedestrians
  - riders on horseback
  - cyclists
  - motorcyclists
- apply the correct procedure at
  - pedestrian crossings

- level crossings (both railway and tramway, where appropriate)
- traffic signals
- road junctions,

You'll need to show

- effective use of the mirrors
- correct use of signals
- alertness and anticipation
- correct use of speed
- observance of speed limits
- expert use of the controls.

For further details of test requirements see page 232–233.

Preliminaries

The examiner won't conduct an eyesight test at the start of your test because you'll have already met the eyesight and medical requirements before your PCV provisional entitlement was granted.

Before you start the engine

The examiner expects that you've checked and prepared your bus for driving and for taking the test. Before you start your engine you must always be sure that

- all doors are properly closed
- your seat is correctly adjusted and comfortable, so that you can reach all the controls easily and have good all-round vision
- your driving mirrors are correctly adjusted
- your seat belt is fastened, correctly adjusted and comfortable, if fitted
- the parking brake is on
- the gear lever is in neutral.

It's best to develop good habits and to practise this routine while you're learning. The examiner won't be impressed if you have to make adjustments during the test that should have been carried out before it began.

After you start the engine

Don't attempt to drive a vehicle fitted with air brakes until the gauges show the correct pressure or when any warning device (a buzzer sounding or a light flashing) is operating.

If you're driving a vehicle with automatic transmission, you should make sure that the safety checks which apply to your vehicle have been carried out.

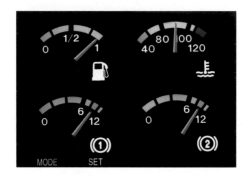

Safety checks

The examiner will ask you to demonstrate or explain how to carry out safety checks on your vehicle before driving. If you're taking a test in a rigid vehicle, the examiner will ask you to demonstrate or explain how to carry out five separate checks. If you're taking a test in a vehicle towing a trailer, the examiner will ask you to demonstrate or explain how to carry out two separate checks. The examiner will also ask you to show the

- location of the fire extinguisher
- fuel cut-off device
- emergency door and how it operates.

Skills you should show

You'll be expected to know how to check that

- your tyres are correctly inflated, have a safe tread depth and are generally safe to use on the road
- your brakes are working effectively and the pedal doesn't have excessive travel
- your vehicle has sufficient oil, coolant and hydraulic fluid
- you have sufficient windscreen washer fluid

- the power-assisted steering is working and that excessive 'play' isn't apparent
- your headlights, tail lights and reflectors are working and clean
- your brake lights are working and clean
- your horn is working
- the wheel nuts and mudguards are secure
- the vehicle has sufficient air pressure
- the kneeling bus device, if fitted, is working correctly
- the service doors and emergency exits are operating correctly
- all cargo doors are secure if towing a trailer.

You'll also be expected to know how to

- check for air leaks
- replace the tachograph disc or operate a digital tachograph
- check the windscreen wipers for wear and that the windscreen is clean
- check the suspension for defects
- check the location of first aid equipment, fire extinguishers and other safety equipment
- load a trailer safely
- ensure that the load is secure.

Faults to avoid

You should avoid

- being unfamiliar with the vehicle you're using on test
- being unable to explain or carry out safety checks on the vehicle you're using on test.

The reversing exercise

You'll be asked to carry out an off-road reversing exercise at the start of the test, whether your test vehicle's coupled to a trailer or not. The examiner will use a diagram of the manoeuvring area to explain the exercise to you. If you take the test with a delegated company examiner, the reversing exercise may consist of reversing into side roads on the left or right during the on-road part of the test.

The diagram opposite shows the area layout for this exercise. The stopping area will have both a solid yellow line and a yellow and black hatched section, and a barrier will be situated at the end of the reversing bay. The barrier is for LGV tests but is left permanently in place.

Starting from a fixed point (cones A and A1), you must keep your vehicle inside a clearly defined yellow boundary line so that

- the offside of your vehicle clears cone B
- you stop with the extreme rear of your vehicle in the 1 metre wide yellow/yellow and black stopping area.

At some centres there's also a steel barrier along part of the boundary.

For vehicles without a significant front overhang, cone A is positioned on the area boundary line. For vehicles with a front overhang, the examiner has the discretion to move the cones. If the front axle is well back from the front of the bus or if it has a limited turning circle, cones A, A1 and B may be moved 1 metre (about 3 feet) further into the area from the boundary line.

The distances

The manoeuvring area is 66 metres long by 11 metres wide.

A to A1 = 1½ times the width of the vehicle.

A to B = 2 times the length of the vehicle.

B to line Z = 3 times the length of the vehicle.

Bay cones C

All vehicles 12 metres or more in overall length, set at 12 metres. Vehicles less than 12 metres set to actual vehicle length.

You won't be told the precise length of the bay, as part of this exercise is designed to assess your judgement of the size of your vehicle.

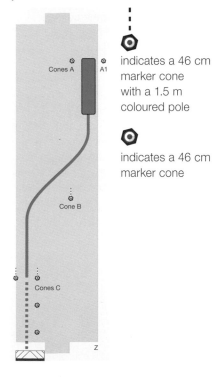

⊙ indicates a 46 cm marker cone with a 1.5 m coloured pole

⬤ indicates a 46 cm marker cone

What the test requires

The exercise is designed to test your ability to manoeuvre your vehicle in a confined space. You must avoid the marker posts and reverse into a clearly defined bay

- under control
- with reasonable accuracy
- with effective observation throughout.

Skills you should show

The examiner will ask you to drive your bus from where you parked it up to cones A and A1. When he or she signals you to do so, drive up to the cones and stop so that

- the front of your bus is between, but not beyond, the cones
- the bus is more or less parallel with the yellow boundary line.

If you don't position the vehicle correctly the examiner may ask you to re-position it.

When you're asked you should then

- steer so that the offside of your bus passes clear of cone B (which has a marker pole)
- reverse across the area at a reasonable pace until the rear of your bus enters the bay formed by cones (the two cones at the entrance to the bay will have marker poles)
- carefully control your use of the accelerator, clutch and footbrake throughout
- steer to position your vehicle accurately

- take effective observation throughout the exercise
- make smooth continuous progress across the area
- stop in the position explained to you by the examiner.

Faults to avoid

You should avoid

- approaching the starting point too fast
- not driving in a reasonably straight line as you approach
- stopping beyond the first marker cones A and A1
- turning the steering wheel the wrong way; turning too much or not enough when starting to reverse
- oversteering so that the front offside wheel travels outside the yellow boundary line of the area
- not taking effective observation or misjudging the position of your vehicle so that it hits (or is about to drive over) cone B and its marker pole
- not taking effective observation or misjudging the position of your vehicle so that it hits (or is about to drive over) the cones or marker poles marking out the bay
- allowing the wheel(s) of your vehicle to ride over the boundary lines of the bay or the area

- incorrect judgement so that the rear of your vehicle, and trailer if applicable, is either short of or beyond the yellow/ yellow and black stopping area
- taking excessive steering movements or 'shunts' to complete the manoeuvre. Since an overall high standard is expected, only a minimal number of shunts will be accepted
- driving down the area ahead of a position level with cones A and A1 when you're 'shunting' (this is because you'll have gone outside the limits set for your vehicle, ie five times its length, after starting the exercise)
- carrying out the manoeuvre at an excessively slow pace.

You should remember that throughout the test the examiner will be looking for effective observation and expert handling of the controls.

Notes

1. You can walk down the inside of the vehicle or get out and have a look at the rear, to judge your position in relation to the yellow stopping area; you can do this once. Make sure that your vehicle is safe before you leave the cab.

2. You can use reversing aids such as a camera but you must still take all-round observation.

The braking exercise

There's no emergency stop exercise in the passenger-carrying vehicle driving test but there is a braking exercise. This will be carried out on-road.

You should make sure that, before you come to the test, there's no loose equipment in the interior of the bus or in luggage lockers. This could fly about and cause injury or damage during the exercise.

What the test requires

Two marker cones approximately 61 metres (200 feet) ahead will be pointed out to you. You should build up the speed of the vehicle to about 32 km/h (20 mph). Only when the front of your vehicle passes between the two markers should you apply the brakes.

You should stop

- quickly
- safely
- under full control.

Skills you should show

Stopping the vehicle

- as quickly as possible
- under full control
- as safely as possible
- in a straight line.

Faults to avoid

You should avoid

- driving too slowly – less than 32 km/h (20 mph)
- braking too soon (anticipating the marker points or the stop signal)
- braking too harshly, causing loss of control
- depressing the clutch too late and stalling the engine
- depressing the clutch well before the brake.

Note

For vehicles fitted with ABS, please refer to the vehicle handbook.

If your bus is fitted with any additional braking controls, such as a retarder, exhaust brake or emergency air brake, you aren't expected to use them in this exercise. This is a test of your ability to stop quickly under normal circumstances.

The vehicle controls

What the test requires

You must show the examiner that you understand what all the controls do and that you can use them

- smoothly
- correctly
- skilfully
- safely
- at the right time.

In particular, the examiner must be sure that you can properly control the

- accelerator
- clutch
- footbrake
- parking brake (handbrake)
- steering
- gears.

Of course, if your vehicle has automatic transmission some of these won't apply to you. You must

- understand what the controls do
- be able to use them competently.

How your examiner will test you

For this aspect of driving there isn't a special exercise. The examiner will watch you carefully to see how you use these controls.

If your vehicle is fitted with cruise control, the examiner will assess your use of it in terms of ecosafe driving. Use the accelerator smoothly; harsh or uncontrolled use wastes fuel.

Accelerator and clutch

The accelerator controls the rate at which the mixture of fuel and air is supplied to the engine. The more you press the accelerator, the more fuel goes to the engine, and more power is generated. Use the accelerator smoothly; harsh or uncontrolled use wastes fuel and produces more harmful emissions.

The clutch is the connection between the engine and gearbox. It's a connection over which the driver has control, but which requires practice in its use.

Skills you should show

You should

- balance the accelerator and clutch to pull away smoothly
- accelerate evenly to gain speed
- release the accelerator smoothly to avoid erratic driving
- depress the clutch pedal just before the vehicle stops
- engage the clutch smoothly when moving away and changing gear.

Faults to avoid

You should avoid

- loud over-revving, causing excessive engine noise and exhaust fumes. This could alarm or distract other road users
- heavy, inappropriate acceleration followed by immediate braking
- making the vehicle jerk and lurch through uncontrolled use of the accelerator or the clutch
- riding the clutch; that is, failing to take your foot off the pedal when you aren't using it
- jerky and uncontrolled use of the clutch when moving off or changing gear.

Use of gears

Using the highest gear possible, matched to the speed of your vehicle and road/traffic conditions, aids fuel economy.

Manual gearboxes

The gears are designed to assist the engine to deliver power under a variety of conditions. The lowest gears may only be necessary if a vehicle is fully loaded or when it's climbing steep gradients.

You should be aware of the manufacturer's advice for the particular vehicle that you drive. Some suggest that first gear should always be used when pulling away, others advise second. Following a manufacturer's advice will minimise clutch and gearbox wear.

Skills you should show

You should

- move off in the most suitable gear
- choose the most appropriate gear for your speed and the road conditions
- change gear in good time before a hazard or junction
- select the correct gear in good time when climbing or before descending a long hill. On gradients it's essential to plan well ahead.

If you leave gear-changing until you're either losing or gaining too much speed you may have difficulty selecting the gear and maintaining control.

Faults to avoid

You should avoid

- taking your eyes off the road when you change gear
- holding onto the gear lever unnecessarily
- selecting the wrong gear
- coasting with the clutch pedal depressed or the gear lever in neutral.

Coasting is particularly dangerous in vehicles fitted with air brakes. The engine-driven compressor won't replace air being exhausted as the brakes are applied, as it's only running at 'tick over' speed.

Automatic gearboxes

Modern vehicles may be fitted with sophisticated gearing systems controlled by on-board computers. These systems sense the load, speed, gradient, etc and select the most appropriate gear for the conditions. On such systems, the driver may only have to ease the accelerator or depress the clutch pedal to allow the system to engage the gear required.

Other automatic gearboxes are controlled by a very simple three-button system

- forward (drive)
- neutral
- reverse.

In spite of this simplicity, it's essential that you learn the correct way to use the system.

Some systems have a 'kick-down' facility, whereby a lower gear can be engaged to allow rapid acceleration (eg for overtaking). This is achieved by pressing the accelerator to the floor.

Skills you should show

You should

- hold the vehicle firmly on the footbrake before pressing 'forward' to engage the drive. Some systems have interlocks that prevent 'drive' being engaged unless the brake pedal is depressed or the doors are closed, etc

- press the selector buttons only when the bus is completely stationary
- make careful use of the accelerator to ensure smooth automatic gear-changing.

Faults to avoid

You should avoid

- engaging 'drive' while the engine revs are above 'tick over'
- letting the bus remain stationary for long periods with 'forward' or 'reverse' engaged
- forgetting to engage 'drive' before attempting to move off
- not making proper use of any 'kick-down' facility.

The footbrake

With all braking systems, it's important to remember that there's a direct relationship between the pressure applied to the footbrake pedal and the braking force exerted on the wheels.

Older vehicles may have vacuum brake systems, which have similar characteristics to air brakes.

Some other vehicles may have a system known as 'air over hydraulic', in which air pressure operates a hydraulic braking system. These are usually lighter vehicles and the system is designed to make the brakes less harsh. Remember that controlled progressive braking is required at all times.

Plan ahead while driving, use engine braking when safe to do so and always be aware of the traffic situation behind.

Skills you should show

You should

- brake in good time
- brake lightly in most situations
- brake progressively
- use the correct technique for releasing pressure on the brake just before coming to rest. This allows you to stop the bus without jerks.

Faults to avoid

You should avoid

- braking harshly
- excessive and prolonged use of the footbrake
- braking and steering at the same time, unless you're already travelling at low speed
- braking in a way that would cause passengers discomfort.

Semi-automatic gearboxes

The system most commonly found on buses and coaches is one whereby the driver has full control over the gear selected, but has no clutch pedal. This is often a 'pneumo-cyclic' gearbox, which consists of a number of electronic relays controlling air systems that make the actual gear changes. The gears are chosen by means.of a 'gate' selector. When coupled with a fluid fly-wheel, this system eliminates the need for the use of a clutch when pulling away, stopping or changing gear. However, smooth changes require some skill and practice to achieve.

Again, the most appropriate method of changing gear will depend on the manufacturer's advice for the particular vehicle. Most advise that, when changing between one gear and another, a brief pause be made when the lever is in neutral. The accelerator should be depressed to a level appropriate for the gear about to be engaged.

Usually, semi-automatic gearboxes are coupled to diesel engines. Thus the amount of time needed in neutral to allow the engine revs to match the road speed needs careful consideration.

Skills you should show
You should

- hold the vehicle firmly on the footbrake before engaging forward or reverse gears from a standstill. Some systems have interlocks that prevent 'drive' being engaged unless the brake pedal is depressed or the doors are closed, etc
- make careful use of the accelerator to ensure smooth gear-changing.

Faults to avoid
You should avoid

- engaging a forward or reverse gear from a standstill while the engine revs are above 'tick over'
- letting the bus remain stationary for long periods with a forward or reverse gear engaged
- forgetting to engage a gear before attempting to move off
- not making proper use of the gear selector and accelerator.

The parking brake

Buses, coaches and minibuses are equipped with one of two types of parking brake.

Mechanical

- Generally found on older or smaller vehicles.

- Comprising a long lever with a button, or more usually, a squeeze-grip release, as in a car. The lever pulls a series of cables that apply the rear (or, more rarely, the front) brakes.

Air-operated

- Fitted to vehicles with air or 'air over hydraulic' footbrake systems.

- Operated by a small lever with a collar or a push-button release.

Skills you should show

You should

- know how and when to apply the parking brake

- apply the parking brake before leaving the cab when you intend to secure the vehicle

- coordinate your use of the parking brake and other controls in order to achieve smooth uphill starts.

Some modern braking systems will apply a parking brake when the vehicle is brought to a stop by the footbrake. The parking brake is released in the normal way. You should know how to operate this system if it's fitted to a vehicle that you intend to drive.

Faults to avoid

You should avoid

- applying the parking brake before the vehicle has stopped

- attempting to move off with the parking brake still applied

- using the 'park' position on the gear selector on automatic vehicles as a substitute for applying the parking brake. Only the gearbox locks when 'P' is engaged – the vehicle may be free to move when the next driver selects neutral to start the engine

- holding the vehicle on the clutch on uphill slopes (in manual buses and coaches). This can cause excessive clutch wear.

The clutch isn't designed to prevent a vehicle weighing up to 18 tonnes from moving backwards. You should always apply the parking brake and carry out the correct uphill start procedure to avoid unnecessary wear and tear on the clutch.

Emergency brakes

All vehicles are required to have at least two braking systems so that failure of one won't prevent the vehicle being brought to rest safely.

Split systems are often fitted to ensure that failure of one part of the normal braking system leaves other parts operational. Fail-safe systems can result in the automatic gradual application of all or some of the brakes if the driver ignores brake warning indicators.

Construction and Use Regulations require the driver to be able to apply all or part of the braking system in the event of footbrake failure. In simple terms this means that if you press the footbrake and nothing happens, you must have another means of stopping. How you do this depends on the system fitted, as follows

- mechanical parking brake: the parking brake can be applied progressively to bring the vehicle to a stop

- emergency brake: a separate lever is provided on some older air- and vacuum-braked buses to allow progressive application of the brakes

- air-operated parking brake: the brake is partially applied to allow progressive application of the brakes.

During your training you should find out which method should be used with the vehicle that you drive. You should practise it in a safe place, preferably off the road and under expert supervision.

You mustn't use this method of braking at any time during your test (unless you actually encounter footbrake failure at that time).

Skills you should show

The braking exercise in the driving test requires a rapid, controlled stop, using the footbrake. It isn't an emergency stop exercise.

Normally it won't be necessary to demonstrate any emergency braking systems.

Faults to avoid

You should avoid

- immediate full application of the brake
- locking the wheels and skidding
- coming to rest heavily in a way that may injure passengers.

Steering

The bus, coach or minibus you drive will probably have power-assisted steering. With power assistance the steering effort required is greatly reduced through the action of an engine-driven pump.

It's generally necessary to take corners more slowly when you don't have the benefit of power assistance, simply because the gearing at the steering wheel is lower and it takes more effort and time to turn it. The danger with power assistance is that the lack of effort required (and, in some cases, the lack of feel transmitted back to the driver) can result in taking corners too quickly. This can put either safety or comfort at risk. You need to be aware of this.

Skills you should show

You should

- place your hands on the steering wheel in a position that's comfortable and which gives you full control at all times

- keep your steering movements steady and smooth

- steer an accurate path and be aware of the 'swept path' that your vehicle will take.

It's particularly important to take the correct path when driving a bus with long overhangs or limited ground clearance.

Faults to avoid

You should avoid

- turning the wheel too early when turning a corner. You risk

  - cutting the corner when turning right, causing the rear wheel(s) to cut across the path of traffic waiting to emerge

  - striking the kerb when turning left

- turning too late. You could put other road users at risk by

  - swinging wide at left turns

  - overshooting right turns

- crossing your hands on the steering wheel (whenever possible)

- allowing the wheel to spin back after turning

- resting your arm on the door.

Remember, the stability of a bus can be affected by cornering too quickly.

275

Other controls

You should understand

- the functions of all controls and switches that have a bearing on road safety, for example
  - indicators
  - lights
  - windscreen wipers
  - demisters
- the meaning of gauges or other displays on the instrument panel, especially
  - air pressure gauge(s)
  - speedometer
  - various warning lights/buzzers
  - on-board computer displays
  - braking systems failure warnings
  - bulb failure warnings
  - gear-selection indicators
- time, speed and distance recording equipment, including
  - operating tachographs
  - completing tachograph charts
  - keeping records
  - the operation of any speed-limiting equipment fitted.

Safety checks

You should also be able to

- carry out routine safety checks on
  - oil and coolant levels
  - tyre pressures
- identify defects, especially with
  - steering
  - brakes
  - tyres
  - seat belts
  - lights
  - reflectors
  - horn
  - rear-view mirrors
  - speedometer
  - exhaust system
  - direction indicators
  - windscreen, wipers and washers
  - wheel-nut security
- understand the effects that any fault or defect will have on the handling of your vehicle.

Warning

Some, but not all, bus manufacturers, fit wheel nuts that tighten clockwise on the nearside of the vehicle and anti-clockwise on the offside. Make sure that you know which thread is fitted to your vehicle before you attempt to tighten them.

It's best to entrust this to trained mechanics, wherever possible, as the consequences of getting it wrong are dangerous; the nuts should always be tightened to the specified torque. Some wheels are spigot-mounted and specialised knowledge is needed when they're being removed or refitted.

Moving off

Balance your use of the accelerator when moving away – how much you depress it will depend on the weight of your vehicle and the circumstances, such as moving off uphill. However, remember that accelerating fiercely wastes fuel.

What the test requires

From a standstill, you must be able to move off safely and under control

- on the level
- from behind a parked vehicle
- on a hill
- uphill and downhill.

How your examiner will test you

The examiner will watch your observation and use of the controls each time you move off.

Level and uphill starts

- Aim to coordinate your use of the controls so that the vehicle remains stationary momentarily when the parking brake is released, ready to move off.
- Check all round for pedestrians and other road users. Move off if it's clear.
- If there's more than a moment's delay between releasing the brake and moving off, reapply the parking brake and repeat the sequence when it's safe to do so.

Downhill starts

- Prevent the vehicle from moving when you release the parking brake by applying the footbrake first.

Angle starts

- Ensure that you apply sufficient steering to pass the parked vehicle safely.
- Ensure that you won't endanger traffic when you move away.

Using the mirrors

Mirrors are one of the best aids to road safety. They help you to avoid causing problems to other road users and allow you to predict when to take action safely.

Try not to think of mirror checks as something you do because you've been told to. The important point isn't that you've looked in the mirrors, but that you've gained additional information to help you to drive safely.

Try to time your mirror checks to allow time to assess what you see before taking any action.

Sequence of mirror checks

Professional drivers develop a technique for checking mirrors while remaining fully aware of what's happening ahead. Whichever method you adopt, the examiner will observe how you use the mirrors and whether you act sensibly on what you see.

When you're on the road, hazards often occur together, or one immediately after another. One may also happen just when the need to begin a manoeuvre to deal with another occurs.

You must ensure that you observe every potential danger and are fully prepared to deal with it, if it occurs.

The sequence of checks has to be adapted as situations develop. In reality, it takes only moments to carry out and should become second-nature without the need to constantly analyse what you're doing.

Order of checks

- Identify the hazard that gives rise to the need to manoeuvre.

- Assess where the greatest potential danger lies in the intended manoeuvre – to the right or to the left of your vehicle. Check that mirror first.

- Check the mirror on the other side.

- As your eyes return to the road ahead reassess the hazard and, if you have an interior mirror that allows you to see what's happening behind, check the position of following traffic.

279

- Check the first mirror again and, as your eyes return to the road ahead, assess what you've seen and signal if necessary.
- Carry out the manoeuvre, if it's still safe to do so, rechecking the mirrors as necessary.

Example: moving out to pass a parked car

You see a parked car some distance ahead.

- The primary danger is that someone may attempt to overtake you as you need to move out. Check the offside mirror.
- Check the nearside mirror.
- Check that the parked car hasn't moved away, or that you'll need to give it extra room because someone's about to get out.
- Will you need to wait for approaching traffic?

- Look to see what traffic is behind you by checking the offside mirror.
- Has the situation ahead changed? Signal right, if necessary.
- Begin to move out if it's safe to do so, or wait if it isn't.
- Keep checking how the situation develops.

What the test requires

Make sure that you use your mirrors effectively

- before any manoeuvre
- to keep up to date with what's happening behind you.

Check carefully before

- moving off
- signalling
- changing direction
- turning left or right
- overtaking or changing lanes
- increasing speed
- slowing down or stopping
- opening any offside door.

Check again in the nearside mirror after

- passing parked vehicles
- passing horse riders, motorcyclists or cyclists
- passing any pedestrians standing close to the kerb
- passing any vehicle you've just overtaken and before moving back to the left.

How your examiner will test you

For this aspect of driving there isn't a special exercise. The examiner will watch your use of mirrors as you drive.

Skills you should show

You should

- establish good habits by
  - looking before you signal
  - looking and signalling before you act
  - acting sensibly and safely on what you see in the mirrors
- be aware that the mirrors won't show everything behind you
- check your nearside mirror every time after passing
  - parked vehicles
  - vulnerable road users
  - vehicles you've just overtaken
- always be as aware of what's happening behind and alongside your vehicle as you are of what's going on ahead
- always be aware of the effect your vehicle has on any vulnerable road users that you may pass.

Faults to avoid

You should avoid

- manoeuvring without checking the mirrors first
- not acting on what you see when you look in the mirrors
- taking action at the same time as looking in the mirrors, instead of as a result of what you see in them
- looking in the mirrors at an inappropriate moment so that you fail to observe changes in the situation ahead.

Always use the MSM/PSL routine

- Mirrors
- Signal
- Manoeuvre
  - Position
  - Speed
  - Look.

Remember, just looking isn't enough. Acting sensibly on what you see is more important.

Giving signals

What the test requires

You must give clear signals in good time so that other road users know what you intend to do next. This is particularly important with long PCVs because other road users may not understand the position into which you need to move

- before turning left
- before turning right
- at roundabouts
- to move off at an angle
- before reversing into an opening.

Neglecting to signal or giving a late or incorrect signal could put other road users and you in danger. This may force them, or you, to take avoiding action such as steering, braking or accelerating to prevent a collision.

You must only use the signals shown in The Highway Code, as any others may be misunderstood. Any signal you give must help other road users to

- understand what you intend to do next
- take appropriate action.

Always check that you've cancelled an indicator signal as soon as it's safe to do so.

How your examiner will test you

For this aspect of driving there isn't a special exercise. The examiner will watch carefully to see how you use signals in your driving.

Skills you should show

Give any signals

- clearly
- at the appropriate time
- by indicator
- by arm, if necessary.

Make sure that any signal you give is visible long enough for other road users to see it and understand its meaning.

Faults to avoid

You should avoid

- giving misleading or incorrect signals
- omitting to cancel signals
- waving on pedestrians to cross in front of your vehicle (there may be a dangerous situation that neither you nor they have seen, towards which you're unknowingly 'inviting' them)
- giving signals other than those shown in The Highway Code.

283

Acting on signs and signals

What the test requires

You must have a thorough knowledge of traffic signs, signals and road markings. You should be able to

- recognise them in good time
- take appropriate action on them.

At the start of the road section of the PCV driving test, the examiner will ask you to continue to follow the road ahead, unless traffic signs indicate otherwise or unless you're asked to turn left or right. You'll be given any direction to turn in good time. If you aren't sure, ask the examiner to repeat the direction.

Skills you should show

Traffic lights

You must

- comply with traffic lights
- approach at such a speed that you can stop, if necessary, under full control
- only move forward at a green traffic light if
  - it's clear for you to do so
  - by doing so your vehicle won't block the junction.

Authorised persons

You must comply with signals given by

- police officers
- traffic wardens
- school crossing patrols
- Vehicle and Operator Services Agency officers
- Highways Agency traffic officers
- any authorised person controlling traffic, eg at road repairs.

Other road users

You must watch for signals given by other road users and

- react safely
- take appropriate action
- anticipate their actions
- give signals to any traffic following your vehicle that may not be able to see the signals given by a road user ahead of you. This is particularly important when a vehicle or rider ahead is intending to turn right, and the size of your vehicle prevents traffic behind you from seeing their signal.

Making progress

The examiner will be looking for a high standard of driving from an experienced driver displaying safe, confident driving techniques. You aren't a learner driver and you won't pass the test if you drive hesitantly or in a way that shows you aren't fully in control of your vehicle.

Because you're an experienced driver and are expected to drive accordingly, you must

- select a safe speed to suit road, weather and traffic conditions
- move away at junctions as soon as it's safe to do so
- avoid stopping unnecessarily
- make progress when conditions permit.

How your examiner will test you

For this aspect of driving there isn't a special exercise. The examiner will watch your driving and will expect to see you

- making reasonable progress where conditions allow
- keeping up with the traffic flow when it's safe and legal to do so
- making positive, safe decisions as you make progress.

Skills you should show

You should

- drive at the appropriate speed, depending on the
  - type of road
  - traffic conditions
  - weather conditions and visibility
- approach all hazards at a safe speed without being unduly cautious or holding up following traffic unnecessarily.

Faults to avoid

You should avoid

- driving so slowly that you hinder other traffic
- being over-cautious or hesitant
- stopping when you can see that it's clear and safe to make progress.

Controlling your speed

What the test requires

You should make good progress when possible, taking into consideration

- the type of road
- the volume of traffic
- the weather conditions and the state of the road surface
- the braking characteristics of your vehicle
- the speed limits that apply to your vehicle
- any hazards associated with the time of day (school times, etc).

How your examiner will test you

For this aspect of driving there isn't a special exercise. The examiner will carefully watch your control of speed as you drive.

Skills you should show

You should

- take great care in the use of speed
- drive at the appropriate speed to the traffic conditions
- be sure that you can stop safely in the distance you can see to be clear
- leave a safe separation distance between your vehicle and the traffic ahead
- allow extra stopping distance on wet or slippery road surfaces
- observe the speed limits that apply to your vehicle
- drive sensibly and anticipate any hazards that could arise
- allow for other road users making mistakes.

Faults to avoid

You should avoid

- driving too fast for the conditions
  - road
  - traffic
  - weather
- exceeding speed limits

- varying your speed erratically
- having to brake hard to avoid a situation ahead
- approaching bends, traffic signals and any other hazards at too high a speed.

Separation distance

Always keep a safe separation distance between your vehicle and the one in front.

What the test requires

You must always drive at such a speed that you can stop safely in the distance you can see to be clear.

In good weather conditions, leave a gap of at least 1 metre (about 3 feet) for each mph of your speed, or a two-second time gap.

In bad conditions, leave at least double that distance, or a four-second time gap.

In slow-moving congested traffic it may not be practical to leave as much space, but you must always be sure that you can stop safely – whatever happens.

How your examiner will test you

For this aspect of driving there isn't a special exercise. The examiner will watch carefully and take account of your

- use of the MSM/PSL routine
- anticipation
- reaction to changing road and traffic conditions
- handling of the controls.

Skills you should show

You should

- be able to judge a safe separation distance between your vehicle and the one ahead
- show correct use of the MSM/PSL routine, especially before reducing speed
- avoid the need to brake sharply if the vehicle in front slows down or stops
- take extra care when your view ahead is limited by large vehicles, such as other buses or lorries.

Watch out for

- brake lights ahead
- direction indicators
- vehicles ahead braking without warning.

Faults to avoid

You should avoid

- following too closely or tailgating
- braking suddenly
- swerving to avoid the vehicle in front, which may be slowing down or stopping
- not leaving side road junctions clear when a queue of traffic stops.

Awareness and anticipation

The traffic situation can change from second to second, depending on the time of day, the location and the density of traffic. Sometimes you can see that a situation is going to turn dangerous. The skilful driver anticipates what might happen.

As the driver of a bus, coach or minibus you must constantly drive with this sense of awareness and anticipation. Ask yourself

- what's happening ahead?
- what are other road users doing, or about to do?
- do I need to
  - speed up?
  - slow down?
  - prepare to stop?
  - change direction?

It's essential to be fully alert at all times and to scan the road ahead constantly. By doing this you'll remain in control of both the situation and your vehicle.

Try to plan further ahead when driving; using the rolling momentum of the vehicle to prevent stopping and moving off again in first gear saves fuel. At roundabouts, look well ahead on approach to assess the traffic situation and fit in safely with the flow of traffic at the junction to prevent unnecessary stops.

In fast-moving traffic you'll need to be constantly checking and re-checking the scene around you. It's essential to recognise well in advance the mistakes that other road users may be about to make.

Hazards

What's a hazard?

When you're moving, a hazard is any situation that could involve adjusting speed or altering course. Look well ahead for

- road junctions or roundabouts
- parked vehicles
- cyclists
- pedestrians or horse riders (on the road or verge)
- pedestrian crossings.

By identifying the hazard early enough you'll have time to take the appropriate action.

When you're stationary, a hazard can be created by the actions of other road users around you. Watch for

- pedestrians crossing in front
- cyclists or motorcyclists moving up alongside
- drivers edging up on the nearside before you make a left turn
- vehicles pulling up close behind when you intend to reverse.

Stay alert and watch what's happening around you.

Hazards – other road users

Skills you should show

Pedestrians

- Give way to pedestrians when turning from one road into another, or when entering premises such as bus or railway stations, schools, etc.

- Take extra care with

    - young children

    - disabled people

    - older passengers

    as they may not realise you won't be able to stop suddenly.

You must be even more vigilant when driving through shopping areas; for example, where there are often large numbers of people waiting to cross at corners. Drive slowly and considerately when you need to enter any pedestrianised areas.

Motorcyclists

Watch for motorcyclists

- filtering in slow traffic streams

- moving up along the side of your vehicle

- especially when you're about to move out at junctions.

> **Remember,** Think once, Think twice, Think bike.

Cyclists

Take extra care when

- crossing cycle lanes

- you can see a cyclist near the rear of your vehicle or moving up along the nearside as you're about to turn left

- approaching any children on cycles

- there are gusty winds.

Horse riders and animals

Remember, the size, noise, lights and sometimes even the colour of your vehicle can unsettle even the best behaved horse. Watch young, possibly inexperienced, riders closely for signs of any difficulty with their mounts. Give horse riders as much room as you can. They may be on the grass verge instead of the road but the same courtesy should be given.

Make several light applications of the brakes as you approach to ensure that the air brake system relief valve doesn't blow off just as you're level with the animal. Avoid revving the engine until you're clear of the animal.

React in good time to anyone herding animals. Look out for warning signs or signals in rural districts.

Faults to avoid

You should avoid

- sounding the horn unnecessarily
- deliberately revving the engine
- flashing your lights unnecessarily
- causing the air brakes to hiss by applying them too heavily
- edging forward when pedestrians are crossing in front of your vehicle
- showing any signs of irritation or aggression towards other road users, especially the more vulnerable.

Hazards – positioning and lane discipline

What the test requires

You should

- normally keep well to the left
- keep clear of parked vehicles
- avoid weaving in and out between parked vehicles
- position your vehicle correctly for the direction you intend to take
- obey road markings, especially
  - left- and right-turn arrows at junctions
  - when approaching roundabouts
  - in one-way streets
  - bus lanes
  - road markings for PCVs or LGVs approaching arched or narrow low bridges.

With long PCVs, straddle lane markings or move over to the left or right only when necessary to avoid mounting the kerb or colliding with lampposts, traffic signs, etc.

How your examiner will test you

For this aspect of driving there isn't a special exercise. The examiner will watch carefully to see that you

- use the MSM/PSL routine
- select the correct lane in good time.

Skills you should show

You should

- use the MSM/PSL routine correctly
- plan ahead and choose the correct lane in good time
- position your vehicle sensibly, even if there aren't any lane markings.

Faults to avoid

You should avoid

- driving too close to the kerb
- driving too close to the centre of the road
- changing lanes at the last moment or without good reason
- hindering other road users by being incorrectly positioned or in the wrong lane

- unnecessarily straddling lanes or lane markings
- using the size of your vehicle to block other road users from making progress
- cutting across the path of other road users in another lane at roundabouts.

Remember, other road users may not understand what you intend to do next. Watch them carefully and ensure that you signal in good time.

Hazards – junctions

The size of your vehicle and the difficulties that may arise when manoeuvring it mean that it's essential to make the correct decisions at road junctions.

Never drive into a situation that you can't see a clear path through. If you drive your vehicle into a blocked road any traffic building up behind will prevent you from reversing out, leaving you in a position from which it's impossible to escape. Similarly, if you need to wait for an obstruction to clear, stop in a position that allows you an escape route if at all possible.

What the test requires

You should

- use the MSM/PSL routine in good time on the approach to junctions

- assess the situation correctly, so that you can position the vehicle to negotiate the junction safely

- take as much room as you need on approach to see the road space available. There may not be enough room for a wide swing in the road that you're entering

- take advantage of any improved vision from the driving position in your vehicle and stop or proceed as necessary

- be aware of any lane markings and the fact that your vehicle may have to occupy part of the lane alongside

- try to position your vehicle in good time in one-way streets

- make sure you take effective observation before emerging at any road junction

- use your mirrors to observe the rear wheels of your vehicle as you drive into and out of the junction
- correctly assess the speed of oncoming vehicles before crossing or entering roads with fast-moving traffic
- always allow for the fact that you'll need time to build up speed on the new road.

If you're crossing a dual carriageway or turning right onto one, don't move forward unless you can clear the central reservation safely. If your vehicle is too long for the gap, wait until it's clear from both sides and there's a safe opportunity to go.

How your examiner will test you

For this aspect of driving there isn't a special exercise. The examiner will watch carefully and take account of your

- use of the MSM/PSL routine
- position and speed on approach
- observation and judgement.

As an aid to remembering the correct routine, think of the word LADEN.

- **L**ook well ahead on approach.
- **A**ssess conditions at the junction.
- **D**ecide when it's safe to go.
- **E**merge from (or enter) the junction safely.
- **N**egotiate the hazard (junction) safely.

Hazards – roundabouts

What the test requires

Roundabouts can vary in size and complexity, but the object of all of them is to allow traffic to keep moving, wherever possible.

Some roundabouts are so complex that they require traffic lights to control the volume of traffic, while at others signals operate at peak periods only.

At the majority of roundabouts, traffic is required to give way to the vehicles approaching from the right. However, at some locations the 'give way' signs and markings apply to traffic already on the roundabout. You must be aware of these differences.

Skills you should show

You should plan your approach well in advance and use the MSM/PSL routine in good time. With buses, it's essential to adopt the appropriate lane, depending on the exit you intend to take and the size of your vehicle.

Lane discipline

You should

- plan well ahead
- look out for traffic signs as you approach
- decide which exit you need to take
- look out for the number of exits before yours
- either follow the lane markings, as far as possible, or select the lane most suitable to the size of your vehicle
- signal your intentions clearly and in good time
- avoid driving into the roundabout too close to the right-hand kerb
- as it isn't always possible to keep your vehicle within road markings, make frequent mirror checks to ensure that you aren't endangering others
- accurately assess the speed and intentions of traffic approaching from the right.

Always watch any vehicle in front when you're about to enter the roundabout. When you see a gap in the traffic, always check to make sure the vehicle in front of you has moved off before you do so. Drivers sometimes change their minds at the last moment. Many rear-end collisions take place in just these circumstances.

Unless lane markings or road signs indicate otherwise you should follow the procedure noted here when turning left or right, including full circle, or when going straight ahead.

Turning left

You should

- check your mirrors
- give a left-turn signal in good time as you approach
- approach in the left-hand lane. With a long vehicle you might need to take up some of the lane on your right, depending on how sharp or narrow the exit turn is
- adopt a path that ensures your rear wheels don't mount the kerb
- give way to traffic approaching from the right, when necessary
- keep checking your mirror(s) as you enter and negotiate the turn, to be sure that no cyclists or motorcyclists are trapped on the nearside or are affected by the overhang of your vehicle
- use the offside mirror to check that no passing vehicle will be hit when the rear overhang swings out as you begin to turn
- continue to signal throughout the turn
- look well ahead for traffic islands/bollards in the middle of your exit road, which will restrict the width available to you.

Going ahead

You should

- approach in the left-hand lane unless blocked or clearly marked for 'left turn' only
- check your mirrors

- not give a signal on approach (other than brake lights, if you need to reduce speed)
- try to stay in the lane if possible; this will depend on the size of your vehicle. If you have to straddle the lanes, do so in good time
- keep checking the mirrors. Be aware that other road users may not anticipate the 'swept path' of your vehicle. Be prepared to stop if they don't, as swerving will normally make matters worse
- indicate left as you pass the exit just before the one that you intend to take
- look well ahead for traffic islands/bollards in the centre of your exit road
- make sure that the rear wheels don't mount the kerb as you leave the roundabout.

Turning right or full circle

You should

- look well ahead and use the MSM/PSL routine in good time
- signal right in good time, before moving over to the right on approach. Watch for any vehicles, especially motorcycles, accelerating up on the offside of your vehicle
- Your position on approach will depend on the size of your vehicle and the layout of the roundabout. If there's a choice of lanes, take up the most appropriate position. This may mean that you have to straddle the lanes
- make frequent mirror checks

- only enter the roundabout when you're sure that it's safe to emerge
- keep checking for traffic coming from your right.

When you need extra space and only one lane is marked for 'right turn', occupy part of the lane to your left. Do this on the approach and through the roundabout.

Don't pull out across the path of any vehicle closely approaching from the right. Not only could the approaching vehicle be travelling at speed, but it could also be moving on a curved course so any sudden braking would be likely to send it into a skid. You should

- use the mirrors to observe traffic coming round with you on the nearside, and also to check that your rear wheels are keeping clear of the kerb on the roundabout itself
- change your signal to 'left turn' as you pass the exit before the one you wish to take.

This procedure is useful when you need to turn a PCV round.

Road surfaces

Roundabouts are junctions where considerable braking and acceleration take place. The road surface can become polished and be slippery, especially in wet weather.

Ensure that all braking and speed reduction is done in good time.

If you can see that it's clear to enter the roundabout, do so – provided you won't cause any traffic coming from your right to brake or swerve.

Cyclists and horse riders

It's often safest for cyclists and horse riders to take the outside path when turning right at large roundabouts. Watch for any signals and give them as much room as you safely can.

Mini-roundabouts

Similar rules and procedures apply at mini-roundabouts as at full-scale roundabouts:

- you should give way to traffic approaching from the right

- because of the restricted space both entering and leaving these locations, it's essential to keep a constant check on the mirrors

- the rear of a long vehicle can easily 'clip' a car waiting to enter a mini-roundabout

- it's most unlikely that PCVs will be able to turn at a mini-roundabout without driving over the marked centre area, but you should try to avoid doing so where possible

- you should position your vehicle so that it doesn't mount the kerb at the entrance or exit.

Double mini-roundabouts

These require even more care and planning, since traffic will often back up from one to the other at busy times. Make sure that there's room for you to move forward and

that, by doing so, your vehicle won't block the whole system.

Although drivers are advised not to carry out U-turn manoeuvres at a mini-roundabout, be alert for any oncoming traffic doing so.

Avoid giving any signals that might confuse. Because of the limited space and the comparatively short amount of time that it takes to negotiate a mini-roundabout, it's important to give only signals that will help other road users.

If you have to drive over a raised mini-roundabout, do so slowly and carefully, so as not to damage your vehicle or cause discomfort to your passengers.

At any roundabout, cancel your signal as soon as you've completed the manoeuvre.

Multiple roundabouts

At a number of (usually well-known) locations, complex roundabout systems have been designed, which incorporate a mini-roundabout at each exit.

The main thing to remember at such places is that traffic is travelling in all directions.

Sometimes mini-roundabouts are sited at what were formerly T-junctions. These junctions can be at a variety of angles, so you should adopt the safest position on approach (even if technically going ahead). Give an appropriate signal to other road users.

Hazards – overtaking

What the test requires

When overtaking, you must

- look well ahead for any hazards, such as
  - oncoming traffic
  - bends
  - junctions
  - road markings
  - traffic signs
  - the vehicle in front being about to overtake
  - any gradient
- assess the speed of the vehicle you intend to overtake
- assess the speed differential of the two vehicles. This will indicate how long the manoeuvre could take
- allow enough room to overtake safely
- avoid the need to cut in on the vehicle you've just overtaken.

How your examiner will test you

For this aspect of driving there isn't a special exercise. The examiner will watch carefully and take account of your

- appropriate use of the MSM/PSL routine
- reactions to road and traffic conditions
- handling of the controls
- choice of safe opportunities to overtake.

Skills you should show

You must be able to assess all the factors that will help you to decide if you can overtake safely, such as

- oncoming traffic
- the type of road (single or dual carriageway)
- the speed of the vehicle ahead
- if you can overtake before reaching any continuous white line on your side of the road
- how far ahead the road is clear
- whether the road will remain clear
- whether your mirror checks show that there's traffic behind about to overtake.

Overtake only when you can do so

- safely
- legally
- without causing other road users to slow down or alter course.

Faults to avoid

You mustn't overtake when

- your view of the road ahead isn't clear
- you would have to exceed the speed limit set for your vehicle on that type of road
- to do so would cause other road users to slow down, stop or swerve
- there are signs or road markings that prohibit overtaking.

Hazards – meeting and passing other vehicles

What the test requires

You must be able to meet and deal with oncoming traffic safely and confidently, especially

- on narrow roads
- where there are obstructions such as parked cars
- where you have to move into the path of oncoming vehicles.

How your examiner will test you

For this aspect of driving there isn't a special exercise. The examiner will watch carefully and take account of your

- use of the MSM/PSL routine
- reactions to road and traffic conditions
- handling of the controls.

Skills you should show

You should

- show sound judgement when meeting oncoming traffic
- be decisive when stopping and moving off
- stop in a position that allows you to move out smoothly when the way is clear
- allow adequate clearance when passing stationary vehicles. Slow down if you have to pass close to them.

Be on the alert for

- doors opening
- children running out
- pedestrians stepping out from between parked vehicles or round the front of other buses
- vehicles pulling out without warning.

Faults to avoid

You should avoid

- causing other vehicles to
  - slow down
  - swerve
  - stop
- passing dangerously close to parked vehicles
- using the size of your vehicle to force other road users to give way.

Hazards – crossing the path of other vehicles

What the test requires

You must be able to cross the path of oncoming traffic safely and with confidence. You'll need to be able to carry this out safely when you intend to

- turn right at a road junction
- enter bus stations or garages on the right-hand side of the road.

You should

- use the MSM/PSL routine on approach
- position the vehicle correctly. The width and type of road and the length of the vehicle will affect this
- accurately assess the speed of any approaching traffic
- wait, if necessary
- observe the road or entrance into which you're about to turn
- watch for any pedestrians.

How your examiner will test you

For this aspect of driving there isn't a special exercise. The examiner will watch carefully and take account of your judgement of oncoming traffic.

Skills you should show

You should

- make safe and confident decisions about when to turn across the path of vehicles approaching from the opposite direction
- ensure that the road or entrance is clear for you to enter
- be confident that your vehicle won't endanger any road user waiting to emerge from the right
- accurately assess whether it's safe to enter the road or entrance
- show courtesy and consideration to other road users, especially pedestrians.

Faults to avoid

You should avoid

- turning across the path of oncoming road users, causing them to
  - slow down
  - swerve
  - brake
- cutting the corner so that you endanger vehicles waiting to emerge
- overshooting the turn so that the front wheels mount the kerb.

Hazards – pedestrian crossings

What the test requires

You must be able to

- recognise the different types of pedestrian crossing
- show courtesy and consideration towards pedestrians
- stop safely, when necessary.

How your examiner will test you

For this aspect of driving there isn't a special exercise. The examiner will watch carefully to see that you

- recognise the pedestrian crossing in good time
- use the MSM/PSL routine
- stop when necessary
- are especially alert when crossings are sited
  - near schools
  - in shopping areas
  - at or near junctions.

Skills you should show

You should

- approach all crossings at a controlled speed
- stop safely, when necessary
- move off when you're sure it's safe to do so.

Controlled crossings

These crossings may be controlled by

- traffic signals at junctions
- police officers
- traffic wardens
- school crossing patrols.

Zebra crossings

These crossings can be recognised by

- black and white stripes across the road
- a row of studs along each edge of the black and white stripes
- tactile paving on both sides of the crossing for partially sighted people
- flashing amber beacons at both sides of the road
- zigzag markings on the road on both sides of the crossing.

You must

- slow down and stop if there's anyone on the crossing
- slow down and be prepared to stop if anyone is waiting to cross or will reach the crossing before you do.

On approach to zebra crossings, slow down and be prepared to stop in good time.

Pelican crossings

The name 'pelican' is an acronym which stands for **PE**destrian **L**ight **I**ndi**CA**tio**N**. These crossings have

- traffic signals that change only after pedestrians have pressed a button on either side of the crossing
- a flashing amber phase to allow pedestrians already crossing to get across safely
- zigzag lines on the road on each side of the crossing
- a 'stop' line painted on the road for traffic waiting at the crossing.

The sequence of the traffic lights is

- red
- flashing amber
- green
- amber
- red.

You must

- stop if the lights are on red or amber
- give way to any pedestrians crossing if the amber lights are flashing
- give way to any pedestrians still crossing when the flashing amber light changes to green.

Puffin crossings

The term 'puffin' is an acronym for **P**edestrian **U**ser-**F**riendly **IN**telligent crossings. This type of crossing has been installed at a number of selected sites and can be identified by

- detectors sited so that the red traffic signal will be held until pedestrians have cleared the crossing
- no flashing amber phase
- traffic lights that operate in normal sequence
    - red
    - red and amber
    - green
    - amber
    - red.

You must

- stop and wait, unless the green light is showing
- drive over the crossing only if it's clear of pedestrians.

Toucan crossings

This name continues the bird theme alongside the two previous crossing types but in this case simply means 'two can cross'. These crossings are mostly found in areas with college or university sites and where there are large numbers of cyclists. They operate in the same way as puffin crossings except that

- cyclists share the crossing with pedestrians without dismounting
- a green cycle light indicates when it's safe to cross.

As with puffin crossings, the traffic lights operate in the normal sequence.

You must

- stop and wait, unless the green light shows
- drive over the crossing only if it's clear of pedestrians or cyclists.

Equestrian crossings

These are especially for horses and riders and have higher controls, a fence along the kerb and a wider crossing area.

Faults to avoid

You should avoid

- approaching any type of crossing at too high a speed
- driving on without stopping or showing awareness of waiting pedestrians
- driving onto or blocking a crossing
- harassing pedestrians by
    - revving the engine
    - making the air brakes hiss
    - edging forward
    - sounding the horn
    - overtaking within the zigzag lines
    - waving them to cross.

Selecting a safe place to stop

What the test requires

When you make a normal stop you must be able to

- select a safe place where you won't
  - cause an obstruction
  - create a hazard
  - contravene any waiting, stopping or parking restrictions
- stop reasonably close to the edge of the road.

How your examiner will test you

At times during the test the examiner will ask you to pull up either at

- a convenient place or
- a particular place; for example next to a lamppost or, in some circumstances, at a bus stop.

This is to demonstrate that you could pull up to allow passengers to board or alight safely.

The examiner will watch your driving and take account of your

- use of the MSM/PSL routine
- judgement in selecting a safe place to stop.

Skills you should show

You must be able to stop in a safe position by

- selecting it in good time
- making proper use of the MSM/PSL routine
- only stopping where you're allowed to do so
- not causing an obstruction
- recognising in good time road markings or signs indicating any restriction
- pulling up close to and parallel with the kerb
- applying the parking brake while the vehicle is stationary
- stopping at the correct place when asked.

Faults to avoid

You should avoid

- pulling up without giving sufficient warning to other road users
- causing danger or inconvenience to any other road users
- parking at or outside
  - school entrances
  - fire stations
  - ambulance stations
  - pedestrian crossings.

You must comply with

- 'no waiting' signs or markings
- 'no parking' signs or markings
- other 'no stopping' restrictions.

Uncoupling and recoupling

What the test requires

If you're taking a test to gain a trailer entitlement, you'll be asked to uncouple and recouple your vehicle, normally at the end of the test. You should know and be able to demonstrate how to uncouple and recouple your vehicle safely. Stopping the engine of your vehicle at the correct time during the exercise isn't only safe but saves fuel and reduces air and noise pollution.

Uncoupling

When uncoupling you should

- ensure that the brakes are applied on both the vehicle and trailer
- set the jockey wheel/prop stand to support the trailer weight
- turn off any taps, disconnect the air lines and stow the lines away safely (where fitted)
- disconnect the electric line and stow it away safely
- release the break-away cable connection
- release the trailer coupling
- drive the tractive unit away slowly, checking the trailer either directly or in the mirrors.

Recoupling

When recoupling

- ensure that the trailer brake is applied
- reverse slowly up to the trailer
- ensure that the vehicle parking brake is applied
- check the height of the coupling
- connect the tow-hitch
- connect the break-away cable
- connect the electric lines
- connect the air lines and turn on taps, if fitted
- raise the jockey wheel/prop stand
- release the trailer parking brake
- start up the engine
- check that the air is building up in the storage tanks (where applicable)
- check lights and indicators.

How your examiner will test you

Your examiner will ask you to perform this exercise where there's safe and level ground. You'll be asked to

- demonstrate the uncoupling of your vehicle and trailer
- pull forward and park the vehicle alongside the trailer
- realign the vehicle with the trailer before recoupling the trailer.

Your examiner will expect you to make sure that the

- coupling is secure
- lights and indicators are working
- trailer brake is released.

Skills you should show

You should be able to uncouple and recouple your vehicle and trailer

- safely
- confidently, and in good time
- showing concern for your own and others' health and safety.

Faults to avoid

Uncoupling

When uncoupling you should avoid

- uncoupling without applying the brakes on the towing vehicle
- releasing the trailer coupling without lowering the jockey wheel/prop stand
- moving forward before the entire correct procedure has been completed.

Recoupling

When recoupling you should avoid

- not checking the brakes are applied on the trailer
- not using good, effective observation of your trailer as you reverse up to it
- leaving the towing vehicle without applying the parking brake
- recoupling at speed.

Don't attempt to move away without checking the

- lights
- indicators
- trailer brake release.

Understanding the rules

Now that the theory test for large goods vehicle and PCV drivers has been introduced, questions on The Highway Code are no longer asked at the end of the practical driving test. However, you'll be expected to

- put its rules into practice when you're driving
- recognise all road signs or road markings that apply to minibus, coach or bus drivers
- show courtesy and consideration towards all other road users.

The Highway Code itself isn't a set of laws; rather a collection of rules reflecting current GB legislation, and offering sound guidance to all road users. Know the rules and use them whenever you drive on the road.

New road signs are introduced from time to time, and the rules set out in The Highway Code may be amended or increased. You should ensure that you're familiar with the most recent edition.

You should also study and be totally familiar with all the signs and road markings set out in the book *Know Your Traffic Signs* (available from TSO). Changes to UK traffic signs will continue to take place over a number of years. It's your responsibility to be aware of any changes as they're introduced.

The test results

Legal requirements of the test

The candidate must show that they're competent to drive the vehicle in which the test is being conducted without danger to, and with due consideration for, other persons using the road. In particular, the candidate must show that they can competently

- start the engine
- move off straight ahead and at an angle
- maintain a proper position in relation to a vehicle immediately in front
- overtake and take an appropriate course in relation to other vehicles
- turn right and left
- stop within a limited distance, under full control
- stop normally and bring the vehicle to rest in an appropriate part of the road
- drive the vehicle forwards and backwards; while driving the vehicle backwards steer the vehicle along a predetermined course to make it enter a restricted opening and bring it to rest in a predetermined position
- indicate their intended actions by appropriate signals at appropriate times
- act correctly and promptly in response to all signals given by any traffic sign, by any person lawfully directing traffic, and by any other person using the road.

If you pass

You'll have demonstrated that you can drive a bus, coach or minibus – without passengers – to the high standard required to obtain a licence.

Your examiner will ask you for your provisional licence so that an upgraded licence can automatically be sent to you through the post.

Once your examiner has taken your provisional licence they'll shred it. You'll be given a temporary pass certificate that will be proof of your success until you receive your new licence.

If you don't want to surrender your licence straightaway you don't have to; for example, if you have yet to take another CPC test. Also, there may be certain circumstances when you won't be able to surrender your licence, eg if you have

- a foreign licence (community licence-holder or NI)
- changed your name.

In these cases you'll have to send your provisional licence, together with your pass certificate and the appropriate fee, to DVLA, and they'll send you your full licence. You must do this within two years or you'll have to take your test again.

You'll also be offered a brief explanation of any driving faults marked. This is to help you overcome any weaknesses in your driving as you gain experience.

After you've passed

You should aim to raise your standard of driving – especially as you'll be driving buses carrying passengers.

Most operators will offer you 'type' training, which will allow you to familiarise yourself with the different vehicles in the fleet.

Your trainer should be able to give you further advice.

If you don't pass

Your driving won't have been up to the high standard required to obtain the vocational driving licence. You'll have made mistakes that either caused, or could have caused, danger on the road.

Your examiner will

- give you a statement of failure including a copy of the driving test report (DL25A), which will show all the faults marked during the test
- explain briefly why you've failed.

You should study the driving test report carefully and refer to the relevant sections in this book.

Show the report to your instructor, who will help you to correct the points of failure. Listen to the advice your instructor gives and try to get as much practice as you can before you retake your test.

Right of appeal

Although the examiner's decision can't be altered, you have a right to appeal if you consider that your driving test wasn't conducted according to the regulations.

If you live in England or Wales you have six months after the issue of the statement of failure in which to appeal (Magistrates' Courts Act 1952 [Ch. 55 part VII, Section 104]). If you live in Scotland you have 21 days in which to appeal (Sheriff Court, Scotland Act of Sederunt (Statutory Appeals) 1981).

section **seven**
ADDITIONAL INFORMATION

This section covers
- Disqualified drivers
- Traffic commissioners and traffic area offices
- Other useful addresses
- PCV licence entitlements
- Minimum test vehicles (MTVs) requirements
- Cone positions
- Glossary
- Road signs
- Index

Disqualified drivers

Retesting once disqualified

Tougher penalties now exist for anyone convicted of certain dangerous driving offences. If a driver is convicted of a dangerous driving offence that involves a period of disqualification, all PCV entitlement is automatically lost regardless of the type of vehicle being driven at the time of the offence.

The decision about whether that entitlement can be regained is a matter for the licensing authority. The options are

- the entitlement may be refused on the grounds that you've shown yourself to be an unfit and improper person to hold a bus or coach driving licence

- the court may require you to take an extended car driving test to regain your category B licence

- you may be required to retake a driving test for each additional category of vehicle that you want to drive

- the additional category(ies) may be restored without any further requirement, in exceptional circumstances.

It's important to remember that a PCV driving licence can't be issued on its own. You must possess a valid, full driving licence entitlement for category B (a car licence) for your category D, D1 or D+E licence entitlement to be valid. If you lose your car licence entitlement you lose your PCV licence with it.

Applying for a retest

If you have to take a category B retest you can apply for a provisional licence at the end of the period of disqualification.

The normal rules for provisional licence-holders apply

- you must be supervised by a person who's at least 21 years of age and has held (and still holds) a full licence for at least three years for the category of vehicle being driven

- red L plates (or D plates, if you wish, in Wales) must be displayed to the front and rear of the vehicle

- driving on motorways isn't allowed

- PCVs may not be driven if you only hold a provisional car licence (category B).

All driving tests can be booked online at **www.gov.uk** or by telephoning the national booking number on **0300 200 1122**. There are higher fees for extended tests, so you must make it clear when you apply which type of test you want.

You can only apply for a provisional category D licence entitlement after you've passed an extended car driving test, if the court has directed you to do so.

317

Traffic commissioners and traffic area offices

Scotland

Level 6
The Stamp Office
10 Waterloo Place
Edinburgh
EH1 3EG
Tel **0300 123 9000**

Area covered:
All Scotland and the Islands.

North-eastern and North-western traffic areas

NE – Hillcrest House
386 Harehills Lane
Leeds LS9 6NF
Tel **0300 123 9000**
NW – Suite 4, Stone Cross Place
Stone Cross Lane, Golborne
Warrington WA3 2SH
Tel **0300 123 9000**

Area covered:
Blackburn with Darwen
Blackpool
Cheshire
Cumbria
Darlington
Derby City
Derbyshire
Durham
East Riding of Yorkshire
Greater Manchester
Halton
Hartlepool
Kingston-upon-Hull
Lancashire
Merseyside
Middlesbrough
North Lincolnshire
North-east Lincolnshire
North Yorkshire
Northumberland
Nottingham
Nottinghamshire
Redcar and Cleveland
South Yorkshire
Stockton-on-Tees
Tyne and Wear
Warrington
West Yorkshire
York

Wales and West Midlands

38 George Road
Edgbaston
Birmingham
B15 1PL
Tel **0300 123 9000**

Area covered: West Midlands

Herefordshire
Shropshire
Staffordshire
Stoke-on-Trent
Telford
Warwickshire
West Midlands
Worcestershire
Wrekin

Area covered: Wales

All of Wales

Eastern

City House
126–130 Hills Road
Cambridge
CB2 1NP
Tel **0300 123 9000**

Area covered:
Bedfordshire
Buckinghamshire
Cambridgeshire
Essex
Hertfordshire
Leicester
Leicestershire
Lincolnshire
Luton
MIlton Keynes
Norfolk
Northamptonshire
Peterborough
Rutland
Southend-on-Sea
Suffolk
Thurrock

Western

Jubilee House
Croydon Street
Bristol
BS5 0GB
Tel **0300 123 9000**

Area covered:
Bath and north-east Somerset
Bournemouth
Bracknell Forest
Bristol
Cornwall
Devon
Dorset

Gloucestershire
Hampshire
Isle of Wight
North Somerset
Oxfordshire
Plymouth
Poole
Portsmouth
Reading
Slough
Somerset
Southampton
South Gloucestershire
Swindon
Torbay
West Berkshire
Wiltshire
Windsor and Maidenhead
Wokingham

South-eastern and Metropolitan London

Ivy House
3 Ivy Terrace
Eastbourne
BN21 4QT
Tel **0300 123 9000**

Area covered:
Brighton and Hove
East Sussex
Greater London
Kent
Medway Towns
Surrey
West Sussex

Other useful addresses

Bus Users UK
Head Office
PO Box 119
Shepperton
TW17 8UX

Tel **01932 232574**
Email **enquiries@bususers.org**
Website **bususers.org**

City and Guilds of London Institute
City and Guilds Head Office
1 Giltspur Street
London EC1A 9DD

Tel **0844 543 0033**
Fax **020 7294 2405**
Email **learnersupport@cityandguilds.com**
Website **cityandguilds.com**

Community Transport Association
Central Support Office
Highbank, Halton Street
Hyde, Cheshire
SK14 2NY

Tel **0161 351 1475**
Fax **0161 351 7221**
Email **info@ctauk.org**
Website **ctauk.org**

Confederation of Passenger Transport UK
CPT Head Office
Drury House
34–43 Russell Street
London WC2B 5HA

Tel **020 7240 3131**
Fax **020 7240 6565**
Website **cpt-uk.org**

Department for Transport (DfT)
Great Minster House
33 Horseferry Road
London SW1P 4DR

Tel **0300 330 3000**
Fax **020 7944 9643**
Website **www.gov.uk/dft**

Disabled Persons Transport Advisory Committee (DPTAC)
2/17 Great Minster House
33 Horseferry Road
London SW1P 4DR

Tel **020 7944 8011**
Email **dptac@dft.gsi.gov.uk**
Website **http://dptac.independent.gov.uk**

Driver and Vehicle Agency (Licensing) in Northern Ireland (DVA)
County Hall
Castlerock Road
Coleraine
BT51 3TB

Tel **0845 402 4000**
Minicom **02870 341380**
Website **dvani.gov.uk**

(9.00 am to 5.00 pm Monday to Friday, except bank and public holidays. Outside office hours you'll receive the option to transfer to the agency's information line which gives basic information.)

Driver and Vehicle Licensing Agency (DVLA)

Customer Enquiry Unit
Licence Enquiries
Swansea
SA6 7JL
Tel **0300 790 6801**
Minicom **0300 123 1278**
Fax **0300 123 0784**
Website **dft.gov.uk/dvla**
(Open 8.00 am to 8.30 pm Monday to Friday,
8.30 am to 5.00 pm Saturday)

DVLA Drivers Medical Group

Swansea
SA99 1TU
Tel **0300 790 6807**
Fax **0845 850 0095**
Email **eftd@dvla.gsi.gov.uk**

GOV.UK

For all official motoring information
and services **www.gov.uk**

Historic Commercial Vehicle Society

Bob Pender
137 Bedgrove
Aylesbury
Bucks
HP21 7TR
Tel **0208 651 0778**
Email **hcvs2011@gmail.com**
Website **hcvs.co.uk**

HSE

Online only at **hse.gov.uk**
Major incident reporting done by phone
0845 300 9923
(8.30 am to 5.00 pm Monday to Friday)

London TravelWatch

Dexter House
2 Royal Mint Court
London EC3N 4QN
Tel **020 3176 2999**
Fax **020 3176 5991**
Email **enquiries@londontravelwatch.org.uk**
Website **londontravelwatch.org.uk**
(9.00 am to 5.00 pm Monday to Friday)

Metropolitan Police Traffic Department

Metropolitan Police Service
New Scotland Yard
Broadway
London SW1H 0BG
Tel **101** (non-urgent enquiries)
Website **http://content.met.police.uk**

Parliamentary and Health Service Ombudsman (the Ombudsman)

Dame Julie Mellor
Millbank Tower
Millbank
London SW1P 4QP
Tel **0345 015 4033**
Minicom **0300 061 4298**
Fax **0300 061 4000**
Email **phso.enquiries@ombudsman.org.uk**
Website **ombudsman.org.uk**
(Open 8.30 am to 5.30 pm Monday to Friday)

Road Operators' Safety Council (ROSCO)
Osborn House
20 High Street
South Olney
Bucks
MK46 4AA

Tel **01234 714420**
Fax **01234 714420**
Email **admin@rosco-uk.org**
Website **rosco-uk.org**

Road Transport Industry Training Board (RTITB)
Access House
Halesfield 17
Telford
TF7 4PW

Tel **01952 520200**
Fax **01952 520201**
Email **rtitb@rtitb.co.uk**
Website **rtitb.co.uk**

Royal Society for the Prevention of Accidents (RoSPA)
RoSPA House
28 Calthorpe Road
Edgbaston
Birmingham
B15 1RP

Tel **0121 248 2000**
Fax **0121 248 2001**
Email **help@rospa.com**
Website **rospa.com**

Transport for Greater Manchester (TfGM)
Transport for Greater Manchester
  Headquarters
2 Piccadilly Place
Manchester
M1 3BG

Tel **0161 244 1000**
Website **tfgm.com**
(9.00 am to 5.00 pm Monday to Friday)

Vehicle and Operator Services Agency (VOSA)
Headquarters
Berkeley House
Croydon Street
Bristol
BS5 0DA

Tel **0300 123 9000**
Fax **0117 954 3212**
Email **enquiries@vosa.gov.uk**
Website **dft.gov.uk/vosa**
(Open 7.30 am to 6.00 pm Monday to Friday
Closed Sat/Sun)

Working on Wheels (working title of the National Playbus Association)
Brunswick Court
Brunswick Square
Bristol
BS2 8PE

Tel **0117 916 6580**
Fax **0117 916 6588**
Email **info@workingonwheels.org**
Website **workingonwheels.org**

PCV licence entitlements

The licence entitlements that you'll require to drive different types of buses, coaches and minibuses are listed here. You must hold full (not provisional) category B entitlement before you can take a test in this group. You must also gain a full category entitlement for a vehicle before taking a second test to add the trailer entitlement (+E). No additional entitlement is required to tow trailers that weigh up to and including 750 kg.

Category	Description	Additional categories covered
D	Any bus including articulated (or bendy bus) with more than 8 passenger seats	D1
D1	Buses with 9–16 passenger seats	None
D+E	Buses towing trailers over 750 kg	D, D1, D1+E
D1+E	Buses with 9–16 passenger seats towing trailers over 750 kg, provided that the combination doesn't exceed 12 tonnes and the laden trailer weight doesn't exceed the unladen weight of the towing vehicle.	D1

If the vehicle you use for your driving test has automatic transmission, your licence entitlement won't include vehicles with manual gearboxes. A vehicle with automatic transmission is defined as a vehicle in which the driver isn't provided with any means whereby he or she may, independently of the use of the accelerator or the brakes, vary the proportion of the power being produced by the engine that's transmitted to the road wheels of the vehicle. This definition includes semi-automatic vehicles, where no clutch pedal exists.

Minibuses may only be driven with a category B licence entitlement within the UK provided

- the vehicle is used by a non-commercial body for social purposes only
- the driver is aged 21 years or over and has held a full car licence for at least two years
- the driver provides his or her services on a voluntary (unpaid) basis
- the minibus weighs no more than 3.5 tonnes (or 4.25 tonnes if specially adapted for disabled passengers).

Minimum age restrictions and entitlements

Age	Category	Restrictions
18	D, D+E	Only permitted to drive when carrying passengers on regular services • where the route doesn't exceed 50 kilometres, or • when not engaged in the carriage of passengers.
18	D1, D1+E	Only permitted to drive within Great Britain.
20	D, D+E	Only permitted to drive within Great Britain.
21	D, D+E	• No restrictions if hold a CPC. • Only permitted to drive non-professionally without CPC.

At age 17, you can drive these vehicles if you're a member of the armed services.

At age 18, you can drive these vehicles if one of the following applies
1) You're learning to drive or taking a PCV test or Driver CPC initial qualification.
2) Having passed a PCV driving test and Driver CPC initial qualification you can drive under any of the following conditions
   - driving on a regular service where the route doesn't exceed 50 km
   - not engaged in the carriage of passengers
   - while undergoing a national vocational training course to obtain a CPC initial qualification
   - driving a vehicle of a class included in sub-category D1.
3) Having passed a PCV test before 10 September 2007 and driving under a bus operator's licence, or minibus permit, or community bus permit and any of the following conditions
   - driving on a regular service where the route doesn't exceed 50 km
   - not engaged in the carriage of passengers
   - driving a vehicle of a class included in sub-category D1.

At age 20, after passing a PCV driving test and Driver CPC initial qualification.

When driving on a regular service within GB the 50 km restriction on route length doesn't apply.

Vehicle types and licence requirements

Type of vehicle	Category required	Notes
People carrier/small minibus with fewer than 9 passenger seats	B	May be subject to taxi or private hire vehicle regulations if used commercially
Minibus or midibus with more than 8 and not more than 16 passenger seats	D1	D1 allows passengers to be carried for hire or reward
Single-deck service bus or midibus with more than 16 passenger seats	D *	
Coaches with more than 16 passenger seats	D *	
Buses towing trailers over 750 kg	D+E	
Supertrams	B	Further qualifications are required to comply with the light rail transit (LRT) systems regulations
Double-deck service buses and coaches (including those with 3 or 4 axles)	D *	
Historic buses and coaches, ie vehicles over 30 years old	D *	In some cases these may be driven with category B entitlement – when not being used for hire or reward, or the carriage of more than 8 passengers
Mobile project and playbuses	C	In some cases these may be driven with category B entitlement
Towing trailers	+ E	In addition to the vehicle category

* This category also includes the entitlement to tow a trailer up to and including 750 kg.

Minimum test vehicles (MTVs) requirements

Any vehicle or vehicle/trailer combination presented for use at test must meet minimum test vehicle standards. These standards are part of European Community legislation on driver licensing. Great Britain, as a member of the European Union, is obliged to comply with these requirements.

All vehicles presented for test must have externally mounted nearside and offside mirrors and seat belts fitted to seats used by the examiner or any person supervising the test.

All vehicles presented for test must be fitted with a tachograph and an anti-lock braking system (ABS). Trailers don't need to be fitted with ABS.

All vehicles should have the relevant 'no smoking' signs on display to conform with the regulations relating to smoking in public places and vehicles used for work purposes.

All test vehicles must also conform to all the requirements shown on page 258.

Stretched limousines and prison vans based on a lorry chassis aren't suitable vehicles for a PCV (category D) test.

PCVs with restricted rear vision such as Highliners and Neoplans are suitable vehicles for test, as the braking manoeuvre is carried out off-road.

All vehicle combinations must operate the appropriate service brakes and utilise a heavy-duty coupling arrangement suitable for the weight.

A vehicle carrying a trade plate isn't suitable for a driving test, as the conditions attached to trade licences don't allow for a vehicle to be used for this purpose.

Minimum test passenger-carrying vehicles

Category	Description
D1	A passenger-carrying vehicle (PCV) with 9–16 passenger seats, with a maximum authorised mass (MAM) of at least four tonnes, of at least five metres in length and capable of 80 km/h (50 mph). Tachograph, ABS, seat belts and examiner mirrors.
D1+E	A category D1 vehicle towing a trailer of at least 1.25 tonnes MAM, with a closed box trailer at least two metres high and two metres wide. Tachograph, ABS, seat belts and examiner mirrors.
D	A passenger-carrying vehicle (PCV) with more than 8 passenger seats, at least 10 metres in length, at least 2.4 metres in width and capable of 80 km/h (50 mph). Tachograph, ABS, seat belts and examiner mirrors.
D+E	A category D vehicle fitted with a tachograph, ABS, seat belts and examiner mirrors. The trailer must be at least 1.25 tonnes MAM, with a closed box trailer at least two metres high and two metres wide.

Cone positions

Ready reckoner: metric measurements

This list of metric measurements should prove useful if you want to practise the reversing exercise.

To calculate the reversing area's layout, identify the length of your vehicle in the left-hand columns and scan across to the right-hand columns for the relevant cone measurements. The cone positions are relative to the base line Z (see diagram on page 263).

Rigid vehicles

Cones A and A1 should be set at three and a half times the vehicle length.

RIGID VEHICLES
All dimensions in metres

Overall length of vehicle	Cone B	Cones A & A1
5.00	7.5	17.5
5.25	7.9	18.4
5.50	8.3	19.3
5.75	8.6	20.1
6.00	9.0	21.0
6.25	9.4	21.9
6.50	9.8	22.8
6.75	10.1	23.6
7.00	10.5	24.5
7.25	10.9	25.4
7.50	11.3	26.3
7.75	11.6	27.1
8.00	12.0	28.0
8.25	12.4	28.9
8.50	12.8	29.8
8.75	13.1	30.6
9.00	13.5	31.5
9.25	13.9	32.4
9.50	14.3	33.3
9.75	14.6	34.1
10.00	15.0	35.0
10.25	15.4	35.9
10.50	15.8	36.8
10.75	16.1	37.6
11.00	16.5	38.5
11.25	16.9	39.4
11.50	17.3	40.3
11.75	17.6	41.1
12.00	18.0	42.0
12.25	18.4	42.9
12.50	18.8	43.8
12.75	19.1	44.6
13.00	19.5	45.5
13.25	19.9	46.4
13.50	20.3	47.3
13.75	20.6	48.1
14.00	21.0	49.0

All articulated vehicles

Cones A and A1 should be set at four times the vehicle length.

ALL ARTICULATED VEHICLES
All dimensions in metres

Overall length of vehicle	Cone B	Cones A & A1
8.00	16.0	32.0
8.25	16.5	33.0
8.50	17.0	34.0
8.75	17.5	35.0
9.00	18.0	36.0
9.25	18.5	37.0
9.50	19.0	38.0
9.75	19.5	39.0
10.00	20.0	40.0
10.25	20.5	41.0
10.50	21.0	42.0
10.75	21.5	43.0
11.00	22.0	44.0
11.25	22.5	45.0
11.50	23.0	46.0
11.75	23.5	47.0
12.00	24.0	48.0
12.25	24.5	49.0
12.50	25.0	50.0
12.75	25.5	51.0
13.00	26.0	52.0
13.25	26.5	53.0
13.50	27.0	54.0
13.75	27.5	55.0
14.00	28.0	56.0
14.25	28.5	57.0
14.50	29.0	58.0
14.75	29.5	59.0
15.00	30.0	60.0
15.25	30.5	61.0
15.50	31.0	62.0
15.75	31.5	63.0
16.00	32.0	64.0
16.25	32.5	65.0
16.50	33.0	66.0
16.75	32.5	66.0
17.00	32.0	66.0
17.25	31.5	66.0
17.50	31.0	66.0
17.75	30.5	66.0
18.00	30.0	66.0
18.25	29.5	66.0
18.50	29.0	66.0
18.75	28.5	66.0

Glossary

ABS Anti-lock braking system (developed by Bosch), which uses electronic sensors to detect when a wheel is about to lock, releases the brakes sufficiently to allow the wheel to revolve, then repeats the process in a very short space of time – thus avoiding skidding.

AETR rules A European agreement concerning the work of crews on vehicles engaged in international road transport (aligned with EU regulations in April 1992). These rules govern drivers' hours and rest periods in specified countries outside the EU. For more detailed information please consult PSV 375 ('Rules on drivers' hours and tachographs: Passenger-carrying vehicles in GB and Europe'), published by VOSA.

Air suspension system This uses a compressible material (usually air), contained in chambers located between the axle and the vehicle body, to replace normal steel-leaf spring suspension. Gives an even load height (empty or laden) and added protection to fragile goods in transit.

Axle weights Limits laid down for maximum permitted weights carried by each axle – depending on axle spacings and wheel/tyre arrangement. (Consult regulations, charts or publications that give the legal requirements.)

BS EN ISO 9000 British Standards code relating to quality assurance adopted by vehicle body-builders, recovery firms, etc.

C & U (Regs) Construction and Use Regulations that set out specifications that govern the design and use of all vehicles.

CAG Computer-aided gearshift system developed by Scania that employs an electronic control unit combined with electropneumatic actuators and a mechanical gearbox. The clutch is still required to achieve the gear change using an electrical gear lever switch.

City of London security regulations Anti-terrorist measures which mean that access to the City of London is restricted to only seven access points, involving closure of several other roads. Full details can be obtained from the Metropolitan Police.

CNG Compressed natural gas.

COSHH Regulations 1988 The Control of Substances Hazardous to Health Regulations 1988 place a responsibility on employers to make a proper assessment of the effects of the storage or use of any substances that may represent a risk to their employees' health. (Details can be obtained from the Health and Safety Executive.)

CPC in road traffic management This Certificate of Professional Competence (CPC) indicates that the holder has attained the standards of knowledge required in order to exercise proper control of a transport business (and is required before an operator's licence can be granted).

Cruise control   A facility that allows a vehicle to travel at a set speed without use of the accelerator pedal. However, the driver can immediately return to normal control by pressing the accelerator or brake pedal.

Double-declutching   A technique employed when driving older PCVs that allows the driver to adjust the engine revs to the road speed when changing gear. The clutch pedal is released briefly while the gear lever is in the neutral position. When changing down, engine revs are increased to match the engine speed to the lower gear in order to minimise the load being placed on the gear mechanism. Note: the construction of modern synchromesh gearboxes is such that this technique can cause damage. At least one major manufacturer has made it clear that the warranty conditions will become invalid if this technique has been used. Refer to the manufacturer and the vehicle handbook, if in doubt.

DPTAC   (Disabled Persons' Transport Advisory Committee) specification. Applied to PCVs to assist passengers with disabilities (for example, bright yellow handrails).

Drive-by-wire   Modern electronic and air control systems that replace direct mechanical linkages.

Driver CPC   The Driver Certificate of Professional Competence indicates that the holder has attained the standards of knowledge required in order to exercise proper control of a large goods vehicle or passenger-carrying vehicle.

Electronic engine management system This system monitors and controls both fuel supply to the engine and the contents of the exhaust gases produced. The system is an essential part of some speed retarder systems.

Electronic power shift   A semi-automatic transmission system, developed by Mercedes, that requires the clutch to be fully depressed each time a gear change is made. This system then selects the appropriate gear.

Endurance braking see **Retarder**

Fluid flywheel   Incorporated in automatic and semi-automatic gear systems, it couples the drive train to the gearbox by use of hydraulic fluid. This allows gear changes, stopping and starting without the need for a separate clutch.

Geartronic   A fully automated transmission system developed by Volvo. There's no clutch pedal. Instead, there's an additional pedal operating the exhaust brake.

HSE   The Health and Safety Executive. HSE produces literature that provides advice and information on health and safety issues at work.

ISO 9000   British Standards code relating to quality assurance adopted by vehicle body-builders, recovery firms, etc.

Jake brake   A long-established system of speed retarding that alters the valve timing in the engine. In effect, the engine becomes a compressor and holds back the vehicle's speed.

Kerb weight (KBW)   The total weight of a vehicle plus fuel, excluding any load (or driver).

'Kneeling' bus   This type of bus uses air suspension to lower the entrance of the bus, while stationary, for easier access – especially useful for disabled passengers

Lamination   A process where plastic film is sandwiched between two layers of glass so that an object, on striking a windscreen for example, will normally indent the screen without large fragments of glass causing injury to the driver.

LEZ (Low Emission Zone)   A specified area in Greater London within which the most polluting diesel-engined vehicles are required to meet specific emissions standards.

Limited-stop service   A bus service operating under stage carriage conditions, but stopping only at specified points.

LNG   Liquefied (compressed) natural gas.

Load-sensing valve   A valve in an air brake system that can be adjusted to reduce the possibility of wheels locking when the vehicle is unladen.

LPG   Liquefied (compressed) petroleum gas.

MAM   Maximum authorised mass, applying to vehicles that include fuel, passengers, etc.

Mobile worker   A mobile worker is defined in legislation as 'any worker forming part of the travelling staff, ie drivers, crew, trainees and apprentices who are in the service of an undertaking which operates road transport services for passengers or goods by road for hire or reward or on its own account'.

PCV   Passenger-carrying vehicle.

Plate   A plate fixed to the vehicle with information relating to dimensions and weights of passenger vehicles. It indicates tyre size, maximum axle weight and maximum loaded weight. Certificates are sometimes referred to as plates when required, with information relating to tachographs, speed limiters, manufacturer's specification and height.

Pneumo-cyclic gearbox   A semi-automatic gearbox, where an electronic or mechanical gearshift operates an air valve system to change gears.

Pre-select gearbox   A gear-change system where the gears are manually selected prior to use and then engaged by pressing a gear-change pedal. It employs a fluid flywheel and no clutch.

PSV   Public service vehicle (official alternative reference for PCV; see page 16).

Range change Gearbox arrangement that permits the driver to select a series of either high- or low-ratio gears depending on the load, speed and any gradient being negotiated. Rarely fitted to PCVs.

Red Routes Approximately 360 route miles (580 km) in the London area have become subject to stringent regulations restricting stopping, unloading and loading. Also being introduced in other major towns and cities.

Re-grooving A process permitted for use on tyres for vehicles over an unladen weight of 2540 kg, allowing a new tread pattern to be cut into the existing tyre surface (subject to certain conditions).

Retarder or endurance brake An additional braking system that may be either mechanical, electrical or hydraulic. Mechanical devices either alter the engine exhaust gas flow or amend the valve timing (creating a 'compressor' effect). Electrical devices consist of an electromagnetic field energised around the transmission drive shaft (more frequently used on passenger vehicles). This type may also be known as 'regenerative' braking, when the energy generated is fed back into the vehicle's electrical storage system (batteries).

Selective or block change A sequence of gear-changing omitting intermediate gears while correctly matching the speed of the vehicle.

Semi-automatic A transmission system in which there's no clutch but the driver changes gear manually.

Splitter box Another name for a gearbox with high and low ratios.

Tachograph A recorder indicating vehicle speeds, duration of journey, rest stops, etc. Required to be fitted to specified vehicles.

TBV Initials of the French (Renault) semi-automatic transmission system that employs a selector lever plus visual display information.

TC Traffic commissioner appointed by the Secretary of State to a traffic area so as to act as the licensing authority for goods vehicle and PSV operators in the area.

Thinking gearbox The term used to describe a fully automated gearbox that selects the appropriate gear for the load, gradient and speed, etc by means of electronic sensors.

Toughened safety glass The glass undergoes a heat treatment process during manufacture so that in the event of an impact (such as a stone) on the windscreen, it breaks up into small blunt fragments, thus reducing the risk of injury. An area on the windscreen in front of the driver is designed to give a zone of vision in the event of such an impact.

Turbo-charged The exhaust gas drives a turbine, which compresses incoming air and effectively delivers more air to the engine than is the case with a normal or non-turbocharged engine.

Turbo-cooled or intercooled Refers to a system where the air from the turbo-charger is cooled before being delivered to the engine. The cooling increases the density of the compressed air to further improve engine power and torque.

Two-speed axle A system whereby an electrical switch actuates a mechanism in the rear axle that doubles the number of ratios available to the driver.

Unloader valve A device fitted to air brake systems, between the compressor and the storage reservoir, pre-set to operate as sufficient pressure is achieved and allowing the excess to be released. (Often heard at regular intervals when the engine is running.)

VEL Vehicle excise licence or road fund licence.

VRO Vehicle registration office, dealing with matters relating to registration of goods vehicles, taxation and licensing.

Walk-round check It's essential that every driver carries out a thorough walk-round check before using a vehicle on the public highway (see page 131).

Waybill A list of passengers, often called a passenger manifest.

WTD (Working Time Directive) This is a European Union directive limiting the number of hours people can work, and determining what breaks should be taken, minimum holiday entitlement, etc. It applies to all kinds of employment, but currently excludes those who are self-employed.

Road signs

You must be aware of the specific road signs that relate to buses and coaches. Those illustrated on this page are currently in use.

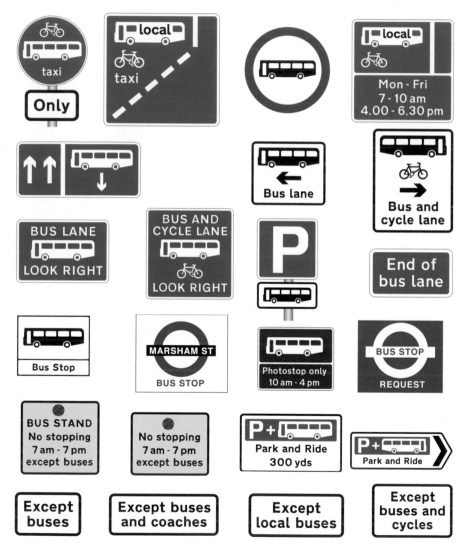

Index

Other Official DSA Publications

Driving
Standards
Agency

The Official DSA Theory Test for Drivers of Large Vehicles

Every official theory test revision question plus the full DSA explanations of the answers. The book includes essential background information on every topic to help you really understand. The CD-ROM provides the closest experience to the multiple choice part of the theory test and includes a digital version of *The Official Highway Code*.

Book	ISBN 9780115532375	£17.99
CD-ROM	ISBN 9780115529047	£35.00

The Official DSA Guide to Hazard Perception DVD

Hazard perception is a vital skill and a key part of today's driving tests. This interactive DVD from the Driving Standards Agency will help you stay safe on the roads. Includes official DSA video clips and tests your responses to hazards.

DVD	ISBN 9780115528651	£15.99

Driving
Standards
Agency

The Official Highway Code

Contains the latest rules of the road and is essential reading for all road users, not just learners. The CD-ROM version is a great interactive alternative to the best-selling book and includes games and quizzes to help bring The Highway Code to life.

Book	ISBN 9780115528149	£2.50
CD-ROM	ISBN 9780115528460	£9.99

Learning The Highway Code with British Sign Language - the Official DSA DVD and Book Pack

DVD and book	ISBN 9780115529849	£9.99

Also available as an eBook from your device's eBook store.

Driver CPC: the Official DSA Guide for Professional Bus and Coach Drivers

This official book is specifically designed to help bus and coach drivers prepare for their initial Certificate of Professional Competence (CPC) by focusing on the syllabus of the Case Studies and the Practical Demonstration Test modules. Includes information on periodic training and ecosafe driving.

Book	ISBN 9780115531644	£9.99
Downloadable PDF	ISBN 9780115531651	£9.99*

information & publishing solutions